CHRISTIAN REALI
THE NEW REAL

Are religion and public life really separate spheres of human activity? Should they be? In this book, Robin W. Lovin criticizes contemporary political and theological views that separate religion from public life as though these areas were systematically opposed and makes the case for a more integrated understanding of modern society. Such an understanding can be underpinned by "Christian realism," which encourages responsible engagement with social and political problems from a distinctively religious perspective. Drawing on the work of Rawls, Galston, Niebuhr, and Bonhoeffer, Lovin argues that the responsibilities of everyday life are a form of politics. Political commitment is no longer confined to the sphere of law and government, and a global ethics arises from the decisions of individuals. This book will foster a better understanding of contemporary political thought among theologians and will introduce readers primarily interested in political thought to relevant developments in recent theology.

ROBIN W. LOVIN is Cary M. Maguire University Professor of Ethics at Southern Methodist University, Dallas, Texas, where he previously served as Dean of the Perkins School of Theology. He is a graduate of Northwestern University and Harvard University and an ordained minister of the United Methodist Church. He was previously Dean at the Theological School of Drew University in Madison, New Jersey, and has also taught at the Divinity School of the University of Chicago. His previous books include *Reinhold Niebuhr and Christian Realism* (1994).

CHRISTIAN REALISM AND THE NEW REALITIES

ROBIN W. LOVIN

Southern Methodist University

CAMBRIDGE
UNIVERSITY PRESS

CAMBRIDGE UNIVERSITY PRESS
Cambridge, New York, Melbourne, Madrid, Cape Town, Singapore, São Paulo, Delhi

Cambridge University Press
32 Avenue of the Americas, New York, NY 10013-2473, USA

www.cambridge.org
Information on this title: www.cambridge.org/9780521603003

First published 2008

Printed in the United States of America

A catalog record for this publication is available from the British Library.

Library of Congress Cataloging in Publication Data
Lovin, Robin W.
Christian realism and the new realities / Robin W. Lovin
p. cm.
Includes bibliographical references and index.
ISBN 978-0-521-84194-8 (hardcover) – ISBN 978-0-521-60300-3 (pbk.)
1. Christianity and politics. 2. Religion and politics. I. Title.
BR115.P7L68   2008
261–dc22   2007045455

ISBN   978-0-521-84194-8 hardback
ISBN   978-0-521-60300-3 paperback

Contents

Preface

More than a decade ago, I wrote a book called *Reinhold Niebuhr and Christian Realism*. The distinction between the man and the method was important to me, as it was to Niebuhr himself. Christian realism did not belong to him alone, though he was its most articulate and influential voice. It is a way of thinking deeply embedded in Christian tradition, and it can be systematically distinguished from other ways of thinking about politics, ethics, and theology available in Niebuhr's time and in ours.

This volume continues that effort to take the way of thinking that Niebuhr represented beyond his own formulation of it. This is not because I think less of Niebuhr, but precisely because I think his Christian realism has been intellectually isolated by more recent developments in philosophy and theology that make it harder for contemporary scholars to appreciate his insights. I have tried to address these problems here by emphasizing the social and political pluralism in the Christian realist tradition and by stressing the theology of responsibility on which his pragmatic approach to moral problems depends. The idea of responsible action connects Niebuhr more closely than I had understood before to his theological adversary, Karl Barth, and to his erstwhile student, Dietrich Bonhoeffer. This book is in some respects an effort to write the theology and ethics we might have had if Niebuhr and Bonhoeffer had each had the opportunity to actually understand what the other was saying. Or perhaps it is an effort to imagine the political philosophy we might have had if John Rawls had continued the line of thinking he explored in his undergraduate thesis at Princeton. (The reader will find that cryptic remark explained near the beginning of Chapter 4.)

I have been encouraged in this work by opportunities to present and discuss it with colleagues in many places, including the Society of Christian Ethics; the Center for the Study of Religion and Conflict at Arizona State University; Simpson College; the Center of Theological Inquiry in Princeton, New Jersey; and a joint meeting of the Society for the Study of Christian Ethics and the Societas Ethica held at Oxford University in 2006. More continuous conversation has been provided by Charlie Curran, Tom Mayo, Beka Miles, Theo Walker, Steve Sverdlik, and other colleagues in the Ethics Colloquy at Southern Methodist University. Douglas Ottati, William Schweiker, and Michael Perry have all been particularly helpful over many years, and I trust they will forgive me if at points I can no longer tell the difference between ideas they have given me and ideas of my own. Oleg Makariev has read, edited, corrected, and questioned this text through many variations, and I am immensely grateful for his loyal assistance during my first five years in my present position. Stephen Riley contributed greatly to the preparation of the final manuscript, and Mark Tarpley assisted with the final editing and prepared the index. Kate Brett at Cambridge University Press has been unfailingly patient, encouraging, and hopeful. I am grateful to all of these people, and to many others whose ideas and interest contributed to the writing of this book and whose work has now delivered it into the reader's hands.

Introduction

Christian realism is a reminder of our limits and an affirmation of our hope. It tells us that our knowledge is imperfect, our plans are incomplete, and our expectations are inevitably distorted by self-interest. We are always trying to overcome these limitations, and we are often partly successful; but our partial successes make it all the more important to remember that the limits remain, mocking our confidence with ironic reversals and threatening our pride with forces beyond our control. Final answers and permanent solutions elude us.

Nevertheless, we live in a meaningful universe. Conflict, violence, and the relentless background drone of anxiety are not the ultimate reality. The coherence of our partial truths and the justice that expresses our imperfect love point to reality in a way that incoherence and injustice do not. So we feel ourselves always obliged to work toward a better approximation of justice and peace, and we cannot rest content merely in prevailing with our own interests.

Everyone experiences this dialectic of power and finitude, meaning and incoherence, hope and anxiety. For some, it signals a need to dig through the distortions of human subjectivity to the hard core of objective fact. For others, the persistence of incoherence and violence suggests that objectivity itself is an illusion, and the only order we will find is the one we make for ourselves.

For biblical faith, however, this unresolved tension in all human experience reveals the nature of ultimate reality and locates our place within it. Biblical faith articulates this revelation by saying both that we are "created in the image of God" and that we are "fallen." We have used the image of God, which is our power to know, imagine, and choose, to separate ourselves from God. As a result, we are unable rightly to choose or to know a good which is nonetheless always present to us, shared by all of us, engaging us in pursuit of its partial and limited realizations, and judging our failures to comprehend it as a whole.

This assessment of the human situation is shared by all Christian theology. What distinguishes Christian realism is the conviction that the best place to see this human condition in ordinary experience is in those large-scale relationships and interactions we call politics. As Edmund Santurri puts it, "Political life displays in a peculiarly transparent way the fallen condition of the world."[1] Although many people center their moral reflections in personal relationships and close communities, Christian realists find the moral life more clearly presented in political problems that show the limits of our understanding, demand higher levels of self-restraint, and demonstrate our dependence on powers and forces outside of our control. Seen from a Christian realist perspective, politics demands our best efforts at the same time that it undermines our self-righteousness. Politics condemns injustice without promising us that good will and sincerity will always be rewarded. "In such a faith, both sentimentality and despair are avoided. The meaningfulness of life does not tempt to premature complacency, and the chaos which always threatens the world of meaning does not destroy the tension of faith and hope in which all moral action is grounded."[2]

Through the work of theologians, preachers, and political thinkers, this Christian realist orientation toward politics shaped the self-understanding of peoples and leaders in the Western democracies just after the Second World War. It helped shape the global order that emerged during those years and lasted to the end of the Cold War. Reinhold Niebuhr was a central figure in these developments, engaged in conversations about events with leading politicians, philosophers, historians, and critics, and also writing books, sermons, and lectures that shaped the public perception of Christianity and its meaning for the modern world.[3]

Niebuhr's Christian realism stressed the role of power in maintaining order and accomplishing political purposes, but he also insisted on the necessity of checking power with countervailing power.[4] Within nations, Christian realism suggested the checks and balances of constitutional democracy as the best way to preserve both order and freedom. Between

---

[1] Edmund Santurri, "Global Justice after the Fall: Christian Realism and the 'Law of Peoples,'" *Journal of Religious Ethics* 33 (2005), 784.

[2] Reinhold Niebuhr, *An Interpretation of Christian Ethics* (New York: Seabury Press, 1979), p. 64.

[3] Heather Warren, *Theologians of a New World Order: Reinhold Niebuhr and the Christian Realists, 1920–1948* (New York: Oxford University Press, 1997); Richard Fox, *Reinhold Niebuhr: A Biography* (Ithaca, NY: Cornell University Press, 1996), pp. 193–248; Martin Halliwell, *The Constant Dialogue: Reinhold Niebuhr and American Intellectual Culture* (Lanham, MD: Rowman & Littlefield Publishers, 2005).

[4] Reinhold Niebuhr, *The Children of Light and the Children of Darkness* (New York: Charles Scribner's Sons, 1960).

nations, a balance of power provided the realistic alternative to utopian plans for world government.

To seek peace through conflict between roughly equal opposing powers seems a risky idea at the outset. Realists come to trust the process through experience over time, but as Niebuhr pointed out, neither secular liberalism nor Marxism supports it in theory. It gains plausibility through the biblical understanding of human nature, which reinforces our experience that there is no single locus of power and authority in this world from which all conflict can be resolved and all questions answered, despite the perennial attraction of imperial claims and comprehensive theories that promise such a center.[5]

Niebuhr's century was one in which lessons about peace had to be learned by reflecting on its absence. Two world wars nearly destroyed the political order that had been maintained by successful modern states since the Protestant Reformation. In the twentieth century, the successful modern state was tested by the forces of imperialism, nationalism, and revolutionary Marxism. Against those challenges, Niebuhr believed the clearest direction was provided not by modern political theory, but by the tradition of the Hebrew prophets. They understood idolatry, and they knew how to defeat it.

The twentieth century was marked by the rise and fall of ideological states that linked absolute power to ultimate good. The Revolution of 1917 transformed the Russian Empire in which the tsar held absolute power into a Soviet Union in which the state held absolute power, ostensibly for the ultimate purpose of bringing about its own dissolution in a proletarian utopia. Mussolini, Franco, and, most successfully, Hitler supplanted faltering governments with a state that promised a new center of authority, adequate to overcome the weaknesses of democracy and the threats of revolution. As European empires faded after the First World War, the Empire of Japan transformed its successful emulation of the nineteenth century European empires into a new imperial ideology that linked religious legitimacy, authoritarian politics, and cultural hegemony. The Chinese completed the cycle of major power transformations with their own communist revolution that ended with the proclamation of the People's Republic of China in 1949.

Although power had tended to concentrate in the hands of the state since the beginning of the modern era, these twentieth century powers demanded more from their people than even the most absolutist modern

---

[5] Reinhold Niebuhr, *Christian Realism and Political Problems* (New York: Charles Scribner's Sons, 1953), p. 100.

states, because they claimed to put their power in service of a greater good. Although the good envisioned was different in each case, these regimes all exercised totalitarian power, demanding not merely obedience, but absolute loyalty, and putting all their people and all their social resources in service of the goal envisioned by their leaders. Institutions, ideas, and persons that could not find a place in service to the new order had to be eliminated.

The link between greater goals and greater power makes logical sense at first. These governments were initially successful in mastering the economic and political dislocations of the time, and both fascist and communist parties gained some following in most Western democracies during the period between the two world wars.

Prophetic tradition, however, knows where the totalitarian claim leads. It leads to a state that not only acts on God's authority, but acts in God's place. The power to unite all good and the authority to silence all opposition belong only to God. The successful modern state has had a different task, important but limited, of securing peace and security within a given territory. Early modern philosophers and jurists, recoiling from the century of religious warfare that followed the Reformation, tended to suppose that intolerance and persecution are the results of religious zealots claiming political power. Democratic theorists through the beginning of the nineteenth century thus supposed that freedom could be secured by the simple expedient of separating religion from politics. But when the totalitarian possibility became a twentieth century reality, its claims were not made by churches, but by states. Prophetic faith was not surprised by this. The sources of idolatry lie in human anxiety and egoism generally, not particularly in religion.[6] Prophetic faith is thus alert to idolatrous claims wherever they occur, and it is suspicious of any power – kingly, priestly, or prophetic – that thinks itself above this temptation.

The most relevant point for twentieth-century Christian realism, however, is that the answer to idolatry is not to emulate it. Faced with totalitarian opponents who are absolutely certain about their cause, Christian realists must be disciplined enough not to claim the same for themselves. This will provoke the anxiety of those who fear their own uncertainty as much as they fear the convictions of their enemies, but faith and political experience concur that a limited, critical assessment of the evil of our foes and limited claims for our own virtue provide effective guidance, even when

---

[6] Reinhold Niebuhr, *The Nature and Destiny of Man: A Christian Interpretation* (Louisville, KY: Westminster John Knox Press, 1996), vol. I, 208–19.

those on the other side insist on seeing the conflict in more ultimate terms. Having learned this lesson with some difficulty in the crisis of the Second World War, Niebuhr and the diplomats and global strategists who shared his realist understanding were determined to handle the looming conflict with the Soviet Union on other terms.

The pride and self-righteousness of powerful nations are a greater hazard to their success in statecraft than the machinations of their foes. If we could combine a greater degree of humility with our stubborn resolution, we might not only be more successful in holding the dyke against tyranny, but we might also gradually establish a genuine sense of community with our foe, however small . . . We shall exploit our opportunities the more successfully, however, if we have knowledge of the limits of the will in creating government, and of the limits of government in creating community. We may have pity upon, but can have no sympathy with, those who flee to the illusory security of the impossible from the insecurities and ambiguities of the possible.[7]

The political strategy of the Christian realist is based on limitation and balance, rather than on a final victory, because the political attention of the Christian realist is focused on what Dietrich Bonhoeffer called "the penultimate."[8] The penultimate is the world of ordinary life seen in anticipation of the ultimate, but not directly participating in it. Concentration on the penultimate requires, according to Bonhoeffer, a rejection both of the radical politics that is willing to destroy anything and everything for the sake of ultimate truth and of the compromises that, by suspending judgment until ultimate truth is fully present, slip by degrees into relativism. The Christian realist shares the radical's dissatisfaction with injustice, but focuses on responsible choices among the concrete possibilities now available.

THE SCOPE OF CHRISTIAN REALISM

The use of Bonhoeffer's *Ethics* to elaborate Niebuhr's understanding of prophetic faith makes a point that needs to be emphasized at the outset. Christian realism is not confined to the work of Reinhold Niebuhr and the American Protestant theologians who took the term upon themselves in the early years of the twentieth century.[9] Christian realism, like William

---

[7] Niebuhr, *Christian Realism and Political Problems*, pp. 30–1.
[8] Dietrich Bonhoeffer, *Ethics*, Clifford J. Green (ed.), Dietrich Bonhoeffer Works, vol. VI (Minneapolis, MN: Fortress Press, 2005), pp. 146–70.
[9] For a history of this Christian realism, see Gary Dorrien, *The Making of American Liberal Theology*, vol. II (Louisville, KY: Westminster John Knox Press, 2003), pp. 435–521.

James's pragmatism, was "a new name for some old ways of thinking."[10] Niebuhr and his colleagues thought of themselves as speaking for a tradition that had its roots in the Hebrew prophets and took shape in Christian theology at least as early as Saint Augustine, who was able to distinguish between an ideal community united in love of God and the penultimate, but nonetheless real communities united by the search for peace.[11] Not all those whom Niebuhr regarded as Christian realists would have recognized themselves in the identification, and not everyone who should be included made it onto Niebuhr's list. Bonhoeffer may have been one Christian realist who did not.[12]

In this book, then, we will be exploring an understanding of Christian realism that is broad in history and in concept. Christian realism belongs to no single author, nor can it be reduced to a single system of ideas. What connects these variations on the realist theme is that they unite political realism, moral realism, and theological realism.[13] The meaning of "realism" is different in each of these uses, and the relationship between them is one of mutual qualification, rather than tight logical implication. They interpret and explain one another, so that a political realist who is also a moral realist views politics differently from a political realist who is not, and a theological realist who is also a political realist probably will not grant moral ideas the same sort of normative force as a theological realist who rejects political realism. The latter might speak of absolute norms or exceptionless moral rules. The former will talk about "the relevance of an impossible ethical ideal."[14] Nothing logically requires a person who holds one of these realisms to affirm the other two. The three realisms are "realistic" in different ways, with regard to different things, but a Christian realist holds all three realisms together.

Political realism analyzes political choices in terms of self-interest and power. Particularly when considering the actions of nations and their leaders, the political realist expects to connect events into a meaningful pattern only by asking how the nation is pursuing its interests over the long run. Larger cycles of history or moral and religious judgments play a role in

---

[10] William James, *Pragmatism: A New Name for Some Old Ways of Thinking* (New York: Longmans, Green, and Co., 1907).

[11] Augustine, *The City of God against the Pagans*, R. W. Dyson (ed.) (Cambridge: Cambridge University Press, 1998), pp. 950–61.

[12] See Reinhold Niebuhr, "*Ethics*, by Dietrich Bonhoeffer," *Union Seminary Quarterly Review* 11 (1956), 57–8.

[13] For a more complete explanation of these three realisms in Reinhold Niebuhr's work, see Robin W. Lovin, *Reinhold Niebuhr and Christian Realism* (Cambridge: Cambridge University Press, 1995), pp. 3–32.

[14] Cf. Niebuhr, *An Interpretation of Christian Ethics*, pp. 62–83.

political understanding only as they can be connected to interests and the search for power to make those interests effective.[15] To be "realistic" in this context means having a keen eye for all the interests that are actually at work in a political situation, thinking clearly about how they relate to one another, and looking beyond rhetoric, proclamations, one's own moral judgments, and other people's ideologies to determine what is actually driving choices and strategies.[16]

A generation of historians, political theorists, and diplomats, exemplified by Arthur Schlesinger Jr., Hans Morgenthau, and George Kennan, urged this political realism on policy makers and strategists for many of the same reasons that the Christian realists urged it on their generation of theologians.[17] After the First World War, idealism led the victorious allies to impose an unworkable peace on the defeated German Empire and to ignore the need to deal realistically with emerging Soviet power. A more stern realistic discipline would be needed after the Second World War, when a defeated Germany would have to be won over quickly as an ally against the full-blown Soviet reality. Democracy could no longer afford the assumption that moral superiority would guarantee victory over a hostile totalitarian power. Western democracies had to understand their own interests and win other nations to share them. They could not engage in a moral crusade to defeat the Soviet Union. They would have to be satisfied with containing and deterring it.

Such political realism ties its analyses closely to concrete political situations and actual political choices. It does not lend itself to speculation about ideal systems of government or to setting up scales of political value that rank governments and institutions against one another in moral terms. Describing the way that competing interest groups negotiate some specific compromise between their claims tells the political realist what is happening in a way that evaluating the result in terms of an abstract standard of justice does not. Political realism forces you to pay attention to the whole range of interests that are actually at work in a situation, rather than just those interests that your ideology or your moral theory tells you are important. So a realist is apt to see forces at work that other people fail to see, or at least forces that other people do not want to talk about.

---

[15] Hans J. Morgenthau, *Politics Among Nations: The Struggle for Power and Peace*, Fourth Edition (New York: Alfred A. Knopf, 1967), pp. 5–8.

[16] Niebuhr, *Christian Realism and Political Problems*, p. 119.

[17] Ronald Stone offers a detailed study of Christian realism in relation to these developments in political thought, especially in the study of international relations. See Ronald H. Stone, *Prophetic Realism* (New York: T. & T. Clark, 2005), pp. 27–55.

In this way of thinking, moral ideals can become interests, too.[18] If nations and their leaders are so committed to democracy that they will risk other interests to support the democratic process or to keep democratic governments from being defeated, then the political realist will have to pay attention to democracy. But to figure out what is going to happen next, the political realist will look at how the interest in the democratic ideal guides decisions, rather than at what the ideal itself prescribes. Political realism, then, is realistic in the eyes-open, feet-on-the-ground, common sense way we say that someone is realistic when he or she pays attention to what is going on and is not misled by vain hopes or baseless fears.

Moral realism is realistic in a different way. Moral realism holds that our moral rules, ideals, and virtues reflect durable features of human nature that really exist, apart from the religious traditions, moral theories, and accumulated practical wisdom on which we draw to talk about them.[19] In contrast to those philosophers who locate the meaning of moral terms in emotive responses to situations, or who suggest that meaningful moral judgments can only arise in a community of discourse that shares a common way of using moral language, the moral realist ties moral meaning to a reality that exists beyond the subjective feelings of those who use moral terms and beyond the systems of language in which they discuss moral judgments with others. Often, this moral realism is a version of ethical naturalism, which holds that meaningful moral language refers to objective conditions required for human flourishing.

A moral realist will qualify the political realist's immediate, concrete focus on power and interests by adding that interests which are incompatible with the conditions for human flourishing or which undermine the communities that sustain those conditions are interests which, sooner or later, will lose out to other interests which have a more realistic grasp of the requirements of human nature. This does not mean abandoning political realism for a utopian program that seeks the ideal conditions for human flourishing, but it suggests that the possibilities and limits of human nature are realities that nations must take into account when deciding what their interests are. Having an accurate account of those possibilities and limitations is an important part of the task of political leadership. Niebuhr sought to provide that account in *The Nature and Destiny of Man*, and he connected it to the task of political realism when he argued that "a free

---

[18] George Kennan, "Morality and Foreign Policy," *Foreign Affairs* 64 (1985), 205–18.
[19] David O. Brink, *Moral Realism and the Foundations of Ethics* (Cambridge: Cambridge University Press, 1989); Russ Shafer-Landau, *Moral Realism: A Defence* (Oxford: Clarendon Press, 2003).

society prospers best in a cultural, religious, and moral atmosphere which encourages neither a too pessimistic nor too optimistic view of human nature."[20] Others who belong to this broad understanding of Christian realism have found Niebuhr's "not too much . . . not too little" formulation too ambiguous to be helpful, but John Courtney Murray, for example, connected his defense of democracy to his Thomist understanding of human nature at the same time that he recognized that political ideals also reflect concrete political interests.[21] Robert Gordis likewise found the emphasis on "original sin" in Niebuhr's account of human nature too extreme for a Jewish interpretation of scripture, but he shared Niebuhr's disillusionment with theology which "stressed the potentialities for perfection in man, or at least for his perpetual and consistent improvement."[22] The moral realism of Niebuhr's theological contemporaries is not marked by their agreement with his political realism, but by the fact that they could discuss their disagreements in terms of an account of human nature that could be traced to biblical sources and confirmed in contemporary experience. In fact, during the 1950s, they often did discuss these questions at Robert Maynard Hutchins's Center for the Study of Democratic Institutions.[23]

Perhaps the most important practical direction provided by this moral realism is the humility and self-restraint that the Christian realist tries to introduce into political discussions. Because our moral concepts formulate ideas about reality that exists independently of our ideas about it, moral realism is not troubled by the idea that the human good is not completely known, or by the fact that our attempts to give a comprehensive account of it may be incomplete. If the language of moral judgment depends on the real conditions of human flourishing, then even those who think they know that language must recognize that they may be mistaken in their moral judgments. Their meaningful moral discourse may make claims about human nature that prove false in longer experience, or that are modified by new technology, or that have to be restated in light of a more inclusive account of whose experience is fully human.

---

[20] Niebuhr, *The Children of Light and the Children of Darkness*, p. viii.

[21] John Courtney Murray, *We Hold These Truths: Catholic Reflections on the America Proposition* (New York: Sheed and Ward, 1960), pp. 19, 30–33.

[22] Robert Gordis, *The Root and the Branch: Judaism and the Free Society* (Chicago: University of Chicago Press, 1962), p. 139.

[23] Leon Hooper, S. J., "Cups Half Full: John Courtney Murray's Skirmishes with Christian Realism," in Eric Patterson (ed.), *The Christian Realists: Reassessing the Contributions of Niebuhr and His Contemporaries* (Lanham, MD: University Press of America, 2003), pp. 159–76; Thomas C. Berg, "John Courtney Murray and Reinhold Niebuhr: Natural Law and Christian Realism," *Journal of Catholic Social Thought* 4 (2007), 3–27.

A moral realist need not claim perfect or complete knowledge of the realities on which moral meanings depend. Recognizing that different people have different moral ideas need not culminate in relativism. A moral realist is likely to be a "fallibilist," holding that moral realities can be known, but that any particular claim to moral knowledge may prove to be false, so that all such claims are in constant need of testing and correction.[24] Someone who ties the meaning of moral language closely to a particular community of moral discourse may see little connection between moral truth and the clash of interests that holds the attention of the political realist, but a moral realist may see that political conflict as one place in which the testing and correction of moral claims can go on. The moral realist who is also a political realist will not surrender moral judgment entirely to that contest of competing interests, but he or she will not completely separate the two realms either.

Finally, Christian realism is also *theological realism*. The realities of interest and power and the realities of human nature are not the whole of reality. The reality of God stands beyond both the world that is susceptible to strategy and power and the enduring realities of human nature. As moral realism holds that there is a moral reality independent of our ideas about it, theological realism holds that our language about God or about the divine is not merely a way of expressing emotions of awe, joy, or terror. Statements about God or the divine can be true or false. Their truth or falsity, moreover, depends on a state of affairs that exists in reality, and not on our ideas about it.[25] This is a strong claim which may have unanticipated implications for believers and nonbelievers alike. On the one hand, religious truth depends on the reality of God, whether or not we know that reality. Consistency with a body of doctrine or a religious tradition may be important for many reasons, but it is not what makes a theological statement true or false. On the other hand, what is true about God is true, whether or not we know it or believe it. When theological realists make statements about God, they are saying something they believe to be true for everyone, not only for those who happen to share the belief. It is often difficult for theological realists to be as dogmatic as those who share their religious traditions would like them to be, or as tolerant of whatever beliefs people happen to hold as a pluralistic society might expect them to be.

Christian realism, however, is not a general philosophical theism, but an affirmation of statements about God drawn from what Niebuhr called

---

[24] See, for example, William Schweiker, *Theological Ethics and Global Dynamics* (Oxford: Blackwell Publishing, 2004), pp. 114–15; also Richard Bernstein, *The Abuse of Evil: The Corruption of Politics and Religion Since 9/11* (Cambridge, UK: Polity Press, 2005), pp. 29–31.
[25] Christopher Insole, *The Realist Hope* (Aldershot, UK: Ashgate Publishing, 2006), pp. 1–5.

"prophetic religion," the tradition that begins with the Hebrew prophets, who saw God both present in and standing in judgment on the human realities with which our moral lives are concerned.[26] For Christians, this realism culminates in Jesus Christ, who makes this divine reality present in the world, reveals God's judgment on it, and finally redeems it for God's own purposes. Theological statements cannot, therefore, be about some realm of divine reality distinct from the world of human experience, nor, for the Christian realist, can statements about reality be about any reality other than the one in which God is present in Christ. "There are not two realities, but *only one reality*," Bonhoeffer insisted, "and that is God's reality revealed in Christ in the reality of the world."[27]

The claim that we live in a meaningful universe is thus closely tied to the reality of *this* God, and sharply distinguished from any system of ideas or plan of action by which we might attempt to make life meaningful on our own terms. The reality of God always sets a limit on historical claims to completeness and finality, and theological realism reinforces the fallibilist approach to moral and political claims that moral realism also requires.[28] But humility and courage are not incompatible virtues, and theological realism may sustain both of them. A struggle for justice against long odds and substantial opposition may make sense only to those who believe that justice will prevail at the end of history.

CHRISTIAN REALISM AND MODERN POLITICS

Niebuhr traced the origins of this combination of political, moral, and theological realisms through Luther, Augustine, and the ethics of Jesus, back to the Hebrew prophets. In that long history, it is the relationship between Christian realism and modern political thought that will primarily concern us in this book. A more detailed account begins in Chapter 2, but it is important at the outset to see how closely Christian tradition and modern political thought are connected. Niebuhr's Christian realism sometimes seems to his critics too much at home with secularism, too heavily involved in that acceptance of existing political realities that Bonhoeffer would call "compromise."[29] We should, however, consider that some of what we call secularism originated in theological assessments of the limits and possibilities

---

[26] Niebuhr, *An Interpretation of Christian Ethics*, p. 22.   [27] Bonhoeffer, *Ethics*, p. 58.
[28] Christopher J. Insole, *The Politics of Human Frailty: A Theological Defense of Political Liberalism* (Notre Dame, IN: University of Notre Dame Press, 2005), pp. 170–7.
[29] Stanley Hauerwas, *With the Grain of the Universe: The Church's Witness and Natural Theology* (Grand Rapids, MI: Brazos Press, 2001), pp. 87–111.

of politics.[30] We should not assume that the way religion, politics, and economics come together for Niebuhr and his contemporaries was simply a reflection of conditions that prevailed in America in the mid-twentieth century. The connections and tensions go deeper into history than that.

The study of politics begins in the West with Aristotle's *Politics*, his account of the deliberations by which we order life in the *polis*, to make human goods and human virtues possible. Rome had made this *polis* larger, and Christianity had made it less final by the time Augustine came along to identify "the lowest common denominators of human existence in the *saeculum*."[31] The human goods we seek together could no longer be the ultimate objects of love, but our common need for peace and order creates something like a commonwealth, nonetheless. Deliberation moves toward more limited spheres of agreement, and the search requires a new kind of moral commitment, because the people who take on its responsibilities now know that it will not make them virtuous or happy.

This more realistic politics also became more complex with the beginning of the modern age, as social institutions became more differentiated. The Reformation meant the loss of the ideal of a unified hierarchy of religious and political authority and led to a clearer differentiation of the church and the emerging modern state. The rapid growth of trade created new financial institutions with their own international networks and patterns of authority. Commercial development and the growth of cities accelerated the differentiation of the household from the world of work, so that the family was no longer identified primarily as an economic unit in a system of agricultural or handcraft production. The rise of modern professions of law and medicine and the development of secular art and literature led to universities, theaters, printing houses, and other institutions of education and culture that were no longer tied directly to the church. Deliberations about the human good now were not only limited and specific. They took place in quite different settings, so that there could be no one system of politics, if politics is the way people organize themselves to make human goods possible.

This social pluralism was reflected in various ways in religious thought. It appears in the Lutheran idea of "orders," in Anglican understandings of an organic society that cannot be reduced to the creations of positive law, in Calvinist theories of "sphere sovereignty," and in Catholic social

[30] Reinhold Niebuhr, *Christian Realism and Political Problems*, pp. 95–103.
[31] Jean Bethke Elshtain, *Augustine and the Limits of Politics* (Notre Dame, IN: University of Notre Dame Press, 1995), p. 91.

teaching regarding "subsidiarity."[32] These ideas are by no means identical, but they point to a religious understanding of modern society that accepts institutional pluralism as integral to an understanding of human good and locates the work of the church as a distinctive task within that framework, rather than apart from it, above it, or incorporated into the program of some other political or cultural authority.

Among these differentiated social contexts in which the search for human goods now goes on, we tend to reserve the term "politics" for the sphere of law and government. In the modern world, politics is concerned with the control of states, and politics among nations is concerned with relations between states. Sometimes, the activities of the state and its agencies are designated as "public," in contrast to a large and undifferentiated "private" sphere that includes religion, culture, commerce, and family life. Politics in this modern sense is primarily about order and security. Its story is a narrative of power and the pursuit of power, the sort of things with which political realists are concerned.

Recent Christian realists, who are also political realists, have generally shared this modern understanding of politics, and in the great conflicts of the twentieth century, the power of states and the control of that power were the central issues. It is important to note, however, that this modern emphasis distorts and narrows our understanding of how society creates and maintains human goods. Politics in the original, Aristotelian sense that Augustine would have recognized still goes on, but we regard this search for human good in businesses, families, churches, schools, and so on as "private," and we do not usually call it "politics," unless we are speaking in a disparaging way of corporate "office politics" or "departmental politics" in a university.

Nevertheless, it is politics, in the original sense of deliberation about how we organize our life together to make human goods possible. To be fully realistic about politics in the twenty-first century, we will have to recover this broader meaning of the word and claim for Christian realism some theologians and political theorists who have thought in these more pluralistic terms. This point is important throughout this book, and I will often remind the reader of it by referring to "modern politics" or "the politics of law and government" when "politics" alone would ordinarily do. When I do refer to "politics" without qualification, the reader will

---

[32] For an overview of these developments in religious thought, see James W. Skillen and Rockne M. McCarthy (eds.), *Political Order and the Plural Structure of Society* (Emory University Studies in Law and Religion, No. 2; Atlanta, GA: Scholars Press, 1991).

note that I am often thinking of a much wider social process that extends beyond the actions of states and includes many things that would generally be thought of as private, or even personal. (Inevitably, I will revert to the ordinary use of "politics" in some extended discussions where the repeated use of qualifiers would become awkward and distracting.)

The rise of the modern state and the development of modern politics complicated the relations between religion and government, but it did not dissolve them. Both church and state accepted the new social pluralism and came to regard it as normative, although churches often gave up the old ideal of a union of sacred and secular authority reluctantly and governments were often tempted toward a utopian or revolutionary politics that put all aspects of the human good in the hands of the state.

Given the tendency of the churches to be a bit reactionary and the temptation of governments to become radical, it is not surprising that church and state often regarded one another warily in the emerging liberal democracies where social pluralism worked best and where the freedom it implied became normative. Church and state each suspected the other of harboring more comprehensive designs that would undermine some aspect of that normative social pluralism. Liberal democracies rarely, if ever, became completely secular or maintained an exclusive religious establishment, but the possibilities haunted them at least into the early nineteenth century, and as we shall see, this controversy shapes the understanding of what is 'public' in modern politics even today.

Such suspicions were largely forgotten in the global conflicts of the twentieth century. Liberal democracy and realistic Christianity discovered how much they had in common. Both valued democracy less for its expectations of civic virtue than for its ways of handling of self-interest and conflict. Both rejected utopian political plans and apocalyptic religious movements, because they saw that utopia and apocalypse are easily exploited by authoritarians. Both understood the importance of power and accepted the necessity of balancing power against power to obtain whatever order might be possible on a global scale and whatever approximation of justice might be achieved in domestic politics. If the liberals were confident that these propositions might all be validated without recourse to religion, realistic Christians like Reinhold Niebuhr and John Courtney Murray traced the origins of democratic politics back to Christian roots. Few at the time regarded this mixing of religious and political reasons as a problem.

Things changed as the external threats receded in the last three decades of the century. A revived interest in political theory renewed questions about religious influences on government, not by questioning the motives of religious leaders, but as a matter of political principle. If democracy means popular sovereignty, then attempts to found democratic government on a religious confession cannot succeed.[33] About the same time, theologians began to challenge the confidence of liberal Protestantism that Christian faith and secular, scientific thought could be reconciled, particularly on matters of human nature and human society. A movement began for direct, public witness to Christian truth, without concessions to the idea that faith ought to make us better citizens or better people. A struggle developed over access to and control of the public square, waged in the pages of academic journals, in the courts, and on happily rare occasions, in physical struggles in the public square itself.

Developments in political theory and in theology have thus contributed to a renewal of the historic tensions between religion and government in the liberal democracies, and efforts to resolve the arguments within the framework of modern politics have proved inconclusive. From a Christian realist point of view, a complete, systematic resolution is impossible and undesirable. The tension between religion and government is inevitable, and it is part of that larger search for the human good which is properly called "politics." Our understanding of the tension is improved, however, by setting it in this larger framework, and in this book Chapter 4, in particular, will be devoted to that reinterpretation.

NEW REALITIES

Things have changed, not only in theology and political theory, but in the political realities that our theories are supposed to help us understand. The changes have been most sweeping in global politics. When the Cold War ended, the strategies of deterrence, containment, and balance-of-power by which realist leaders had successfully managed the superpower rivalry became obsolete. It was suddenly unclear who had enough power to require consideration and counterbalance. Fragmentation of empires was the order of the day. The new forces which emerged included established states like the members of the old Warsaw Pact, who could now operate more independently, but also nationalist movements like the Bosnian Serbs or the Tamil Tigers, who might press for the breakup of the states in which they lived. At the low end of the spectrum of organization and resources,

---

[33] Franklin Gamwell, *Politics as a Christian Vocation* (Cambridge: Cambridge University Press, 2005), pp. 69–70.

fundamentalist networks and terrorist organizations challenged established states for the control of territory, whereas at the high end, multinational corporations took advantage of increased global trade and new technologies to gain greater independence from local authorities in the countries where they operate.

In ways that became apparent only after what Niebuhr called "the structure of nations and empires"[34] had collapsed, realism had depended on successful modern states to control a whole range of other economic, political, and cultural forces and especially to keep those forces off the global stage, so that politics at that level could be viewed as a problem of relations between states with competing interests and goals. Those who understood the elegant simplifications of that theory best also knew that it was limited to a particular period in history.[35] The theory would work only as long as nation states occupied the key role in organizing the multiple, competing forces of religion, commerce, and culture within their borders and as long as they could prevent those forces from constituting transnational movements and institutions beyond the easy reach of state power. That order had lasted a long time before realist political theorists came along, but many now believe that the order no longer exists in the way required for the theory to work. They are less clear about how to understand what is coming next.

Christian realists are reluctant to make predictions, but eager for understanding. In this book, we will try to comprehend these new realities by taking a longer look at the history that got us to this point and a broader look at the conduct of politics. We will see how interactions between social contexts of government, religion, business, family, and culture shape the search for the human good, first in more local, less differentiated ways and then on a global scale.

We will begin with an examination of the disputed legacy of Christian realism itself (Chapter 1). With the end of the Cold War, we lost the set of circumstances that held a variety of Christian thinkers in consensus on a realistic understanding of politics and society and allied them with a liberal understanding of modern democracy. Christian realism itself has become disputed territory, with rival understandings of the realist legacy competing for attention and adherents. Some whose background and convictions might predictably have made them Christian realists now reject the label, whereas former critics of Christian realism find themselves, perhaps to their

[34] Reinhold Niebuhr, *The Structure of Nations and Empires* (New York: Charles Scribner's Sons, 1959).
[35] Cf. Hans J. Morgenthau, *Politics Among Nations*, p. 9.

own surprise, drawing on realist lessons to explain what has gone wrong with the quasi-apocalyptic interpretations of recent events.

Understanding those differences requires a longer perspective on the history of Christian realism (Chapter 2). By returning to its origins in Augustine's theology, we will see more clearly how Christian realism contrasts with other Christian ideas about faith and society. By tracing a new idea of secular authority that emerged from the Protestant Reformation, we will understand the close connections between Christian realism and the development of modern politics, but we will also find resources for a more pluralistic understanding of society that becomes increasingly relevant as the role of the state changes and other social forces are transformed into global powers of a different sort.

Creating a framework for this new, pluralist Christian realism will require extensive rethinking of the understanding of politics and society that Christian realists and liberal theorists created together and that has now become a source of tension between them (Chapters 3 and 4). A pluralistic understanding of society that includes multiple centers of responsible action gave the Christian realists their best response to ideologies that brought all politics under a single authority, although few writers in theology or Christian ethics have given this social pluralism the development it requires. That task is made more urgent by the intellectual changes that have set liberal theory and Christian theology at odds over the requirements of modern politics. What both liberal theory and unapologetic Christianity want is to maintain their own integrity, but it is not clear that either can do that in a politics that includes both of them and allows for only one public forum. Pluralistic Christian realism suggests that a more comprehensive view of politics allows us to maintain both the integrity of various discussions of the human good and the relationships between them.

This is not just a question of reconciling theology and political theory. It allows us to understand what is happening to politics on a global scale (Chapter 5). The balance of power between states by which realistic diplomats, strategists, and theorists sustained a global order through the Cold War era must now be turned to balancing a variety of social forces that now move easily across the international boundaries that previously kept all of them reasonably well under state control. The relations between religion, state, and business are especially important in this new reality, because religious movements and global corporations are claiming the dominant role that has until now clearly belonged to states. Peace and security may now require balancing those forces on a global scale with the same realism that was once devoted to balancing the power of states.

Christian realism takes an interest in all of these questions, from the intricacies of political theory to the complexities of global politics. It has never been withdrawn from the world or content to repeat one solution to all of the world's changing realities. But from Augustine's time, too, it has not seen the vicissitudes of human nature as the last word on human destiny. A restatement of Christian realism for a new century must return in the end to the reminder of limits and the affirmation of hope with which we began (Chapter 6). Beyond the limits of our knowledge, imagination, and love that become so evident in the realities of politics, Christian faith sustains our hope that we live in a meaningful universe. But a meaningful universe, if the Christian realists' statements about God are true, imposes its own limitations on politics, and we will want to conclude by asking what we can say about what those limitations are and how we might continue to say it in a pluralistic, global politics.

CHAPTER I

Reflections on the End of an Era

THE CRISIS

At the end of 1933, the future looked grim for the social and political order that had dominated the world at the end of the nineteenth century. Europe had destroyed a generation of its youth in a disastrous war and disrupted the world economy, and the effects were still being felt more than a decade later. The only signs of recovery seemed to be in Russia, Germany, and Japan, places that had abandoned democracy and capitalism for a communist or nationalist vision that would be spread by revolution or by conquest.

In light of those political and historical realities, Reinhold Niebuhr abandoned the sentimental hope of the Social Gospel that Christian ideals would change social realities for the better. Realism required a harder look at the pervasive self-interest of the rich and the need for power of the poor. Like early Christian apocalyptic or Marxist revolutionary theory, Christian realism also seemed to require a recognition that civilization had arrived at the end of an age. The foundations of social life had been so disrupted that conventional wisdom and established expectations could no longer guide responsible action.[1]

This theme distressed many of Niebuhr's Christian readers, who still wanted to see the Gospel as a strategy for social transformation, but Niebuhr repeated the point even more forcefully a little more than a year later in *Reflections on the End of an Era*.[2] Marxist revolutionaries might be subject to their own delusions, and nationalist and imperialist tyrants were simply evil, but the world of bourgeois democracy was coming to an end. What Christians needed was an independent Christian ethic, sufficiently freed from the assumptions of a dying civilization to guide action under the new

---

[1] Reinhold Niebuhr, *Moral Man and Immoral Society* (Louisville, KY: Westminster John Knox Press, 2001), pp. 155–6.
[2] Reinhold Niebuhr, *Reflections on the End of an Era* (New York: Charles Scribner's Sons, 1934).

conditions that were just beginning to become clear.[3] Christian realism was meant to be that independent Christian ethic.

Niebuhr's anticipation of the end of an era of bourgeois culture continued at least to the eve of the Second World War,[4] but the world that emerged on the far side of the crisis was hardly the one that Niebuhr had anticipated. A judicious postwar application of American diplomacy and economic power through the Marshall Plan restored economic order to Europe more quickly than the punitive terms of the Versailles Treaty had done after the First World War, and it was a capitalist economic order, at that. A policy of containment and balance of power halted Soviet expansion at least as effectively as military force might have done. The liberal democracies embarked on a period of unprecedented cooperation and economic growth, contradicting Stalin's interpretation of Marxist theory, which predicted a return to ruinous wars between competing capitalist powers and anticipated that the last half of the twentieth century would be the Soviet moment.[5]

Liberal democracy and market economics fared better in the twentieth century than either Marxists or political realists might have expected at the beginning. This ought to make us cautious about Christian realism as a tool for predicting the future, but it seems nevertheless that we begin the twenty-first century on the far side of the historical transition that Reinhold Niebuhr saw looming before him at the beginning of the 1930s. It may be as difficult now to say exactly what has ended as it was to predict the details of that ending before the fact.

For some, liberal democracy and market economics have survived their great test and emerged triumphant to shape the human future for the next period of history. Unencumbered by empire and authority, choice and efficiency will rule the world. The globalization of trade and commerce will bring unprecedented freedom and prosperity, after the initial dislocations necessary to align markets and governments to these new realities. Others see the dislocations but expect quite different results for those who are left behind by these developments.[6] They anticipate a long period of structural poverty, widening gaps between rich and poor, and increased political and environmental instability, unrelieved by any effective limits on the market

---

[3] Reinhold Niebuhr, *An Interpretation of Christian Ethics* (New York: Seabury Press, 1979), p. 1.

[4] See, for example, his address to the Oxford Conference on Church, Community, and State in 1937, published in Reinhold Niebuhr, *Christianity and Power Politics* (New York: Charles Scribner's Sons, 1940), pp. 203–26.

[5] Robert Service, *Stalin: A Biography* (Cambridge, MA: Harvard University Press, 2005), pp. 503–04, 565–7.

[6] Joseph E. Stiglitz, *Globalization and Its Discontents* (New York: W. W. Norton, 2002).

forces now released from political control and unthreatened by revolutionary opposition.

What all agree is that these changes are so fundamental that they cannot be managed entirely by diplomats and trade negotiators. They are changing politics within nations as well as among them, as people return to their most basic ideas about society and human purposes to find guidance for dealing with these new realities. Each of these views of our present situation has its own academic theorists, its political leaders and strategic planners who see the world through its lens, and its commentators, bloggers, analysts, and editorialists who urge the public to think in its terms. We will consider many of them more specifically as we proceed.

To begin, however, we need to see the variety of ways available to interpret Reinhold Niebuhr's legacy for our time. Niebuhr's ways of thinking still seem illuminating to many people, perhaps even more today than in the years just after his death in 1971. But something has changed, too. The world to which he spoke is not our world, and how we understand Christian realism depends in large part on where we think the transition lies and what, exactly, we think has ended. If what ended was the Cold War, we may need to rethink the meaning of security in a world that is now dangerous in different ways from the dangers Niebuhr knew. If what ended was the conflict between freedom and totalitarianism, we will have to learn what freedom means in a world where we cannot easily define it by pointing to places where it is absent. If what ended was the era that we have lived in since the Reformation and the rise of the modern state, we will have to ask what it means to be realistic when the most familiar social and political realities have disappeared or taken different forms. Niebuhr's ways of thinking still seem illuminating to many people. The problem is that holding his different ways of thinking together proves more difficult than he made it appear.

TWENTY-FIRST-CENTURY REALISMS

We can organize this complex field of possibilities by identifying four kinds of contemporary Christian realism:

1. First, there is the antirealist, uncompromising politics of the Christian Witness. We should perhaps not think of this as a version of Christian realism at all, except that it is so clearly shaped by its explicit rejection of the Christian realist understanding of faith and politics. Once the moral confusion of modern ideas of freedom, justice, and human rights has

been recognized, the critical task of Christian ethics is to disentangle the Christian witness from the web of connections that the Christian realists wove to link prophetic faith to American democracy. What Christians need to think and do in the face of the new realities becomes almost a mirror image of the way the Niebuhrians faced the political world of their day.

2. The Antiutopian Realist stakes a more direct claim to the legacy of Christian realism. These are the people most likely to ask, "Where is Reinhold Niebuhr when we need him?" Their company is large and growing, and includes theologians, political theorists, commentators, and international relations experts.[7] They share a Niebuhrian emphasis on the persistence of evil in social and political life, and they urge us to keep our expectations for human progress appropriately limited. They remind us that governments must be prepared to use power to restrain evil. That is what government is for. Antiutopian Realists differ over whether governments and political activity can accomplish much more than that, but they agree that without the rough approximations of peace and order that power can impose, nothing else would be possible.

3. The Counterapocalyptic Realist, by contrast, warns that those who are in charge of maintaining approximate peace and order are likely to over-estimate their own virtue and exaggerate the wickedness of their opponents. In Niebuhr's work, antiutopian and counterapocalyptic ideas are two sides of the same coin, offering a realistic vindication of democratic order while avoiding an exaggerated account of democratic virtues.[8] Under the stress of changing global realities and the changing role that America plays in the world, this balanced assessment tends to break apart, with the Counterapocalyptic Realists urging restraint on the same forces that Antiutopian Realists are eager to set free to restore peace and order.

4. The Pluralist Realist recognizes both the importance of order and the limits of virtue in a way that locates this appropriation of the Niebuhrian legacy uneasily between the Antiutopian Realist and the Counterapocalyptic Realist, but the Pluralist Realist is less inclined to view present crises in apocalyptic terms. New global realities are seen as further developments in a struggle between religious, economic, political, and cultural

---

[7] For a survey of some of these political analyses, see Paul Elie, "A Man for All Reasons," *Atlantic Monthly* 300 (November 2007), 82–96.

[8] This is seen most clearly in Reinhold Niebuhr, *The Children of Light and the Children of Darkness* (New York: Charles Scribner's Sons, 1960), pp. 9–33.

forces that have shaped the modern world from the beginning. In the aftermath of the Reformation and the collapse of feudal society, those who shaped politics at the beginning of the modern era wanted order. Their success produced diversity. They wanted peace. Their success got them freedom. What they learned was that no power – political, economic, or religious – can be trusted to settle every question. So a realist committed to peace and freedom has to ask not "Who should win?" but "How do we sustain the conflict?"

These four positions – the Witness, the Antiutopian, the Counterapocalyptic, and the Pluralist – make different judgments about the current state of world politics. The range of possibilities for Christian realism today can be delineated by considering each position in more detail, and we should do that before coming to any conclusions about the possibility of a contemporary Christian realism that would be as united in its vision as the Niebuhrian realism of the mid-twentieth century.

THE WITNESS

Will Herberg, Niebuhr's Jewish counterpart in interpreting the relationship between religion and American society, described a consensus on the "American Way of Life" that embraced the major faiths and derived much of its moral authority from them. Herberg had few illusions about the depths of this moral commitment. He understood that the "American Way of Life" tended to put religious traditions at the service of patriotism and personal fulfillment, but he also shared a Niebuhrian hope that even weak moral aspirations might eventually lead to greater justice. Because all moral ideals are flawed and limited, the question becomes whether the ones we have available have some capacity to change prevailing practices. Herberg thought that the almost universal acknowledgement of the American consensus might create an opening for religious activity that "could in the longer view transform the inner character of American religion and bring it closer to the faith it professes."[9]

If that hope seemed plausible to many Christians and Jews in 1955, it is a measure of how much things have changed in half a century that some theologians now regard it as one of the worst illusions perpetuated by their Protestant forebears. Unlike nostalgic forms of popular religion that yearn for the good old days or Christian political activists who want to restore

---

[9] Will Herberg, *Protestant, Catholic, Jew* (New York: Doubleday and Company, 1955), p. 289.

the religious foundations of law and government, these theologians are happy to leave the American way of life behind for good. Its loss is not the result of political and social changes that might be reversed. Nor was the American consensus the result of a compromise with secular realities that the theologians have now suddenly decided to revoke. The world promised by Herberg's "American Way of Life" never really existed. Christians can no longer cherish the illusion of a widely shared way of life that also meets the requirements of faith. They can only offer a witness to religious truth left suddenly aware that it has no home in this world.

In recent Christian ethics, Stanley Hauerwas best represents this position of the Witness, and he is also the most clear about how his theological views differ from those of Christian realism. According to Hauerwas, the truths of Christian faith must be held in a community formed by a shared narrative, which shapes individual character and makes shared moral judgments possible. To follow the crucified and risen Christ demands disciplines of peaceableness, patience, and forgiveness that do not come naturally. Witnesses are formed by living in a community that listens to that narrative and accepts its judgment on their lives.[10]

Hauerwas's move to a narrative ethics marks an important departure from the moral realism that is part of the complex of Christian realist ethics. For him, the human good is determined by the narrative, in contrast to moral realism, which locates human good in objective, natural conditions that are imperfectly and fallibly comprehended by narratives, traditions, and working agreements that we use to discuss the good. Hauerwas dismisses this moral realism, rather than directly denying it. It is, of course, the case that every human community requires certain objective conditions and commitments if it is to survive and prosper. In that sense, theological virtues of faith, hope, and love that sustain the church are also perfectly "natural" virtues, too. But what we can learn about human good from the moral realist's examination of community is a pale reflection of the rich, precise meanings that these virtues take on in the context of the Christian narrative.[11]

Liberal democracy, according to Hauerwas, is structured around a commitment to these vague, general, and "natural" virtues, and it tries to insulate political life from potential conflicts caused by people bringing their identity-forming narratives into the public square. As a result, liberal

---

[10] Stanley Hauerwas, *The Peaceable Kingdom* (Notre Dame, IN: University of Notre Dame Press, 1983), pp. 102–11.
[11] *Ibid.*, p. 103

democracy lacks a narrative strong enough to sustain a community and form a virtuous people. The flaw is inherent in the system. It is not something that might be corrected by rediscovering a narrative in our history or by identifying a civil religion that provides a basis for community in a nation of rugged individualists.

Hauerwas deals with Reinhold Niebuhr's realism primarily by subsuming it under the larger program of liberal democracy. Niebuhr's work shares the general failings of liberalism, with the result that Niebuhr's once powerful attempt to connect Christian faith and moral realism collapses in the general loss of confidence in a political community built on natural virtues. "In an odd way, Niebuhr's work now represents the worst of two worlds: most secular people do not find his theological arguments convincing; yet his theology is not sufficient to provide the means for Christians to sustain their lives."[12] Hauerwas's argument for dismissing Niebuhr in this way relies heavily on evidence that Niebuhr was influenced early in his theological education by the philosophy of pragmatism and by William James's account of religious experience. We might ask whether this is an adequate account of Niebuhr's mature theology in *The Nature and Destiny of Man*. Certainly, pragmatists from John Dewey, Sidney Hook, and Morton White to, more recently, Richard Bernstein, have raised philosophical questions about Niebuhr's theological claims.[13] They do not recognize in him the pragmatist that Hauerwas sees so clearly.

Our present purpose, however, is not to defend Niebuhr against Hauerwas's interpretation of his work, but to see what becomes of Christian realism when one treats it as part of a more general criticism of political and theological liberalism. First, Hauerwas warns that liberalism's efforts to maintain neutrality between competing narratives may lead to the suppression of religious identity in public life. Religion is irreducible to individual goals and interests, so liberalism adopts cultural strategies and perhaps even legal restrictions that force religion out of public life. Christian realists may even cooperate in this neutralization of religion, given their commitment to the liberal project. In this, Hauerwas joins a more widely shared complaint. Stephen Carter has argued that there is a bias against religion among cultural elites that belittles faith and obscures its importance to our history and culture.[14] Richard Neuhaus contends that Americans have privatized

---

[12] Stanley Hauerwas, *With the Grain of the Universe: The Church's Witness and Natural Theology* (Grand Rapids, MI: Brazos Press, 2001), p. 139.

[13] See Richard Bernstein, *The Abuse of Evil: The Corruption of Politics and Religion Since 9/11* (Malden, MA: Polity Press, 2005), p. 61.

[14] Stephen Carter, *The Culture of Disbelief* (New York: Basic Books, 1993).

religion and excluded religious ideas, symbols, and values from public discourse.[15]

Hauerwas's disillusionment with liberalism runs deeper, however. Neuhaus and Carter hope to create a climate in which religion can more easily find expression in the public square. Hauerwas is skeptical that it belongs there at all. Public religion has a hard time remaining authentically religious. Liberalism, lacking a narrative of its own that could inspire commitment to the public good, is apt to adopt any powerful religious narrative that is publicly available and press it into service for its own purposes. This is the problem of "Constantinianism." "Put simply," Hauerwas says, "Constantinianism is the attempt to make Christianity necessary, to make the church at home in the world, in a manner that witness is no longer required."[16] A political order that welcomes Christianity into public life has probably reduced Christianity's distinctive identity to a few harmless civic virtues that support loyalty to the state and good functioning of the government.

What, then, are those who understand politics in these terms supposed to do? The short answer is that they are to live their faith in community with one another and in witness to the world. "The first task of Christian social ethics," for Hauerwas, "is not to make the 'world' better or more just, but to help Christian people form their community consistent with their conviction that the story of Christ is a truthful account of our existence."[17] Becoming that kind of community is not an enabling exercise for people whose real task is justice and peace in the world. Becoming that kind of community is the most that Christians can accomplish. Witness is not an exhortation to the wider society to become more moral, more just, or more like the Christian community, as though such a thing were possible. Witness is the integrity of the church's claim to be what it is.

As Hauerwas sees it, it is risky to take witness much beyond this point. Because the Christian narrative sets the terms on which the church's witness can be true, a witness does not expect to appear truthful, or even understandable, to a society that does not share the narrative. The loss of moral realism radicalizes the idea of witness by insisting that it is impossible to render Christian truth comprehensible apart from the Christian narrative.

---

[15] Richard J. Neuhaus, *The Naked Public Square* (Grand Rapids, MI: Eerdmans, 1984).
[16] Hauerwas, *With the Grain of the Universe*, p. 221.
[17] Stanley Hauerwas, *A Community of Character* (Notre Dame, IN: University of Notre Dame Press, 1981), p. 10.

It is not a matter of learning from experience when to speak to the world and when not to. The effort to communicate a narrated truth outside of its narrative context never works.

This has some odd results. Hauerwas begins his most important public lectures by repeatedly assuring his audience that they will find his perfectly straightforward statements of traditional Christian teaching incomprehensible.[18] In a world of narrated truth, it is apparently impossible that someone might understand and yet disagree. Because the narrative creates the truth for those who participate in its community, the alternatives are assent or unintelligibility.

Hauerwas, however, sometimes writes as though the community of witnesses were not only misunderstood, but also under threat. The task is not just to help people form a community of shared truth, but to "become a polity that has the character necessary to survive as a truthful society" in the wider context of American public life.[19] It is not clear whether this is a contingent, historical judgment on the present state of liberal democracy or an element of the theological narrative. Hauerwas believes that the failure of the liberal project has pitched American society into an anxious and idolatrous search for alternative sources of meaning. His analysis at this point comes very close to Niebuhr's Augustinian view of politics, though Hauerwas thinks that Niebuhr could not have seen this crisis coming, because he was too closely identified with the assumptions of American society in his day.[20] One might argue, by contrast, that Hauerwas is so committed to his portrait of Niebuhr as a Jamesian liberal that he fails to recognize the family resemblance between his critique of liberal democracy and the Christian realist assessment of democracy's characteristic illusions.

What is clear is that Hauerwas believes that in today's world, with democratic governments engaged in a tightly orchestrated effort to sustain public confidence, a church that holds back on the margins of the public square and fails to offer the expected endorsement will be seen as a threat. In that situation, the power of public authority will in turn become a threat to the church. "For the idolatry most convenient to us all," Hauerwas writes, "remains the presumed primacy of the nation-state."[21] At least that is where Hauerwas thinks we are. It may be that the Christian realist turned Witness believes this is where we will always be.

---

[18] Hauerwas, *With the Grain of the Universe*, p. 15.   [19] Hauerwas, *A Community of Character*, p. 3.
[20] Hauerwas, *With the Grain of the Universe*, pp. 139–40.
[21] Hauerwas, *A Community of Character*, p. 110.

THE ANTIUTOPIAN REALIST

In contrast to the Witness, who largely abandons moral realism, the Antiu-topian Realist finds moral realism an important resource in times of social disorder and moral confusion. Sorting things out begins with recognizing particular, concrete events for what they are. Jean Bethke Elshtain made this the starting point for her understanding of the events of September 11, 2001, and for her evaluation of the American response. Particular, concrete events must first be recognized for what they are. Flying airplanes into skyscrapers to cause indiscriminate death, destruction, and public horror is terrorism. To call it murder confuses it with ordinary criminality. To call it martyrdom veils the concrete evil with a fabric of interpretation. Interpretation is essential, but interpretations work only if the concrete events are seen at the outset for what they are. Get the facts wrong, and the narrative as a whole will be false.[22]

Elshtain traces her moral realism at this point back to Reinhold Niebuhr, who held that it is possible to make discriminating moral judgments about particular events, even when it is clear that all parties in the situation fall short of the demands of ideal justice. Niebuhr's understanding of politics was centered on power, and power inevitably exaggerates its own goodness to achieve its goals. This, Niebuhr believed, is already apparent in the bib-lical stories of Jesus and the teaching of the prophets. "If one realizes to what degree every civilization, as a system of power, idealizes and rational-izes its system of power and how these rationalizations invariably include standards of morals which serve the moral and spiritual pride of the ruling oligarchy, it is apparent that an attack upon Pharisaism is really an attack upon the final and most confusing and dishonest pretension of power."[23] Maintaining the ultimate standard of judgment that dissipates the confu-sion and reveals the pretense is the particular task of religious ethics, but that vocation does not require the theologian to give up the ordinary moral task of drawing distinctions between greater and lesser evils, nor should it prevent us from recognizing evil when we encounter it. Thus, Niebuhr cautioned against illusions of American virtue in the years after the Second World War and called for a more multilateral approach to global problems, but when the Soviet Union sent troops into Hungary in 1956, Niebuhr

---

[22] Jean Bethke Elshtain, *Just War against Terror: The Burden of American Power in a Violent World* (New York: Basic Books, 2003), pp. 9–19.

[23] Reinhold Niebuhr, *The Nature and Destiny of Man: A Christian Interpretation* (Louisville, KY: Westminster John Knox Press, 1996), vol. I, 225.

condemned the invasion and heaped scorn on Karl Barth's "eschatological" theology that found such alternations in political systems beneath its notice.[24]

What particularly interests Elshtain are the political effects of this lack of realism. Those who incorporate particular historical events into a larger narrative about the inevitability of violence and the corruptions of all forms of power are apt to suppose that moral insight alone will eventually bring all of the equally guilty parties to repentance. Although those who hold to secular narratives of progress may be driven to despair by recurrent wars and human aggression, those who anticipate a religious redemption are paradoxically susceptible to utopian illusions that peace can be achieved without the need for discriminating judgments about relative good and evil, and without the need for concrete measures to enforce those judgments against evildoers. In such utopias, Elshtain observes, "politics disappears. The conflict and reconciliation of human wills that is politics no longer mars the beatific landscape. One way or another, the 'eschatological moment' of the Kingdom of God at the end of time is brought down to earth, secularized, placed within time, and embraced as a realizable goal – despite the fact that over the long course of humankind's bloody history nothing remotely approximating this vision has ever been attained."[25]

It is this utopianism that Elshtain found pervasive in American religious responses to the events of September 11. Church leaders seemed unable to arrive at a condemnation of the terrorist attacks that was not qualified by a more general confession of guilt and an acknowledgment that religious and political alternatives to violence had failed. From a Niebuhrian perspective, this indiscriminate judgment is correct as far as it goes, but it cannot be the last word, because it offers no guidance for the appropriate use of power to respond to particular evil. Elshtain was not the only political theorist to call attention to this issue. Kenneth Anderson observed immediately after September 11 that preachers wanted " . . . to maintain the moral purity of pacifism while still sounding relevant to the real world of conflict, sin, and death. They recognized the inevitability of armed retaliation, but elided the question of its legitimacy."[26] Without that evaluation of realistic responses to specific events, theology drifts toward utopian dreams of a moral resolution without specific judgment or action.

---

[24] Reinhold Niebuhr, *Essays in Applied Christianity*, D. B. Robertson (ed.) (New York: Meridian Books, 1959), p. 186.
[25] Elshtain, *Just War Against Terror*, p. 127.
[26] Kenneth Anderson, "Language, Law, and Terror," *Times Literary Supplement*, No. 5138 (September 21, 2001), 13.

The efforts of Antiutopian Realists to guide judgment and action in the months after September 11, 2001, centered on relating just war criteria to the new realities of international terrorism. Opinions differed over how to pursue Al Qaeda in Afghanistan and Pakistan, and Antiutopian Realists differed more sharply over the American invasion of Iraq in 2003. They could agree, however, that this was where the moral and theological issues come into focus. In the aftermath of the terrorist attacks, the United States had responsibilities to its own people and to global civilization. Using force to repel aggression was part of the government's obligation to its citizens. Measuring that force against criteria of discrimination and proportionality was an obligation to the international community. Utopians might imagine a different world in which force would be unnecessary, or where international organizations would be in a position to make effective judgments about its use. In the real world, those choices fall to the governments of nations, which may aspire to a grander role in history, but which earn their legitimate powers by providing their citizens with security and order. By the events of September 11, Jean Bethke Elshtain wrote, "we are reminded of what governments are for."[27]

What governments are for is security against external aggression and internal disorder. They provide a limited justice, which makes people neither good nor loving, but keeps their vices and injustices from threatening the welfare of their neighbors or the stability of society. Utopians may want more than this, but Antiutopian Realists will keep a watchful eye on the main task, lest those who are responsible for security and limited justice become distracted. What modern Christian realists understand better than their Reformation-era forebears is that rulers need advice as well as power, and constitutional limits as well as legitimate authority.[28] So the theologian cannot avoid going beyond the general prophetic condemnation of all unrighteousness to some specific advice about how imperfect and not altogether virtuous leaders ought to use the power that is placed in their hands. The Witness will complain that those who offer their governments reasons for war and violence are less than true Christians,[29] but Antiutopian Realists will reply that they have a witness of their own to maintain. It is a witness that articulates the limits that fallen human nature imposes on politics and insists that political leaders conduct their office within those boundaries.

---

[27] Elshtain, *Just War against Terror*, p. 46.
[28] Cf. Niebuhr, *The Children of Light and the Children of Darkness*, p. 44.
[29] Cf. Stanley Hauerwas and Paul J. Griffiths, "War, Peace, and Jean Bethke Elshtain," *First Things* 136 (2003), 41–7.

Glenn Tinder articulates the connection between this Antiutopian understanding of politics and Christian belief:

One reason for the powerful appeal of the ideal of justice lies in the vision it represents – a vision of perfect worldly order... Even though Christians have shared [that vision], it is essentially Hellenic, depending on the sense that being is primarily order rather than history... that understanding the order of being is the proper work of the intellect, and that reconstructing it, in the world around, is within the scope of human powers. These premises are in conflict with the Christian understanding of things.[30]

From this perspective, the Witness is simply wrong to see realistic theology and political power entwined in a Constantinian embrace. The Antiutopian Realist sees the interaction of faith and politics as a continuing tension. Religious judgments are always in danger of being dismissed, ridiculed, or even persecuted, but prophetic religion nevertheless provides the critical self-limitation that keeps a political community from overreaching and overconfidence. Christian realism persists in public discourse, not because it is always welcome, but because when its critical function fails, the corruption or failure of the political system itself follows not far behind. Antiutopian Realists enter into the discussion about power and the use of force as full participants. An appropriate sense of the limits of politics keeps them from expecting too much. An appropriate anxiety about what will happen if politics loses this critical self-limitation keeps them involved.

The Antiutopian Realists have recently been joined by a number of political theorists, policy analysts, and commentators who find the warning about the limits of politics timely, whether or not they share the theology behind it. The apparent failure of the Bush administration to achieve the easy establishment of democracy that it anticipated in Iraq has led to a recalculation of the advantages and limits of "superpower" status, even when there is only one nation that enjoys it. Some of these observers explicitly recall the political realism of American policy immediately after the Second World War and Niebuhr's role in shaping it.[31]

In those postwar years, a careful calculation of the national interest and a recognition of the limits on American power and American virtue led to a global strategy of cooperation and containment, rather than aggressive expansion into other areas of the globe. By contrast, some policy makers

---

[30] Glenn Tinder, *The Political Meaning of Christianity: An Interpretation* (Baton Rouge: Louisiana State University Press, 1989), pp. 64–5.

[31] Anatol Lieven and John Hulsman, *Ethical Realism* (New York: Pantheon Books, 2006), pp. 55–83; Peter Beinart, *The Good Fight* (San Francisco: Harper Collins, 2006), p. 16.

greeted the end of the Cold War with an expansionist realism that saw apparently unchallenged American power as an occasion for the spread of American ideals. Lawrence Kaplan and William Kristol emphasized this new attitude when they wrote in 2003, "After we have already seen dictatorships toppled by democratic forces in such seemingly unlikely places as the Philippines, Indonesia, Chile, Nicaragua, Paraguay, Taiwan, and South Korea, how utopian is it to imagine a change of regime in a place like Iraq? . . . With democratic change sweeping the world at an unprecedented rate over the past decades, is it truly 'realistic' to insist that we quit now?"[32] Subsequent events have suggested a more restrained version of realism, even to many who at first supported the idea that America could fight terrorism by aggressively spreading democracy.

There was no consensus on policy or strategy among these Antiutopian Realists. Some, like Elshtain, continued to support the Iraq War as necessary for American self-interest and security. Others argued that Iraq marked the failure of American hegemony and proposed a new policy of multilateral cooperation and the strictly limited resorting to military intervention. What seems to unite them, however, is the Antiutopian recognition that governments, given sufficient power, can provide security and order; but even when they have a great deal more power than they strictly need, they cannot guarantee peace and justice. Those who carry these reflections beyond the implications for policy and strategy often conclude with Reinhold Niebuhr that the reasons for this lie in human nature and the way it shapes and limits human community.[33]

THE COUNTERAPOCALYPTIC REALIST

The changes in the world that were dramatized by the events of September 11 elicit other responses, alongside antiutopian questions about the realistic use of power. Most notably, there is the apocalyptic vision of the terrorists themselves. Their leaders, as nearly as we can determine from their taped messages and a tardy reconstruction of their thinking after the fact, see themselves engaged in a struggle to reshape the whole human world, rejecting the corruptions of the West and overthrowing the states which modernity brought into being and which now sustain modern life by their power. No clear plan connects the acts of terror and the end of the West.

---

[32] Lawrence F. Kaplan and William Kristol, *The War over Iraq: Saddam's Tyranny and America's Mission* (San Francisco: Encounter Books, 2003), p. 111.

[33] Jean Bethke Elshtain, "Against the New Utopianism," *Studies in Christian Ethics* 20 (2007), 52–4.

Like other acts of religious violence, they anticipate the end of the present order of events, rather than working within it.[34]

Muslim intellectuals have pursued their own development of what we might call an Islamic political realism to refute the religious justifications of this apocalyptic violence and turn the legitimate grievances and resentments of Muslims back into the channels of political action.[35] There is little that Western Christian realists can contribute directly to this reassessment. The Antiutopian Realists simply reject the jihadists' apocalyptic narrative and move to gather the forces that will restore security and prevent future terrorist violence. The Counterapocalyptic Realists, however, are concerned with a Western apocalypse that has emerged as a reaction to the jihadist one.

At the popular level, this Western apocalypse seems to grow from a lost sense of control over events and lost hope for the future. The spiritual and psychological impact of terrorist attacks is compounded by a series of brutal civil conflicts and devastating humanitarian crises. All these events are made present in a vivid way by instantaneous communications and twenty-four-hour news channels. Signals of global climate change intimate that we may have already done irreversible damage to our environment. Even natural events – earthquakes, tsunamis, and threats of pandemic disease – are incorporated into a general sense that the order of things is dissolving and that the ordinary language of planning and evaluation is quite inadequate to the occasion.[36]

Thus, we experience again something like the uncertain times in which Christianity spread rapidly across the Roman Empire and appreciate in new ways the apocalyptic passages in the New Testament. We also begin to understand why an apocalyptic understanding of Christianity "has been embraced down the ages by humble, generous, and hopeful believers as giving them guidance to living lives of faith in hard and terrifying times."[37]

Today, this narrative sometimes takes explicitly the form and language of fundamentalist Christianity, in which widespread immorality and the apparent triumph of evil become signs of the "end-time" in which God is about to act. Other versions of the apocalypse are thoroughly secular,

---

[34] Mark Juergensmeyer, *Terror in the Mind of God: The Global Rise of Religious Violence* (Berkeley: University of California Press, 2000), pp. 162–3.

[35] See, for example, Olivier Roy, *Globalized Islam: The Search for a New Ummah* (New York: Columbia University Press, 2004), pp. 41–57; Tariq Ramadan, *Western Muslims and the Future of Islam* (New York: Oxford University Press, 2004), pp. 158–61.

[36] Duncan B. Forrester, *Apocalypse Now?* (Aldershot, UK: Ashgate Publishing, 2005), pp. 49–64.

[37] *Ibid.*, p. 52.

focusing on ecological catastrophes that might bring an end to civilization as we know it. But apocalypse is also sometimes political. Counterapocalyptic theologians detect in the speeches of political leaders and the slogans of the "War on Terrorism" an appropriation of the language of ultimacy also found among the fundamentalists. The use of force against the powers of evil, the promise of decisive action that will end the ambiguities of history, and a conviction that any appearance of failure must be illusory invest the actions of government with an importance that transcends politics and history. As Catherine Keller puts it, "The unknowable gains daily in end-time density: How will our 'defensive' aggressions produce security and not endless war? Might the terrorists get nuclear weapons? smallpox?... The uncertainty lurches at moments toward the unbearable. Yet it is the tone of *certainty* that rings apocalyptic: the certainty of what is evil – and so of 'our' goodness."[38]

What the Counterapocalyptic Realist rejects is the coupling of this apocalyptic certainty with political power. Apocalyptic thinking allows a leader to claim the present as a time of unprecedented risk and unique opportunity. Ordinary critical questions do not apply in apocalyptic time, and past experience offers no guidance and no meaningful warnings. Everything depends on fidelity to the vision of the future, and the leader claims to dispose of lives and resources without accountability to standards that belong to an old age that is passing away.

In those circumstances, the role of biblical faith is to insist that "the end is not yet."[39] One need not minimize the danger and violence, the "wars and rumors of wars," nor deny the signs that the prevailing order of things is breaking up. Unlike the Antiutopian Realist, the Counterapocalyptic realist feels no urgency about maintaining order. But apocalyptic thinking must not be used to increase the authority of the powers that already are. When that happens, the urgent task of theologians is to force apocalyptic claims by the leaders of nations back into the limits of ordinary politics, where success and failure can be measured and accountability can be reestablished.

Reinhold Niebuhr was as concerned with these apocalyptic exaggerations of America's role in the world as he was with America's necessary part in maintaining international order. Duncan Forrester reminds us that Niebuhr resisted the "Manichaean" strain in American politics that tried to turn the Second World War and Cold War rivalry with Soviet communism into a

---

[38] Catherine Keller, *God and Power: Counter-Apocalyptic Journeys* (Minneapolis: Fortress Press, 2005), p. 12.

[39] Matthew 24:6.

struggle of light against darkness. The real threat, from Niebuhr's point of view, is unchecked power and the pride which inevitably accompanies it. Niebuhr saw real evil in Hitler and Stalin, but democracies are also susceptible to evil. The superiority of democracy was not its moral purity, but the more realistic and effective ways it had devised to keep the evil under control. "Theologians should," Forrester writes, "in this context, be asking hard questions about the only surviving superpower and its purposes and practices from long before 9/11."[40]

Catherine Keller calls our attention to Niebuhr's warning toward the end of *The Irony of American History* that Americans might be tempted by the frustrations and ambiguities of modern life to bring them to an end with one apocalyptic exercise of technological power.[41] Until the Soviet Union acquired the nuclear capacity to maintain "mutually assured destruction," the possibility of terminating the rivalry by an American "preventive war" remained under discussion. Niebuhr recognized this for what it was – not only a strategic error, but a moral temptation.

Our foreign policy is therefore threatened with a kind of apoplectic rigidity and inflexibility. Constant proof is required that the foe is hated with sufficient vigor. Unfortunately, the only persuasive proof seems to be the disavowal of precisely those discriminate judgments which are so necessary for an effective conflict with the evil, which we are supposed to abhor.[42]

The theologians are not alone in their warnings about the dangers of apocalyptic thinking in high places. Michael Ignatieff recognizes the unprecedented problems that global terrorism poses for political leaders, but he argues that it is precisely because of the extremity of the threat that their actions must remain open to the ordinary processes of review and evaluation. Confronted with a new kind of danger, an official may issue orders and limit freedoms in ways that test the limits of legitimate authority. What a democracy cannot accept, however, is a claim by political authority that the new conditions place these actions beyond the reach of legislative inquiry and judicial review.[43]

Political realists generally are likely to be antiapocalyptic, as they are antiutopian. What distinguishes the Counterapocalyptic theologians from other political realists is that they affirm apocalyptic thinking by the poor

---

[40] Forrester, *Apocalypse Now?*, p. 7.   [41] Keller, *God and Power*, p. 28.

[42] Reinhold Niebuhr, *The Irony of American History* (New York: Charles Scribner's Sons, 1952), pp. 146–7.

[43] Michael Ignatieff, *The Lesser Evil: Political Ethics in an Age of Terror* (Princeton, NJ: Princeton University Press, 2004), pp. 145–70.

and powerless as strongly as they condemn it among the powerful. In the hands of the powerful, a narrative that sees the world coming apart is an invitation to set things right by force. In the hands of the powerless, it is a promise of liberation from existing powers, whom the apocalyptic situation always shows to be less powerful than they think they are. The disturbing signs and portents at the dawn of the twenty-first century do indeed threaten new forms of tyranny and political chaos, but our times hold promises as well as threats. We will not understand that unless we see things through the eyes of those who view events from outside the centers of power and security. For them, apocalyptic events become a sign of hope that something else is possible. Hope sustains those who have no stake in the present, even when they have no realistic reasons to expect anything better in the future.

Counterapocalyptic Realism thus emphasizes a side of Niebuhr's work that he himself tended to balance with an antiutopian stress on the risks inherent in revolutionary change.[44] Counterapocalyptic Realists recall the younger Niebuhr, who wrote at the conclusion of *Moral Man and Immoral Society* that "justice cannot be approximated if the hope of its perfect realization does not generate a sublime madness in the soul."[45] Three-quarters of a century later, Counterapocalyptic Realists remind us that this "madness" is itself an important part of the reality of the human condition, which has generated changes of historic proportions that cannot be accounted for by the standard realist explanations. When twentieth-century Christian realism reached the zenith of its influence, the world was dominated by a superpower conflict that seemed destined to last indefinitely into the future. Realistic expectations, on this antiutopian account, had to be trimmed to fit the dangers of such a world and the overriding need for stability. Injustice could be exposed and evil could be criticized, but injustice and evil would often have to be endured because the powers behind them were beyond the reach of public criticism, or because they were so essential to global stability that we could not risk opposing them.

On the basis of those estimates, we might still be waiting for the end of legal segregation, especially in parts of America where it was honored by long custom and local expectations had adjusted to it. Martin Luther

[44] Eyal Naveh, *Reinhold Niebuhr and Non-Utopian Liberalism: Beyond Illusion and Despair* (Brighton, UK: Sussex Academic Press, 2002), pp. 117–41.

[45] Reinhold Niebuhr, *Moral Man and Immoral Society: A Study in Ethics and Politics* (Louisville, KY: Westminster John Knox Press, 2001), p. 277.

King's movement should have stalled out against massive white resistance. The "velvet revolution" at the end of the 1980s should have been crushed like the 1956 uprising in Hungary. The Berlin Wall should not have fallen, and Nelson Mandela would in all likelihood have died in prison.

The mid-century realists would not have wanted those outcomes, of course, but their way of understanding the balances of power, the ambiguities of change, and the ironies of history would have led them to expect those results, or something like them. So the question that the Counterapocalyptic Realist puts to us is, "Who is unrealistic?" Those who hope for changes that transcend predictable results? Or those who expect institutional inertia to control the pace of events because everyone prefers present order to uncertain possibilities?

The Counterapocalyptic Realist gives more attention than the Antiutopian Realist to the narrative that sustains hope, but the Counterapocalyptic Realist is a political realist nonetheless. Catherine Keller, Duncan Forrester, and other Counterapocalyptic Realists would agree with Jean Bethke Elshtain that what government is for is to deliver approximate justice through systems of security and order. Where Elshtain worries about utopian critics of government who might deprive it of the power it needs to complete those tasks, the Counterapocalyptic Realists are more concerned about the mounting evidence that governments at the turn of the twenty-first century are grasping for an apocalyptic mission that obscures their failures to deliver even approximate justice and postpones accountability for those failures until they have completed their new task of bringing an end to evil. Given the scope of that task and the real limits on their power, apocalypse now means that accountability will be delayed indefinitely.

THE PLURALIST REALIST

Events since September 11, 2001, have revealed sharp differences among those who claim the legacy of Christian realism. In Niebuhr's work, antiutopian and Counterapocalyptic ideas work together to define an indispensable, but limited role for democratic powers and democratic politics in an emerging world order. Uncertainties about the future tend to set today's Antiutopian and Counterapocalyptic Realists at odds over today's politics. The Pluralist Realist seeks to resolve some of these differences by tracing them farther back into the past. First, the Pluralist Realist looks to 1991, rather than 2001, to orient our understanding of the world. The changes in global politics at the end of the Cold War made America the target of the terrorists, made Afghanistan available to them as a base of operations, and continue to shape the world situation today.[46]

The globalization of commerce after the Cold War accelerates the independence of business from political constraints. States become relatively less powerful in a world aligned in trading blocs, rather than ideological empires. Commerce in goods in turn increases the traffic in ideas, making it far more difficult for governments to control the flow of information or exercise a monopoly on persuasion. Books, journals, films, and Internet communications flow with increasing ease across borders. Individuals join professional associations, academic disciplines, and interest groups that create new identities that transcend nation and ethnicity. Even the resurgence of religious identity that exercised such a powerful influence shaping the events of 9/11 can be seen as part of these developments.

Those who understand events in this "post-1991" perspective are political realists, as Niebuhr defined the term. They have a "disposition to take all factors in a social and political situation, which offer resistance to established norms, into account, particularly the factors of self-interest and power."[47] What they see, in ways that Niebuhr himself perhaps did not, is that the forces at work include more than states and governments. Self-interest is not always national self-interest, and military power is not always the decisive form of power. This way of looking at contemporary events may conveniently be called Pluralist Realism, to emphasize the diversity of forces that come into consideration and the more complex picture of political life that results.

Max Stackhouse and Dennis McCann were among the first to recognize that the end of the Cold War would change the shape of Christian social ethics.[48] Stackhouse has subsequently argued that in this reconstruction, "we must acknowledge the declining power of the state and the increasing power of nongovernmental groups – including, above all, the religious institutions that are before our very eyes and beneath our very noses."[49] Once everything is no longer seen in terms of superpower rivalries and competing economic systems, we are able to pay attention to the range of

---

[46] William J. Dobson, "The Day Nothing Much Changed," *Foreign Policy* No. 156 (September/October 2006), 2–25.
[47] Niebuhr, *Christian Realism and Political Problems*, p. 119.
[48] Max Stackhouse and Dennis McCann, "A Post-Communist Manifesto," *Christian Century* 108 (January 16, 1991), 1, 44–7.
[49] Max L. Stackhouse, "Christian Social Ethics in a Global Era: Reforming Protestant Views," in Max Stackhouse (ed.), *Christian Social Ethics in a Global Era* (Abingdon Press Studies in Christian Ethics and Economic Life, No. 1; Nashville, TN: Abingdon Press, 1995), p. 58.

institutions and ideas that actually shape life in a modern society. Reductive ideological analyses lose their appeal, and the rich variety of social and ethical themes offered by theology can again become part of public discourse.

William Schweiker has a similar assessment of the political importance of this institutional pluralism, although he is more ambivalent about its implications for ethics, especially as pluralism is closely tied to globalization. When systems interact on a global scale, people may suddenly find their moral world fragmented. More precisely, they may realize that they have been living in a fragmented moral world for some time, although the fragmentation was obscured by a personal identification with state and ideology that becomes increasingly difficult to maintain in a global marketplace and a global culture.

We can now state more pointedly the ethical problem of pluralism. Contemporary people around the world mostly live in highly differentiated societies wherein social subsystems (market, law, etc.) entail diverse ways of knowing and valuing. The interaction of social subsystems brings about shifts in those frameworks of knowing and valuing and shapes the moral imagination: the economy, for example, must adjust to legal practice; educational systems (sad to say) are increasingly permeated by the logic and value of the economic market. These shifts in knowing and valuing reach from the level of individual consciousness to the relations among communities and nations… Given the shifts in thinking and valuing, it seems impossible to offer any comprehensive beliefs about human existence. Moral codes are disconnected from beliefs about reality.[50]

Confronted with this state of affairs, the Pluralist Realist adopts a strategy that is directly opposite that of the Witness. The Witness turns to a comprehensive narrative that unifies the community formed around it. Christians may not be able to escape dealing with the differentiated social subsystems in which everyone now lives, but the Witness says they can ignore them in their search for moral order and meaning in life, because they know in advance that none is to be found there. Narrated truth creates moral meaning. Fragmentation is meaningless. The Pluralist Realist, by contrast, begins with the experienced variety of human goods, and seeks them where they are to be found. Whatever goods or evils really exist for human life are created and sustained in these complex and differentiated systems of relationships, and it is in that multiplicity of contexts that we must seek whatever unity our moral life will have. Pluralist Realism includes a commitment to moral realism, but moral realism under the conditions

---

[50] Schweiker, *Theological Ethics and Global Dynamics*, p. 31.

of modern life requires us to attend to the diversity of goods and to make comprehensive claims very cautiously.[51]

Just how far Pluralist Realism can move in the direction of a comprehensive understanding of the human good is an important question. The answer largely determines whether and how the competing versions of Christian realism surveyed in this chapter can be reintegrated. How far must Counterapocalyptic Realism be removed from the concrete realities of power in order to sustain hope? At what point, by contrast, does the real fragmentation of life in modern society render the integration of a moral universe that theological realism requires implausible or unbelievable? Can specific moral judgments about concrete events be liberating? Are expectations that rise above order and security always utopian?

The answer also affects how Christian realism relates to other ways of thinking about ethics and politics. Contemporary political theories often understand religion as a "comprehensive doctrine" that provides the believer with a consistent understanding of all aspects of the human good. The question then becomes how persons who hold these "comprehensive doctrines" can participate in a political community which will, under the conditions of modern life, necessarily include a wide variety of these beliefs.[52] Pluralist Realism suggests, however, that the "fact of reasonable pluralism"[53] that characterizes the modern political situation may, in part, be a religious contribution to politics and not entirely a political solution to a religious problem.

To understand how this is so, the Pluralist Realist must work back through history before 1991, before the Cold War that unified the political vision of an earlier generation of Christian realists, even before the origins of modern liberal democracy. An earlier experience of fragmentation preceded the era of the successful modern state, just as today's fragmentation may mark the beginning of an era of globalization. Then as now, the conflicts were not new, but a new awareness of them changed the way that European Christians thought of their common life. A Christian understanding of politics unified by the authority of church and empire and an Aristotelian understanding of politics unified by the search for the human good gave way to a political realism that defined the task of government in other terms. To succeed, government would have to be about the search

---

[51] *Ibid.*, p. 28.

[52] We owe this way of formulating the problem especially to John Rawls, but it has been widely taken up in other discussions. See John Rawls, *Justice as Fairness: A Restatement* (Cambridge, MA: Harvard University Press, 2001), p. 9.

[53] *Ibid.*, p. 3.

for security and order that the Antiutopian Realist stresses today. It was in the aftermath of the Reformation and in the formation of the modern state that we learned what we now think that government is for. It is a lesson we remember every time that utopian illusions about government are dispelled and apocalyptic promises go unfulfilled.

But that redefinition of politics that confined it narrowly to the work of government in the context of the modern nation state did not end the search for the human good. In the modern world, people invented more ways to pursue, create, and maintain human goods, more ways to acquire and distribute them, more ways to reflect on them and evaluate them than any civilization had ever done before. In that new mix of institutions and activities, the specific task of government was to coordinate the pursuit of interests in a way that provided order and security for everyone. Soon enough, that became the meaning of 'politics,' and only antiquarians remembered that it had once meant something more. But in the shops, and the offices, and the factories, in universities, and theaters, and museums, in the new domestic life of families, and the new ways of religious life in churches, human goods were imagined and created. These new institutions competed with one another for loyalty and resources, and they made demands on one another and on the individuals who participated in them. The process of claim and counterclaim went on, and successful states learned quickly enough that imposing too much order on these conflicts had high costs.

Catholic social thought resisted the Reformation idea of a secular political authority, but the tradition of Thomas Aquinas also experienced the differentiation and fragmentation in social life that mark the modern age. The idea of a unity of all good that culminates in union with God remained the great underlying truth of history, but more distinct and limited forms of human good came to be understood as in their own ways analogical to this ultimate common good. Because each form of human relationship and each sphere of human good participates in this analogy, all of them are important, and none of them is absolute. David Hollenbach has explicated this "pluralistic-analogical" understanding of the human good in ways that make an important contribution to contemporary Pluralist Realism and anchor it more firmly in the ecumenical Christian tradition.[54]

---

[54] David Hollenbach, *The Common Good and Christian Ethics* (Cambridge: Cambridge University Press, 2002), pp. 129–36. For the relationship between Reformed theology and this Thomist tradition, see David Fergusson, *Church, State, and Civil Society* (Cambridge: Cambridge University Press, 2004), p. 46.

The world of 1500 is not the world after 9/11 or the world in the age of globalization, but the "highly differentiated societies wherein social sub-systems (market, law, etc.) entail diverse ways of knowing and valuing" that Schweiker describes already existed in forms recognizable to us, and recognizable to the people who lived in them, at the beginning of the modern era. That is why Stackhouse finds the theological tradition of social "spheres" or "orders of creation" useful in explaining the pluralism of institutions that flourish alongside government and increasingly exercise their own forms of power apart from it.[55] Ongoing competition, tension, and even open conflict between these fragments of social life are essential to any order worth having. Our idea of good order – of a good society, locally or globally – must incorporate ambiguity, uncertainty, and competing values. Under the conditions of modern life, the search for human good can only proceed in fragments, and the good itself can only be understood when we see some kind of unity beyond the fragmentation.

That is how the Pluralist Realist seeks to understand the tensions between narrative and concrete judgment, between order and apocalypse, between security and hope that have divided those who share the legacy of Christian realism. Both pluralism and realism suggest that it would be a mistake to want those tensions to disappear. The future must be seen in terms of how we will live with them. Nevertheless, a broader conception of Christian realism and a longer view of its history suggests that we have more experience in facing these problems than we might at first think.

[55] Max Stackhouse, "Public Theology and Political Economy in a Globalizing Era," *Studies in Christian Ethics* 14 (2001), 70–1.

CHAPTER 2

A Short History of Christian Realism

REALITY AND RESPONSIBILITY

The Christian realisms that we explored in the previous chapter call for further exploration of their history. The increasing complexity of global relationships and the sharp differences that separate our world from the world that Reinhold Niebuhr knew make different understandings of Christian realism inevitable, but the lines along which these interpretations divide reflect older and deeper controversies in Christian theology and ethics.

Christians have always lived in the tension between ultimate reality and immediate responsibility. From the beginning, they have expected God's ultimate victory over all conditions that threaten the meaning of life and deprive human action of purpose. Christians measure choice and action by this hope, and not by the chances of success or failure. Thus, theologians as different as Stanley Hauerwas and Reinhold Niebuhr have affirmed that doing Christian ethics requires thinking eschatologically.[1] This accounts for the persistence of apocalyptic movements and ideas in lived Christian faith, even in a secular, scientific age. It also helps to explain why today's Counterapocalyptic Realists are so urgent in rejecting a political apocalypse that puts the recreation of the world in the hands of the powerful. To do that destroys the distinctive hope that Christian eschatology has always offered to the poor.

Christian hope, however, is not only eschatological. The world which God will finally rule is also God's creation, which means that it is from the beginning ordered toward that end. No contingent victory over primordial chaos, no subjugation of recalcitrant, preexistent matter was required to set this order in place. Likewise, the interests we pursue, the communities we

---

[1] Reinhold Niebuhr, *Faith and History* (New York: Charles Scribner's Sons, 1949), p. 214; Stanley Hauerwas, *The Peaceable Kingdom: A Primer in Christian Ethics* (Notre Dame, IN: University of Notre Dame Press, 1983), pp. 83–5. See also Paul Ramsey, *Deeds and Rules in Christian Ethics* (New York: Charles Scribner's Sons, 1967), pp. 108–09.

create, and the goods we seek are not merely a local order of our own making. Rightly understood and rightly ordered in relation to each other, they form a whole. Life need not be lived at cross-purposes, in conflicts where every good achieved requires the elimination of rival claimants. Nor need human life be a struggle against nature, as though reality were alien or indifferent to human purposes. "Distant though it may be from typical attitudes of the present day," Glenn Tinder reminds us, "the idea that the human and the natural are in fundamental accord is one of the major themes in the philosophical traditions of the West . . . A sign of this harmony is found in the familiar, age-old idea of natural law; the moral and the natural in their depths are at one."[2]

For Christian realists, the question becomes what evidence we can expect of this ultimately meaningful world in immediate human experience, which bears down with equal and undeniable force on those who are Christian realists and those who are not.[3] Conflict between persons, groups, and nations remains central to much human experience. In the narrative of history, the clash between good and evil follows no certain course, and even the good things that we pursue often seem to be in conflict with one another – freedom against commitment, compassion against accountability, justice against reconciliation. Because the order ultimately belongs to God and moves toward a conclusion that lies beyond our lives and even beyond nature and history themselves, how we should live often will not be immediately clear to us.

One way to deal with these realities is a utopian Christianity that seeks fulfillment of history within history, rather than beyond it. That version of Christian hope has taken many forms, but it flourished first during the rapid spread of Christianity across the Roman Empire. Although second-century Christians often saw Christian faith and Roman power in a confrontation that presaged the end of history, by the middle of the fourth century, the Roman emperor was a Christian, and some people – especially those for whom Rome was the world – concluded that God was closing the gap between history and ultimate reality from history's side. For Eusebius of Caesarea, the first great historian of the early church, Constantine's conversion marked the beginning of a new age in Rome's history and in God's dealings with humanity. "Old troubles were forgotten, and all irreligion

---

[2] Glenn Tinder, "Against Fate," in Robert P. Kraynak and Glenn Tinder (eds.), *In Defense of Human Dignity: Essays for Our Times* (Notre Dame, IN: University of Notre Dame Press, 2003), pp. 38–9.

[3] Tinder, "Against Fate," pp. 11–12. See also James Gustafson, *Ethics from a Theocentric Perspective* (Chicago: University of Chicago Press, 1981), pp. 195–235.

passed into oblivion; good things present were enjoyed and those yet to come eagerly awaited."[4]

Events, however, quickly undermined this unity of ultimate reality and imperial order. At the end of the fifth century, Pope Gelasius I could still write to Emperor Anastasius in Constantinople of a world in which royal and priestly power jointly ordered human affairs, but he was reminding him of an ideal that had, from the papal point of view, already ceased to function.[5] The emperor, in turn, might have received this as something like a summary of the Constantinian system which he had inherited, but it is doubtful that he thought any longer of the old capital and its bishop as being at the actual source of political order. Rome had become an idea, rather than a place. Through the following centuries, others would claim that idea for themselves.[6]

In any case, those engaged in practical affairs had more urgent problems to sort out, and in Western Europe, they could hardly regard the fulfillment of history as an accomplished fact. Rapidly changing realities forced some Christian leaders in the West to think seriously about mundane matters of politics, and it is in those circumstances that we may locate the origin of that combination of theological conviction with realistic politics that we now call Christian realism. The Roman imperial system had already begun to break down before the time of Gelasius I, and the church found itself involved in questions of order on a local scale. Bishops settled questions of law, as well as matters of faith. Their power balanced and sometimes overshadowed that of the emperor's Roman officials, who were increasingly cut off from central authority and isolated from one another. For very practical reasons, Christian interest in political problems began to grow, and the close ties between Christian politics and the imperial system began to loosen.[7]

---

[4] Eusebius, *The History of the Church*, G. A. Williamson (trans.) (London: Penguin Books, 1989), p. 332.

[5] See Oliver O'Donovan and Joan Lockwood O'Donovan (eds.), *From Irenaeus to Grotius: A Sourcebook in Christian Political Thought* (Grand Rapids: Eerdmans, 1999), p. 179: "Two there are, august Emperor, by which this world is ruled: the consecrated authority of priests and the royal power."

[6] In Eastern Christianity, the "Third Rome" at Moscow symbolized a unity of faith and order that now receives new attention with the revival of Orthodox Christianity in Russia. See Nicolai N. Petro, *The Rebirth of Russian Democracy: An Interpretation of Political Culture* (Cambridge, MA: Harvard University Press, 1995), pp. 61–77. In the West, the Holy Roman Empire claimed *Pax Romana*, imperial power as the source of universal peace and stability, until its dissolution in 1806, and it has been claimed at least metaphorically by those who have spoken of a *Pax Britannica* or a *Pax Americana* ordering the world in the late nineteenth and late twentieth centuries, respectively.

[7] Peter Brown, *Augustine of Hippo: A Biography* (Berkeley: University of California Press, 2000), p. 138.

Alongside the widening gaps in Roman political authority, there was an even older deficit in political thought. Rome had created a system of law and government, but it had no new way to think about politics on an imperial scale. For that, Christians and pagans alike were thrown back on resources drawn from the Greek city-states and the Roman republic, mediated through Stoic philosophers. The political problem remained as Plato and Aristotle had defined it: to determine what kind of life is best for human beings and to order a city that makes that life possible. Ambrose of Milan, who had been first a Roman magistrate and then a Christian bishop, adapted Cicero's republican politics to provide a model of leadership for Christian clergy.[8]

It fell to Augustine of Hippo, teacher of rhetoric in Milan, Christian convert, and pupil of Ambrose, to complete this Christian appropriation of political philosophy, rethinking the relationship between faith and politics and becoming in the process the first great Christian realist.[9] His understanding of how Christian hope relates to immediate responsibility appears most clearly in a great theological study of history, philosophy, and politics, his *City of God*.[10]

According to Augustine, the philosophers had it right that all persons, Christians and pagans, seek a kind of political good that Augustine calls "peace," but Augustine is too much the realist to suppose that this is a disinterested, rational search. People seek what they desire, not what reason tells them is good. So Augustine's realistic politics provides a better description of the communities that people actually create than Cicero's natural law or Plato's good. Bands of thieves are political communities, too, on this definition.[11] Nevertheless, all human communities, which Augustine collectively calls "the earthly city," seek some kind of peace, and they can all be understood in those terms.

Here Augustine parts company with Christian thinkers who dismiss the goods of the earthly city or set them in dualistic opposition to the goods

---

[8] Ambrose, *De Officiis*, Ivor J. Davidson (ed.) (Oxford: Oxford University Press, 2001).

[9] Cf. Reinhold Niebuhr, "Augustine's Political Realism," in *Christian Realism and Political Problems* (New York: Charles Scribner's Sons, 1953), pp. 119–46.

[10] For the relationship between Augustine's theology and his realistic politics, see the fine account recently published by Kristen Deede Johnson, *Theology, Political Theory, and Pluralism: Beyond Tolerance and Difference* (Cambridge: Cambridge University Press, 2007), pp. 140–82.

[11] Augustine, *The City of God Against the Pagans*, R. W. Dyson (ed.) (Cambridge: Cambridge University Press, 1998), p. 934. Cf. Plato *Republic* I, 351–3. See also Jean Bethke Elshtain, *Augustine and the Limits of Politics* (Notre Dame: University of Notre Dame Press, 1995), p. 22.

sought by Christians. The human search for peace is frustrated by conflict and, in the end, defeated by death, but the goods that people seek are real goods, precisely because all of them are created by God. If the history of the earthly city is a tale of disappointment, conflict, and death, that is not because its citizens seek bad things, but because they do not know how to order the goods they seek in relationship to one another or how to relate them to God. Christians do a better job of being moral realists, because they know how to order the many things that are good in relation to God, who alone holds the multiplicity of goods in unity and provides the possibility of enjoying them securely and permanently.[12] "The Christian of *City of God*," writes James O'Donnell, "is the one who has all the virtues of the classical world and none of its vices."[13]

Nevertheless, Christians do not seek true peace isolated in their churches, while others seek an approximation of it by their own lights in the markets, baths, and amphitheaters. Christians may have insights that others lack, but the conditions for earthly peace are such that the others cannot be ignored, even when they are ultimately mistaken. The distinction between the two cities is, as Paul Weithman says, eschatological rather than political.[14] It is what they hope for that separates Christians from their neighbors, not the immediate realities of their daily lives.

This is true as a matter of sociological fact. Christians are found in every earthly city, and, like the people of Israel who were dispersed in exile among the Babylonians, they seek and share many of the same goods that their neighbors seek for their own peace and well-being.[15] But there is a theological truth here, too, and it captures in Augustine's terms the attentiveness to the details of reality with which Christian realism begins. Christians in this world do not immediately understand all good things in relation to God's goodness with the clarity and certainty that they hope to know in the end. Christians do not come into the world equipped by nature with a complete knowledge of all goods in relation to God. They begin in the same state of ignorance as everyone else. Because people love the goods they have chosen in their ignorance, they do not give them up lightly, even when their relationship to God helps them to see what the real good is. Augustine, unlike Plato, thinks that even those who know the good will have to struggle all their lives to do it.[16]

---

[12] Augustine, *City of God*, p. 961.

[13] James J. O'Donnell, *Augustine* (New York: HarperCollins, 2005), p. 252.

[14] See Paul Weithman, "Augustine's political philosophy," in Eleonore Stump and Norman Kretzmann (eds.), *The Cambridge Companion to Augustine*, (Cambridge: Cambridge University Press, 2001), p. 237.

[15] Augustine, *City of God*, p. 962.   [16] *Ibid.*, p. 963.

Even when Christians succeed in that struggle, God's ultimate purposes may remain obscure. In a world where they are surrounded by false gods and misunderstood goods, Christians must be bold to use the powers of judgment that their faith has taught them, but they dare not equate their own judgments with God's final verdict at the end of history.[17]

Most important for Augustine, this realism is not the occasion for musing about the ambiguities of history. It is the starting point for an active moral life. Christians are called to full involvement in the life of the earthly cities where they find themselves.[18] They understand themselves as "on pilgrimage" or "in exile," in the sense that their happiness does not ultimately depend on the politics of this city. But pilgrims and exiles are not mere spectators. They are involved as people who raise families, earn a living, hold property, and plan for the future. Like the exiles whom Jeremiah advised to pray for the peace of Babylon, Christians pray and work for the places where they live, because as the prophet said, "in her peace is your peace," meaning, Augustine added, "the temporal peace of the meantime, which is shared by good and bad alike."[19]

Through his reflections on how the two cities are related, Augustine understood how Christian hope could engender human responsibility for a concrete political situation. Christian hope begins with God, and it will be complete only when every political achievement is past. But Christians are not for that reason excused from living peacefully and well with their neighbors. Rather, because their hope is already set on the only glory worth having, they are freed from pursuit of worldly honors to focus on contributions to the common good. "For it is not out of any desire for mastery that they command; rather, they do so from a dutiful concern for others: not out of pride in ruling, but because they love mercy."[20]

Perhaps more relevant to our discussion is the fact that this understanding applies to every earthly city. By using Babylon as his image for the place of political responsibility, Augustine rejected the idea that Christians accept these tasks because they are Romans, and Rome has a special destiny in God's providential plan. Rome is simply the available place where Christians can work for a peace that they can share with their neighbors. The city where Christians live and for which they pray is not the Rome of Constantine and Eusebius, but neither is it the Babylon of the early Christian apocalypse. This is a Babylon which one can pray for, and not only pray to be delivered

[17] *Ibid.*, pp. 48–9.
[18] Michael Banner, "Christianity and Civil Society," in Simone Chambers and Will Kymlicka (eds.), *Alternative Conceptions of Civil Society* (Princeton, NJ: Princeton University Press, 2002), p. 116.
[19] Augustine, *City of God*, p. 962.   [20] *Ibid.*, p. 942.

from it. As R. A. Markus puts it, "Of the two traditions represented in Christian thinking, the Eusebian and the apocalyptic, as we might refer to them for the sake of convenience, Augustine followed neither."[21]

Christian realism begins by thus heightening the tension between ultimate reality and concrete responsibility, where others had sought to resolve it. Augustine saw that both are necessary to the Christian moral life, and he refused to let Christians live entirely in one or the other. In his time, that meant not allowing people who were confident of God's ultimate judgment escape responsibility for proximate choices. Modern people have become accustomed to resolve this tension in the opposite way, leaning toward the secular idea that politics focuses more effectively on the present by systematically eliminating reference to the ultimate. Augustine raises the possibility that it is precisely the certainty of ultimate judgment that allows one to take immediate problems seriously.

Compared to the philosophers he discusses in Book 19 of the *City of God*, Augustine had a higher estimate of the ultimate good available to human beings and lower expectations for their achievements in this world. This made him realistic in the important sense that he could pay more attention to what was actually happening in political life. Violence, ignorance, and evil did not have to be explained away, and so could be described more candidly.

Augustine was, by general consent, the first great "realist" in western history. He deserves this distinction because his picture of social reality in his *civitas dei* gives an adequate account of the social factions, tensions, and competitions which we know to be well-nigh universal on every level of community; while the classical age conceived the order and justice of its *polis* to be a comparatively simple achievement, which would be accomplished when reason had brought all subrational forces under its dominion.[22]

Because of his realistically lowered expectations, Augustine was also more sympathetic to the struggles of ordinary people to acquire whatever

---

[21] R. A. Markus, *Saeculum: History and Society in the Theology of St. Augustine*, revised edn. (Cambridge: Cambridge University Press, 1988), p. 56. This understanding of Christianity and society in Augustine has been vigorously criticized by Oliver O'Donovan and others who see Augustine championing a stronger Christian opposition to the powers and orders of history. Franklin Gamwell, by contrast, sees Augustine as more deferential to established political order and lacking, along with the rest of early Christianity, any developed idea of a Christian political vocation. See Oliver O'Donovan, "The Political Thought of *City of God* 19," in Oliver O'Donovan and Joan Lockwood O'Donovan (eds.), *Bonds of Imperfection: Christian Politics, Past and Present* (Grand Rapids, MI: Eerdmans, 2004), pp. 55–9; and Franklin Gamwell, *Politics as a Christian Vocation: Faith and Democracy Today* (Cambridge: Cambridge University Press, 2005), pp. 9–21.

[22] Niebuhr, "Augustine's Political Realism," pp. 120–1.

approximations of virtue might be available to them. The Christian bishop required a more catholic answer to the old philosophical question about whether a life of leisure, a life of action, or a combination of the two is the best life. A Christian might pursue any of these ways, provided also that "he loves the truth and performs the duties of charity."[23] We see here just a hint of the three orders of church, government, and family in which later theologians would say that the Christian life could be lived. This realistic acknowledgment of the diversity of lives and contexts is a striking departure from the urgent philosophical question about which one way of life is best. It will become very important in our subsequent exploration of Christian realism, but Augustine does not develop it into a full-fledged account of the diversity of social institutions.

CHRISTIAN IDEALISM

For those who, like Augustine, saw the forms of Roman urban life as the best available model of earthly peace, the worst was yet to come. Augustine died in 430, as the Vandals were looting the estates and cities of Roman Africa. In all the West, both north and south of the Mediterranean, there would soon be little left of the society that Ambrose and Augustine had understood and led. What a realist with a little more ironic distance might recognize, however, was that these invaders were not totally alien. They had lived on the edges of Roman civilization for generations, and many of them were Christians, although in Augustine's time they often followed a different, hostile Arian theology that added the fuel of religious hatred to the fires of ethnic conflict. The irony was that these "barbarians" soon came to see themselves, and not the defeated Latins, as the heirs of Roman power and glory.

Where declining Roman elites and modern historians alike have seen a patchwork of predatory barbarian kingdoms clashing in a Dark Age of ignorance and disorder, there were at the time people with imagination, intellect, and a gift for leadership who saw the old ideal of imperial order and Christian faith, undiminished by the grim realities of the moment. Increasingly, the leaders who maintained this vision were in the church, rather than gathered around the ruler, but they maintained the ideal unity of royal and priestly power that had been taught by Gelasius I and codified by Justinian. Gregory the Great (ca. 540–604) assimilated the rulers of the Germanic kingdoms to Justinian's Byzantine order. Their conversion to

---

[23] Augustine, *City of God*, p. 948.

Catholic Christianity and their adoption of elements of Roman law placed them in continuity with the Roman order that had preceded them.[24]

The theologians who came after Augustine and saw the church through the transition into the Middle Ages adopted his moral and theological realism, but not his political realism. Or perhaps we should say that their realistic political strategy required a different kind of political theology. They adopted Justinian's law that gave the emperor temporal control over the church, and Gregory the Great elaborated that into a general obligation of Christians to obey their temporal rulers, whose authority came directly from God and not from the people.[25] The result is a normative understanding of Christian society, enduring through the vicissitudes of history and applicable everywhere in the Christian world. If the model seems, especially from a later Western perspective, to enlarge imperial authority at the expense of the church, we must remember that the churchmen who extended its reach in the West were also its principal interpreters. The emperor in person was distant and increasingly irrelevant, but the imperial constitution could be used to settle important political questions on terms set by the religious leaders' understanding of it. Christians are no longer exiles praying for the peace of whatever Babylon they find themselves in for the moment. They are part of an imperial order which is also a Christian order. Although this is not the realized eschatology of Eusebius, who sees all evil and irreligion banished, it is a Christianity that knows the right way to organize church and society for the temporal and eternal welfare of the people. Call it, if you will, a Christian political idealism, to distinguish it from the political realism that we have seen in Augustine.

The differences between the two are not as sharp as we might at first suppose. No doubt many of these Christian political idealists thought they were echoing Augustine, not contradicting him, when they set out the requirements of a Christian political order. We may distinguish the types, however, by saying that the Christian political idealist holds that there is a political order which all Christians should recognize as normative. That order encompasses both church and state and sets the terms for their relationships with one another. It also establishes the rights and obligations

---

[24] On Gregory the Great (ca. 540–604), see O'Donovan and O'Donovan, *From Irenaeus to Grotius*, pp. 195–203; R. A. Markus, "The Latin Fathers," in J. H. Burns (ed.), *The Cambridge History of Medieval Political Thought* (Cambridge: Cambridge University Press, 1988), pp. 116–22; Harold Berman, *Law and Revolution: The Formation of the Western Legal Tradition* (Cambridge, MA: Harvard University Press, 1983), p. 568.

[25] O'Donovan and O'Donovan, *From Irenaeus to Grotius*, p. 190; R. W. and A. J. Carlyle, *A History of Medieval Political Theory in the West*, vol. I (Edinburgh: William Blackwood & Sons, 1927), p. 159.

of the people who live in it. Exceptions required by prevailing political realities may be recognized, and deviations from the ideal may be considered better or worse in relation to one another, but the way things should be is not in doubt. The Christian political idealist sees the normative model as universal and encompassing. The relationships between the basic elements of any society are part of a normative order, and conflict between the church and secular rulers is a sign that this order has broken down.

This Christian idealism became central to papal teaching and legal theory through the Middle Ages and beyond.[26] It should not be understood in radical opposition to Augustine's Christian realism, but as a different way of developing it. What both Christian realists and Christian idealists share through the centuries is an Augustinian conviction about the pervasiveness of sin and the fragility of any system of earthly peace. Both groups are suspicious of utopian claims that the ideal Christian order has been achieved and awaits only full implementation or universal extension. Both likewise reject apocalyptic or sectarian proclamations that the goods of this life are slated for imminent destruction or have become so corrupt that Christians can have no part in the pursuit of them. The idealist, however, puts the emphasis on a comprehensive ordering of these goods that is part of the truth which the church teaches, whereas the realist focuses on specific goods found in particular social settings. The realist is concerned with goods that many different people seek for all sorts of reasons. These goods thus maintain a powerful influence on choice and action in concrete situations, although they may not be easily ordered into a comprehensive structure that unifies a whole society or transcends cultural and historical boundaries.

Despite the localized reality of social life in premodern Europe, it was the idealistic understanding that prevailed in the church's teaching. The successors of Gregory the Great elaborated a universal system of religious authority structured by canon law. By the time of Pope Gregory VII (1073–1085), the church possessed a system of administration and a system of law which secular rulers, dependent on a combination of armed force and local custom, could scarcely comprehend. The idea of a polity ruled by law was bequeathed to the modern West by the church, which found in that idea a means to enforce its understanding of social and political relationships, even against the superior physical power of kings and emperors.[27] Against this idealized understanding of the Christian polity, rulers could

---

[26] See, for example, Wilhelm G. Grewe, *The Epochs of International Law*, Michael Byers (trans.) (Berlin: Walter de Gruyter, 2000), pp. 40–8.

[27] See Harold Berman, *Law and Revolution: The Formation of the Western Legal Tradition* (Cambridge, MA: Harvard University Press, 1983), pp. 85–119.

assert themselves only by creating their own idea of law and secular authority, culminating in the beginnings of modern states modeled on the order of the church.[28] The differentiation of church and state into separate systems of authority that might oppose one another in principle – as distinct from personal power struggles between popes and emperors or kings and bishops – was thus, paradoxically, the product of the church's idea of a universal Christian order. The church continued to assert its claim to judge all conflicts in light of its own ideas of order, but it had to explain itself, increasingly, in terms of distinct spheres of royal and papal power. Once that framework was established, it was possible to articulate other ways of understanding the relationship between the spheres and thus to take the first steps toward what would emerge as modern understandings of church and state. The ideal relationship set out in the papal teaching became a map of disputed territory. Not for the last time, the result of Christian idealism was a conflict that could best be understood in realist terms.

REFORMATION REALISM

Like others of his time, Martin Luther looked increasingly to local princes who were beginning to exercise something like sovereign authority over their territories to provide order and restrain evil. In his 1523 treatise *On Secular Authority*, Luther wrote, "If there were [no law and government], then seeing that all the world is evil and that scarcely one human being in a thousand is a true Christian, people would devour each other and no one would be able to support his wife and children, feed himself, and serve God. The world would become a desert."[29]

What Luther saw in a different way was the relationship between order and good in this kind of political community. Because order requires effective restraint of evil even more than it requires promotion of the good, a ruler must first be prepared to undertake the difficult and sometimes deadly work of restraining evil. Too much princely interest in virtue or piety may actually distract from the main task at hand, so people must regard the effective use of force as itself noble and worthy of honor. Luther suggests that this corresponds to God's intentions for politics.

You should know that a prudent prince has been a rare bird in the world since the beginning of time, and a just prince an even rarer one. As a rule, princes are the greatest fools or the worst criminals on earth, and the worst is always to be

---

[28] *Ibid.*, p. 113.
[29] Martin Luther, "On Secular Authority," in Harro Höpfl, ed. *Luther and Calvin on Secular Authority* (Cambridge: Cambridge University Press, 1991), p. 10.

expected, and little good hoped for, from them, especially in what regards God and the salvation of souls. For these are God's jailers and hangmen, and his divine wrath makes use of them to punish the wicked and maintain outward peace . . . It is his divine will and pleasure that we should call his hangmen 'gracious lords', fall at their feet and be subject to them in all humility, so long as they do not overreach themselves by wanting to become pastors instead of hangmen.[30]

Secular rulers achieve results by power, not by wisdom, and only spiritual authority can work an inward moral transformation. "Therefore care must be taken to keep these two governments distinct, and both must be allowed to continue [their work], the one to make [people] just, the other to create outward peace and prevent evil-doing. Neither is enough for the world without the other."[31]

Luther's idea of secular authority reflected new realities with which his contemporaries had to live. Feudal relationships that medieval Christian idealism incorporated into a chain of God-given authority from the highest level to the lowest had broken down. A new kind of sovereign authority had emerged, holding exclusive power over a wide swath of territory and answering to no power beyond itself. While no one really wants a fool for a prince, Luther's extreme assertion that most of them are fools highlighted the reality that personal virtue and wisdom do not matter in the way that classical and Christian political thinkers had supposed. Politics simply cannot be about personal virtue. The requirements of peace are too important to make them dependent on good people.

Luther thus arrived by a quite different route at an understanding of princely authority that paralleled the advice offered by early political realists to the rulers of Italian city-states. The learned scholars of the newly revived classical learning knew that the ancient sources praised rulers for their virtues, but those who paid attention to the actual course of events noted that the appearance of virtue could be a more effective instrument of political purposes than the real thing. "Therefore," as Machiavelli summed it up, "a ruler who wishes to maintain his power must be prepared to act immorally when this becomes necessary."[32] If politics is about good lives and virtuous leaders, it makes no sense to talk about political success by vicious means. But if politics is about the effective use of power, then what would be a vice in the merchant, the banker, or the priest may well be the key to the prince's success.

---

[30] Luther, "On Secular Authority," p. 30.   [31] *Ibid.*, p. 12.
[32] Niccolò Machiavelli, *The Prince*, Quentin Skinner and Russell Price (eds.) (Cambridge: Cambridge University Press, 1988), p. 55.

Luther's idea of secular authority was radical, and neither he nor the Protestant princes fully implemented it in practice. His statement that princes must not try to be pastors seemed at the time a radical infringement on the medieval ideal of princely authority, and the princes themselves clearly preferred the Peace of Augsburg (1555) that made them the arbiters of religious choice within their borders and protected them from outside religious interference. *Cujus regio, ejus religio*[33] did not quite come up to Christian idealism's image of local rulers protecting the universal faith of a universal church, but it was a close enough approximation for princes who increasingly understood their authority in modern terms as the final word within a sovereign territory.

The Augsburg settlement did not extend to Reformed churches and rulers, but in Geneva, Jean Calvin had his own reasons to give the civil authority a strong role in protecting true faith and maintaining proper orders of worship and sacraments. Calvin's theology was at this point closer to the medieval ideal than Luther's, but he also assigned civil order a high place among human goods. Those who would dispense with the authority of government take away our human nature. "Mankind derives as much benefit from [civil order] as it does from bread, water, sun, and air, and its dignity is far greater than any of them."[34]

It is precisely this dignity, however, that provides the theological ground for the distinct vocation of the civil magistrate. Here, Calvin's understanding that the civil ruler has a calling quite different from that of the pastor parallels Luther's understanding of the prince's authority, although his language is characteristically more moderate. It would not do to speak of civil authorities as God's hangmen, from whom nothing good was to be expected in matters of faith, particularly in Geneva, where the magistrates were chosen from among the members of the reformed church. Calvin expected the Reformation to improve Christian society in ways that would make the working relationship between pastors and magistrates a harmonious one. Luther, by contrast, warns us to expect the worst, and then brightens that picture with images of what a wise prince with good counsel might be able to do.

Nevertheless, it was for the reformed church and society of Geneva that Calvin formulated a functional distinction between civil and religious authorities in terms of the questions they might answer and the constraints

---

[33] The Latin phrase summarizes the principle laid down by the Peace of Augsburg that the religion of the ruler is the official religion of the state.

[34] Jean Calvin, "On Civil Government," in Harro Höpfl (ed.), *Luther and Calvin on Secular Authority* (Cambridge: Cambridge University Press, 1991), p. 50.

they might employ. Leaders of the church considered questions of faith and applied moral admonitions and the sanctions of church discipline, including exclusion from the sacraments. Civil authorities considered questions of law and applied the coercion of physical force. Although Calvin has higher aspirations than Luther for the moral and religious elevation of this community as a whole, the distinction between the two kinds of authority required to hold the community together is, as David Fergusson points out, very similar to Luther's, and it may have been devised as an alternative to more theocratic ideas in other Swiss cities.[35]

The distinction between civil and religious authority was present in Calvinism from the beginning, but it grew sharper in the English-speaking world, where the Reformed faith often had to maintain its position against civil authorities who held to other ideas. Eventually, among Presbyterians in North America, the distinction became the basis of demands for religious freedom and strict neutrality on the part of the civil authorities toward religious controversies.[36]

Both theology and political experience thus contributed to a Reformation realism that came to stress the freedom of individual conscience and its independence from secular authority. No doubt both Luther and Calvin would have been shocked by the idea of a religiously neutral secular authority, but it was on the basis of their ideas that some churches eventually demanded that neutrality as a necessary condition for religious integrity.

This religiously contentious society was also becoming more complex socially. Later understandings of secular authority reflected these social changes as well as the theological reconsideration. Growing cities and expanding trade required more government than was needed in an earlier economy of local agriculture. Powerful armies with new kinds of weapons and tactics threatened order from without and required highly organized defenses. A growing system of police, courts, laws, and taxes was needed to maintain order within.

In its initial Lutheran formulation, the idea of secular order was strongly authoritarian. A Christian prince should not rely too much on laws or councilors. The best ruler will maintain a stern justice, conformed not to the letter of the law, but to the specifics of the situation.[37] The Lutheran

---

[35] David Fergusson, *Church, State, and Civil Society* (Cambridge: Cambridge University Press, 2004), pp. 39–41.

[36] Jeffrey H. Morrison, *John Witherspoon and the Founding of the American Republic* (Notre Dame, IN: University of Notre Dame Press, 2005), p. 108.

[37] Luther, "On Secular Authority," pp. 42–3.

Reformation as a whole, however, reveals a more considered judgment about the requirements of order and the structures of law. The complex circumstances of modern life make order a more urgent problem, but it is just that complexity which makes it impossible for the ruler to maintain order by personal authority alone.[38] It is a curious point of connection between Luther's treatise on secular authority and England's King James I that both insisted that a wise Christian prince should rely more on his own reason than on law. Luther's lawyers set him straight on that point, as did the king's eminent jurist, Sir Edward Coke, who pointed out that the law has its own reason:

True it was that God had endowed his Majesty with excellent science and great endowments of nature; but his Majesty was not learned in the laws of his realm of England, and causes which concern the life, or inheritance, or goods, or fortunes of his subjects, are not to be decided by natural reason, but by the artificial reason and judgment of the law, which law is an act which requires long study and experience, before that a man can attain to the cognizance of it.[39]

Order in the modern state requires many people with different skills and virtues working on it at once, guided by a pattern of law that extends across distance and time. Legal formulae and public ceremonies may maintain the fiction that these agents of law and order are servants of the ruler, but the reality is that they increasingly serve an abstract sovereign authority, rather than an individual ruler's will. A realistic account of order thus came to include limits on the ruler's power as well as a sharp distinction between order and the ruler's virtue. The initial formulations of Christian political realism were authoritarian in ways that medieval theology could not imagine, because Reformation realism lacked an ideal political order against which existing arrangements might be measured. Nevertheless, when the requirements of order are seen in light of the developing requirements of the modern state, with its extensive networks of commerce and the variety of its institutions and social relationships, order increasingly takes the form of a government limited by law and deriving its legitimacy from the consent of the governed. The image of the prince who maintains order by unlimited authority over life and goods gives way to the image of a democratic legislature, constrained by a constitutional understanding of its own limited purposes.

[38] See John Witte, *Law and Protestantism: The Legal Teachings of the Lutheran Reformation* (Cambridge: Cambridge University Press, 2002), pp. 105–17.

[39] Quoted in Edward S. Corwin, *The "Higher Law" Background of American Constitutional Law* (Ithaca, NY: Cornell University Press, 1955), pp. 38–9.

THE SUCCESSFUL MODERN STATE

Thus, there emerges from the Reformation era a new kind of political realism that Augustine himself never quite conceived. The good of peace provides a point of unity for all members of the civil community, virtuous and vicious, Christian and non-Christian, but a realistic assessment of the limits of civil peace focuses attention on the distinctive requirements of order, and politics is redefined from that starting point.

Luther, as we have seen, narrows the range of politics by excluding from the ruler's authority anything that depends on religious truth or spiritual well being. The relevant point for our purposes is not how Luther assigns specific things to either the spiritual or the secular realm, but the idea that the secular realm functions under its own rules, fitted to its own purposes and increasingly differentiated as a formal system of law from the personal authority of the ruler. In this realm where evil is restrained and order is maintained, faith and love provide no guidance, and the attempt to introduce them brings chaos, usually with bad results for the people who believe in faith and love. "And so to try to rule a whole country or the world by means of the Gospel is like herding together wolves, lions, eagles and sheep in the same pen . . . The sheep would certainly keep the peace and let themselves be governed and pastured peaceably, but they would not live long."[40] Political realism, by contrast, grants government the kind of authority it needs to fulfill its purposes and keeps that coercive power distinct from all other goods and values that might be pursued in other ways.

As this modern politics develops, Luther's differentiation between secular and spiritual authorities is transformed into the complementary realms of "public" and "private." Ideas about human good then belong to the private realm, where people make choices about religion, business affairs, marriage and family relations, education, and more. Where these choices do not intrude on public order, government has no authority over them and no wisdom to offer about them. The goods sought in private, likewise, have no claim on the powers of government to see that they are achieved.

Subsequent thinkers did not draw the lines exactly where Luther did. For him, secular authority extended over everything related to earthly life and goods, whereas spiritual authority governs matters of eternal life and relationship to God. Locke or Jefferson would have agreed that government and its laws have no power to decide religious questions, but they would

---

[40] Luther, "On Secular Authority," pp. 11–12.

also have identified a great many choices related to earthly life and goods that were similarly irrelevant to the government's distinctive functions of peace and order. Edmund Burke would have included "public prosperity" among the concerns of government, along with public peace and public order, but it was equally important for him to know the distinctive purposes of government, which determine the reach of government's authority, but also set limits on it.[41]

Wherever the boundary is drawn, however, the principle is that the two sorts of choice must be kept distinct. Private choices about the good cannot be put into effect by the power of government without disastrous consequences, any more than the Gospel of love could replace the sword wielded by Luther's secular authority, though as this realistic way of thinking develops in a more worldly direction, it seems that the group danger from the sword is not the true Christians, but the peaceable sheep in the secular fold, who would be attacked by the faithful, using government's public powers to impose their private choices about religion and virtue on others. As John Locke saw it, even the most vigorous defenders of religious truth "do hardly ever let loose this their Zeal for God, with which they are so warmed and inflamed, unless where they have the Civil Magistrate on their side."[42]

This was quite different from earlier political ideals that gave rulers moral authority and gave government a moral purpose. Government now existed to secure peace, and although peace required the rule of law, rather than arbitrary authority, peace also seemed to require that law know its own purposes and not offer its powers to those who were pursuing other goods. What everyone could agree on was the necessity of these distinctive goods of order and security, which only a government operating under these new rules that characterized the modern state could provide. The historic questions of politics – what other goods there might be, and how those goods were related to the goods of order and security, and to each other – could no longer be public questions, though people would, of course, continue to explore the questions and pursue the goods privately, on the terms that seemed best to them. The surprising thing turned out to be that they were able to do it so successfully.

Theologians and lawyers, believers and skeptics, princes and people thus argued their way to the idea of a sovereign state whose authority was limited

---

[41] Edmund Burke, "Thoughts and Details on Scarcity," in R. B. McDowell (ed.), *The Writings and Speeches of Edmund Burke*, vol. IX (Oxford: Clarendon Press, 1991), p. 143.

[42] John Locke, *A Letter Concerning Toleration*, James Tully (ed.) (Indianapolis: Hackett Publishing, 1983), p. 32.

by law. That kind of government proved equal to the task of providing an effective replacement for the old order of religious unity and feudal obligation that had broken down. Indeed, it made possible a good deal more. Luther's orderly government under which a person would have peace in which to "support his wife and children, feed himself, and serve God" began to offer family life, food and drink, and possibilities for worship, education, inspiration, and amusement on a scale Luther himself could not have conceived.

Within the framework of security provided by the modern state, spiritual and intellectual pursuits could thrive. Educational and cultural institutions grew and developed apart from the religious context that had sustained them in medieval Europe. The cultural changes begun during the Renaissance accelerated and spread more broadly into the population as the technology of printing made books widely available. The arts moved from ecclesiastical and aristocratic patronage to public performances and exhibitions.

Economic life expanded, fueled by growth in trade and the exploitation of new colonial resources. The growth of cities allowed money, as well as ideas, to circulate more quickly. People put their material security to practical use, creating new goods and new kinds of professions and corporations to organize economic life. Indeed, associations and institutions of all kinds flourished and multiplied, given a base of security and material resources in which to grow. The successful modern state, designed by people who were seeking peace and order, thus provides a setting in which they can pursue goods that are more abundant and complex than the need for security, taken by itself, would suggest. Indeed, where the modern state is working well, people may hardly think about security at all, as they open the castle gates, landscape their moats, go about their business on the highways, and draw up the legal documents that lock in their expectations of future gain.

Perhaps most important for our purposes was the development of a political order that could manage conflicts between these rapidly developing institutions and give political expression to the diversity of ideas and interests that the new, differentiated institutional contexts supported. To become the prevailing form of political organization, the modern state had to overcome the threat of disorder posed by strongly held religious ideas. Security seemed to require that sovereigns have power to dispose of religious conflicts without interference or appeals to higher authority, just as they were able to deploy coercive force within their realms without worrying about competing forces mounted by local barons or distant emperors. Providing a sovereign authority strong enough to make good on the claim *cujus regio, ejus religio* seemed essential at the beginning of the modern period. Yet the striking thing about the next two centuries was that peace prevailed, even while opinions multiplied. Religious differences persisted. Sects proliferated as education and communication enabled more people to formulate their own beliefs. New educational, business, and cultural institutions created their own constituencies with interests and ideas often quite different from the feudal or ecclesiastical institutions from which they emerged.

Ironically, the security that the modern state created gave rise to the sort of diversity of beliefs, institutions, and authorities that the sovereign's authority was supposed to suppress. Conventional wisdom had it that diversity threatened security, but here diversity and security developed side by side, and both survived. The end result was higher expectations. Life should not only be secure, but also prosperous and free.

We need not sort out all of the causes behind this transformation to appreciate the irony: A realistic way of thinking that reduced politics to the requirements of security created the political conditions for the most rapid expansion of goods, choices, and possibilities in human history. The grim recognition that people would not follow virtuous rulers as readily as they would obey strong ones gave way to new ways of thinking about goods and virtues in ordinary lives. Where Luther would not trust providence or politics to provide him with a wise prince, eighteenth-century moral sense theorists would consult an "honest farmer" to test ideas about moral relationships.[43]

POLITICS FOR THE PUBLIC

A good deal of attention has been given to what happens to religion as a result of this modern differentiation of public and private life. It may be more important to consider first what happens to politics, because people with this modern understanding of authority and order clearly cannot engage in politics in the Aristotelian sense of deliberation on the best human life and the ordering of community in ways that make that life possible. Or, to be more precise, they cannot connect that political deliberation to the authority of government. In private, of course, people are free to spend endless hours in Aristotelian political discussions. Nor should we suppose that in a free society this will be done entirely in dinner table conversation or sectarian study groups. University lectures, op-ed columns, and books about

---

[43] Francis Hutcheson, *An Inquiry into the Original of Our Ideas of Beauty and Virtue,* Wolfgang Leidhold (ed.) (Indianapolis: Liberty Fund, 2004), p. 112.

religion and politics are all part of what John Rawls called the "background culture."[44] Much can be accomplished there, but it should not be confused with the work of legislation, adjudication, and administration by which the coercive power of government is brought to bear on the problems of public order.

Indeed, it would be risky under these modern conditions to connect politics and government even in the more limited way that Augustine thought a workable commonwealth could be organized around common objects of love. Augustine recognizes that this consensus is always fragile, precisely because it never finds the one true good around which all other loves might be organized. The irony of the modern experience is that the more successful a government is at creating the conditions of peace under which people can pursue the goods on which they happen to agree, the more different goods they will produce, and the more opportunities they will have to quarrel over how those goods are to be understood and valued in relation to one another. The success of their Augustinian politics always imperils their Augustinian peace.

The modern solution, which Luther's distinction between spiritual and secular authority already anticipates, is that politics in the Aristotelian or Augustinian sense, politics that concerns human goods and the common objects of love, must be rigorously separated from the work of government. Aristotelian politics becomes private, as religion becomes private. We have obscured this momentous shift by continuing to use the word "politics" for activities associated with government and, indeed, to use the word especially for activities associated with getting and keeping the power that belongs uniquely to modern governments. But politics in the public sphere that the modern world has set apart for the distinctive tasks of peace and order must mean something quite different from Aristotelian politics, because the things with which Aristotelian politics is most concerned have been removed from that sphere.[45]

The new understanding of politics is reflected in the changing under-standings of secular authority from Luther's time to our own. For Luther, the secular ruler had an unchallengeable authority over life and goods, an authority necessary to the order that the ruler was divinely instituted to maintain. Subsequent developments quickly transferred that authority

---

[44] John Rawls, *Collected Papers*, Samuel Freeman (ed.) (Cambridge, MA: Harvard University Press, 1999), p. 576.

[45] For another view of the consequences of Luther's political thought, see Dietrich Bonhoeffer, *Ethics*, Dietrich Bonhoeffer Works, vol. VI. (Minneapolis, MN: Fortress Press, 2005), p. 113.

from the ruler's arbitrary will to the enactments of law, but modern theories of legal positivism still reflect the basic Reformation era idea that if you allow an unruly people to inject their different ideas about what the human good is into their discussion of what the law is, chaos will follow. Limits on the authority of rulers and lawmakers came in the form of distinctive rational requirements of law, rather than goods that had to be respected. Principles of universality and reciprocity were traced back to Roman maxims or formulated as categorical imperatives, but the idea in various forms was that rules of procedure or rational consistency provide the primary test of legal authority. Henceforward, the ruler would have to maintain justice as well as peace, but justice would be defined in rational terms that did not require agreement on goods. The commonwealth was secured by agreement on principles of justice, not by common objects of love.

Citizens of the successful modern state are not like Luther's Christians, willing to accept whatever disposition the sovereign makes of their lives and worldly goods, so that they may witness to a spiritual good which promises something far better. Nor are they like Hobbes's subjects, submitting to the judgments of the sovereign lest they suffer something worse in an unrestrained state of nature. Citizens of the successful modern state belong, rather, to a Lockean civil society, seeking a sovereign protector from foreign enemies and an impartial judge who will follow the rule of law and to spare them the "inconveniences" of having to enforce their claims for themselves.[46] The justice they seek comes not from an authority who will tell them what the right ordering of goods is, but from someone who will settle their claims fairly, according to rational principles of justice that the parties have accepted for themselves. This justice requires what later theorists would identify as the priority of right over good.[47] Instead of awarding the goods at issue to the most virtuous, the modern judge tries to balance competing interests fairly, without deciding which side has made the best choices.

At least that is how politics in the successful modern state appears once it has been rendered consistent by liberal political theory. Liberal theory in all its variations translates the Reformation idea of secular authority into a government structured by law and subject to reasoned judgment. Liberal theory makes sense of the emergence of a new kind of politics in which everyone participates in the exercise of secular authority by using reason

[46] John Locke, *Two Treatises of Government*, Peter Laslett (ed.) (Cambridge: Cambridge University Press, 1988), p. 276.
[47] John Rawls, *A Theory of Justice* (Cambridge, MA: Harvard University Press, 1971), p. 31.

to establish and anticipate the requirements of justice. Modern politics need not be authoritarian, because the requirements of order are known to reason and can be embodied in law, to which those who hold power can be held accountable. But modern politics cannot be Aristotelian, because the requirements of order dictate a justice that is not tied to questions about the good. Those questions are part of the background culture, appropriately discussed in private settings.

REALISM AND LIBERALISM

It is not difficult to trace a line of theological criticism that parallels the development of this liberal understanding of politics. From sixteenth-century Dominicans and Jesuits who criticized Luther's account of secular authority to postmodern theologians who deconstruct the rationalism of liberal political theory, significant Christian thinkers have simply rejected the premises of liberalism as incompatible with a Christian understanding of politics.

The Christian idealism which shaped Catholic political thought through the Middle Ages could not easily surrender the Aristotelian idea of politics, which had been linked more closely to Augustine's ideas about the good by the work of Thomas Aquinas. From that perspective, the liberal priority of the right over the good could only be seen as a sign of moral confusion, and the development of an expansive public sphere of liberal politics in which determinations of justice are made without reference to a fixed order of human goods is a formula for social dissolution, rather than a requirement of peace and stability.

Papal social teaching, especially, rejected any accommodation with liberal political ideas until late in the nineteenth century,[48] and conservative Catholic thinkers have continued to resist the idea of a neutral public order. From their point of view, democratic procedures alone are unable to produce true justice, which requires a just ordering of goods in relation to one another. Indeed, democratic procedures are unlikely to work over the long run unless the people who act in this public realm are shaped by Christian theological convictions.[49]

[48] Peter Steinfels, "The Failed Encounter: The Catholic Church and Liberalism in the Nineteenth Century," in R. Bruce Douglas and David Hollenbach (eds.), *Catholicism and Liberalism: Contributions to American Public Philosophy* (Cambridge: Cambridge University Press, 1994), pp. 19–44.
[49] Emmet John Hughes, *The Church and Liberal Society* (Princeton, NJ: Princeton University Press, 1944), pp. 35–51; John Murray Cuddihy, *No Offense: Civil Religion and Protestant Taste* (New York: Seabury Press, 1978).

By contrast to this political idealism, once Reformation realism had clearly drawn the line between spiritual and secular authority, the way was open for some Christians to withdraw from the work of government and leave secular authority to others. The Swiss Brethren, Mennonites, and other Anabaptist groups rejected both the benefits and the burdens of governments and sought to create Christian communities that would maintain their own peace by purely spiritual means. Seeing clearly what kind of politics is going to be possible in the modern world, they concluded that it has nothing to do with Christian faith and focused their religious energy elsewhere. This position continues to be important, as our discussion of the "Witness" in the previous chapter shows, but the characterization of this movement as a rejection of "Constantinian" Christianity obscures its historical origins. Both the natural law jurisprudence that emerged in Catholic thought and this sectarian Protestant rejection of government and politics are responses to the understanding of secular authority that arose with the Reformation. Christian idealism and sectarian radicalism found themselves equally unable to inhabit the political world of a strictly secular authority, whether that authority is Luther's prince, who knows that he is nothing more than God's glorified hangman, or a liberal, democratic legislature, which provides impartial justice while maintaining neutrality between competing ideas of the human good.

Christian realism, however, was too closely involved in the emergence of the idea of secular authority simply to reject the modern politics that grew from it. Order and security were extremely important to the Reformers, and their dire predictions of what would happen to human life if those who preached Christian freedom from the restraints of government gained the ascendancy read like today's warnings about the effects of global warming. A world in which order and security are lacking becomes uninhabitable. Precisely because the civil peace that Augustine saw as essential to any human society had now clearly become the exclusive business of government, Reformation realism insisted on the dignity and authority of that government, and this support continued through the emergence of more legal, liberal, and democratic forms of secular authority.

Christian realism diverges from political liberalism only after modern politics takes a sort of utopian turn in the nineteenth century. As democratic institutions developed and liberal societies prospered, expectations for what could be accomplished under a properly organized government grew. A whole range of needs might be supplied by commerce. Arts, culture, and education would flourish. Justice, administered according to neutral principles, would begin to approximate the human good, without the necessity to come to agreement about the good itself. Eventually, a properly organized society would not only restrain evil, as Luther and Calvin insisted it must. A properly organized society would eliminate evil by creating public conditions under which it would no longer be possible. The constraints that law puts on behavior, when finely tuned, can accomplish the desired results. In America, at least, theological and scientific versions of this utopian idea moved together. Walter Rauschenbusch articulated it in its most developed form: "If the twentieth century could do for us in the control of social forces what the nineteenth did for us in the control of natural forces, our grandchildren would live in a society that would be justified in regarding our present social life as semi-barbarous."[50]

This expansive, utopian view was always at variance with more realistic Christian themes about the persistence of evil and history's ironic reversals of human achievements. When events conspired at the beginning of the twentieth century to refute the predictions of continual progress, some theologians were ready with a different account of what had happened in the catastrophe of the Great War and what we might expect in the future. It was at this point that the long tradition of Christian realism became a self-conscious movement, identifying itself by name.

Reinhold Niebuhr was not the first to speak of "theological realism" or "Christian realism," but he became its public voice, and he achieved this role in large part by explaining that Christian realism not only rejects the assumptions of previous theology, but condemns the easy conscience of an entire culture. The problem with the liberal Protestantism of the American mainstream, he wrote in 1935, is that it joins forces with secular utopianism by reducing the demands of the Gospel to "prudential rules of conduct which the common sense of many generations and the experience of the ages have elaborated."[51] It then appears that Jesus's command to love your neighbor as yourself demands no more than what a reasonable accommodation of the neighbor's needs requires.

Therefore, the first step toward a realistic Christian ethics is to make a distinction between love and justice. This requires a recognition of the radical demands of love, which can be seen in Jesus's imprudent and unreasonable commands: Take no thought for your life . . . take no thought for tomorrow . . . lend without expecting repayment . . . give everything you have. It also requires an appropriate lowering of expectations for justice. "The ethic of Jesus does not deal at all with the immediate moral problem

---

[50] Walter Rauschenbusch, *Christianity and the Social Crisis* (New York: Macmillan, 1907), p. 421.
[51] Reinhold Niebuhr, *An Interpretation of Christian Ethics* (New York: Seabury Press, 1979), p. 63.

of every human life – the problem of arranging some kind of armistice between contending factions and forces."[52] Even the most fragile social peace is a difficult achievement. Justice names the equilibrium between competing forces that allows that peace to become relatively stable and durable. Justice, to put the matter in theological terms, "is the approximation of brotherhood under the conditions of sin."[53]

Niebuhr speaks of justice as an approximation of love, but this does not mean that it is simply a partial or less demanding application of Jesus's commands. The requirements of justice have their own integrity, and cannot be reduced to a partial list of what love in its fullness would require. Justice must be determined by attention to concrete details of historical situations. There are principles of justice that enable us to locate the balance between competing forces and to understand which direction the interests and powers at work in a situation are driving events. Niebuhr's principles are interpretative or "regulative" principles, which set the parameters within which we may expect to find competing interests arriving at a reasonable accommodation to one another. Those who value stability will work to keep social conflict within those boundaries. Those who have a realistic grasp of Christian ethics will call the results "justice," without confusing them with the requirements of love.[54]

Niebuhr's principles of justice are less determinative than the principles of John Rawls's theory of justice. Rawls would no doubt have found Niebuhr's equilibrium between liberty and equality too vague to provide any normative guidance, and Rawls's derivation of the principles of justice would question Niebuhr's way of relating justice and love. We will have occasion to consider the differences between Christian realism and liberal theory in more detail in later chapters. At the outset, however, it is important to note one thing that Niebuhr has in common with Rawls and the other liberal theorists. They share the idea that justice provides norms for a distinctive sphere of life that is governed by different expectations from those that mark the highest aspirations of personal life or a comprehensive achievement of human good. This distinction depends on a kind of political realism that we first see clearly in the way the Reformation realists separated spiritual and secular authority. Although sectarian and idealist Christian critics rejected this realism at the outset, political liberalism and

---

[52] *Ibid.*, p. 23.
[53] Reinhold Niebuhr, *The Nature and Destiny of Man*, vol. I (Louisville, KY: Westminster John Knox Press, 1996), p. 254.
[54] For an account that gives more attention to the nontheological sources of Niebuhr's political realism, see Ronald H. Stone, *Prophetic Realism* (New York: T. & T. Clark, 2005), pp. 10–26.

Christian political realism developed together until the twentieth century, when the failure of revolutionary ideologies and utopian expectations led both theologians and political philosophers to reassess the role of religious ideals in public, political discussions. In some respects, political liberalism and Christian realism decided to blame one another for the failures of utopianism.

Of course, both sides continued to reject utopianism, but by the end of the twentieth century, there were few real utopians left to oppose. Utopianism was an idea to accuse other people of holding. Antiutopian Christian realists detected utopianism among theologians and preachers who were reluctant to use force to restrain the spread of communism or to resist evil in the war on terrorism. Secular political realists made similar criticisms of those who wanted to rely on the United Nations or on multilateral agreements to keep the peace. Likewise, both political liberalism and Christian realism rejected a new sectarian activism that sought to redefine the political order in moral and religious terms and questioned whether a justice that differs from divine law is worth pursuing.

JUSTICE AND HOPE

Christian realists and liberal theorists remain united in their rejection of utopian thinking that replaces the carefully worked out requirements of justice with a moral language that transcends the available political options. Realists and liberals begin to eye one another warily, however, when systems of justice are challenged by those who find the available political options insufficient.

People on the margins of society often assert needs that cannot be met by a more evenhanded application of prevailing ideas of justice. Of course, they may be denied access to courts or lack influence in the legislature, but this is not the root of the problem. The root of the problem is that the prevailing idea of justice itself diminishes their humanity and limits their possibilities. They are slaves, illegal immigrants, members of an inferior race, or followers of an alien religion. Giving them justice, if justice continues to see them that way, will only make their situation worse. They seek a society that defines its justice in different terms.

They do not, however, typically make their demands in philosophical terms that challenge the accepted principles of justice, especially when their suffering has been long and the prospects for immediate change are not great. They claim a justice that is closer to divine love, and they claim it, not as a utopian alternative to the prevailing idea of justice, but as a divine judgment on it. They sustain hope by an appeal to God, precisely because no power within the framework of justice in their society can deliver the justice they seek.

At this point, Christian realists and liberal theorists share a problem faced by all politics shaped by Reformation realism's idea of secular authority. Order and justice, which are the purposes of politics, require a single system of sovereign authority in each state. To secure order, the judgments of secular authority must stand, without a higher legal authority to which they might be appealed or a moral authority by which they might be invalidated. Even for those who know their opposition to be right, Calvin insists, there is no recourse but to "obey and suffer."[55]

Luther and Calvin qualified this position, for otherwise their Reformation would not have survived the opposition of the secular authorities arrayed against it. Secular authority cannot be purely arbitrary. It must rule by law, and it may be challenged where the law itself provides these opportunities.[56] As secular authority becomes more liberal, constitutional, and democratic, citizens regularly use legislation or litigation to hold the immediate judgments of the authorities accountable to recognized principles of justice.

What happens, though, when the prevailing idea of justice itself is questioned? How can one argue for the freedom of slaves, or the rights of minorities, or protection of the poor when the law itself affirms that slaves are property, establishes classes and categories of citizenship, or remains silent about economic and social rights? If the liberal version of the idea of secular authority distinguishes between religious and moral ideals that some people may hold in private and the principles of justice to which everyone must appeal in public discussion, how can there be a moral or religious challenge to the shared, public understanding of justice? Both the liberal political philosopher who distinguishes public from private reasons and the Christian realist who distinguishes justice from love want to establish a framework in which a shared, public discourse can settle ordinary questions of justice and policy without pausing to consider unreasonable, impractical, or eccentric demands.

The problem is that public reason itself must determine what is reasonable, practical, and public, because it recognizes no higher authority to which those determinations might be referred or appealed. Rawlsian liberals

---

[55] Calvin, "On Civil Government," p. 82.
[56] Quentin Skinner, *The Foundations of Modern Political Thought*, vol. II (Cambridge: Cambridge University Press, 1978), pp. 189–238.

and Niebuhrian realists alike seem to be back in the uncomfortable position of the Reformers, preaching obedience to secular authority while the lawyers look for constitutional loopholes that might permit resistance to authorities whose ideas of what is reasonable definitely do not include Reformation.

The intellectual problem becomes more difficult over time. Everyone knows that public understandings of justice have changed, often in ways that seem conclusively better. Although slavery was once a disputed question, it now seems impossible to use accepted principles of justice to argue that persons can be property. Equal rights of citizenship now preclude all sorts of social distinctions that were once regarded as entirely appropriate. Claims to a minimum standard of food, housing, and medical care are in many places regarded in the same way as the right to equal treatment under the law. No one doubts that such changes in the public understanding of justice occur. The question is whether we can make sense of them using a theory of justice which also says that it is unjust to change basic provisions of the law for reasons other than those that everyone could reasonably accept.[57]

John Rawls acknowledged that these historic changes are rarely explicable as the strict working out of neutral principles of justice in arguments limited to public reasons. In the United States, the end of slavery and legalized discrimination depended heavily on leaders who aroused the public to action by religious ideas. So it appears to Rawls that Abraham Lincoln and Martin Luther King Jr. spoke within the requirements of public reason, even though their greatest words invoked divine justice in judgment against prevailing law and morality. The religious language that shaped abolitionism or the civil rights movement was necessary at the time to bring about social transformations required by the principles of justice, and may for that reason be regarded as consistent with the requirements of public reason.[58] Exceptional cases stretch the language, if not the logic, of public reason, and at least in retrospect, we can recognize the validity of arguments that cannot always be made decisively in the public terms available at a critical time in history.

In contrast to the normative sufficiency that Rawls generally finds in the principles of justice defined by public reason, Niebuhr suggests that the pressure toward a "higher justice" is constant, not occasional or exceptional.

---

[57] John Rawls, *Political Liberalism* (New York: Columbia University Press, 1996), pp. 212–20; Rawls, *Collected Papers*, pp. 573–614.
[58] John Rawls, *Political Liberalism*, pp. 247–51.

A theory of justice must either settle for an endorsement of conventional moral expectations or place itself in a dialectical relationship with an impossible moral ideal.[59] At least some accommodation must be made for the illusion that perfect justice is possible, or the realistic standard of justice will become nothing more than a justification of privilege. Especially in his early work, Niebuhr acknowledges that admitting this illusion into the politics of liberal democracy will encourage fanaticism. "The illusion is dangerous because it encourages terrible fanaticisms. It must therefore be brought under the control of reason. One can only hope that reason will not destroy it before its work is done."[60]

The requirements of public reason which John Rawls articulated four decades later seem designed, by contrast, to exclude not only fanaticism, but also the more moderate forms of coercion that occur when widely shared religious and moral expectations are incorporated into law, enforced by courts, and imposed on those who aspire to public leadership. From Rawls's point of view, there is little difference between the repressive moral order imposed by a fundamentalist fanatic and a system of justice imposed by Christian realists who think that a moderate application of the law of love will make their fellow citizens better people for it.

Once Rawls's idea of public reason became an important criterion of what should and should not be said in political arguments, liberals began to suspect that Niebuhrian realists, with their constant references to the still-relevant "impossible ideal," were ready to by-pass the requirements of public reason with a quick and vague appeal to the ultimate law of love. Christian realists who shared many of the values of liberalism argued, by contrast, that liberal theorists were destroying hope and denying history by excluding from politics the language of aspiration that has led to many important advances in justice. It aggravates the conflict between liberal theorists and Christian realists on this point that the language of aspiration is often religious, but that is not the main issue. The main issue is whether language which appeals to a different understanding of justice has any place in the public discussion of what justice requires.[61]

The question has generated a large literature, but few conclusions. In general, the more cautious participants in the debate uphold the terms of public reason and argue that the only aspirations we should admit to public

---

[59] Niebuhr, *An Interpretation of Christian Ethics*, p. 64.

[60] Reinhold Niebuhr, *Moral Man and Immoral Society* (Louisville, KY: Westminster John Knox Press, 2001), p. 277.

[61] See Jeremy Waldron, "Religious Contributions in Public Deliberation," *San Diego Law Review* 30 (1993), 817–48.

discussion are those which can at least retrospectively be explained in those terms. The more adventurous would allow people to argue in whatever way they wish. The lines that divide the cautious from the adventurous do not coincide neatly with who is religious and who is not.

Christian realism does not begin with a clear position on this question. Niebuhr says very little about how the impossible ideal which is always relevant to concrete, historical choices becomes relevant to the public discussion of them. The utopian or the fanatic simply disrupts the discussion by demanding realization of the ideal. The more reasonable realist brings more concrete ideas to the table, but the realist's sense of possibility has been expanded by reading the same scriptures that moved the fanatic to action. And of course, Niebuhr supposed that all the others in the public discussion knew those scriptures, too, whether or not they shared his religious convictions. The whole literature about what is public and what is not would have baffled him.

Seen in a broader historical perspective, that debate is in any case an argument among antiutopian political realists who continue together to work out the implications of Reformation realism's idea of political authority. The successful modern state has allowed the development of a public, political discussion broader in scope, more open, and more effective in transforming society than anything a Reformation realist could have anticipated. Liberal theorists now view these transformations primarily as the work of public reason, which keeps political discussions from being captured by ideals that demand unreasoned assent and foreclose the exploration of new possibilities. Christian realists assert that these transformations demonstrate the continued relevance of religious and moral ideals, which prevent premature satisfaction with the achievements of public discussion and keep us from reducing the hope of the poor to conventional justice and generosity. Does public reason admit the possibility of a justice which might exceed conventional expectations? Does the dialectic between love and justice have any place in reasoned public discussions? Perhaps these questions cannot be completely answered within the context formed by legislation, litigation, and the work of government.

BEYOND SECULAR AUTHORITY

The differentiation of secular political authority from an ideal unity of religion and government marks the beginning of modern politics and creates the space in which both political liberalism and antiutopian Christian realism have grown. It is within that space that they now argue with one another about the integrity of public reason and the relevance of Christian hope. It is important space, but it was not the only space open to discussion, even at the beginning of the modern era. Already with Augustine's realism came the recognition that Christian life takes different forms.[62] Some resemble the philosopher's ideal of the contemplative life or the active life. Others are centered on more practical concerns. These ways of life represent enduring concerns of faith, rule, and domestic life, but they also take on transient forms dictated by culture and circumstances. If the distinction between "public" and "private" can be traced back to Luther's dualism of religious and secular authority, the reflection on these multiple forms of Christian life takes its start from another Lutheran idea: the three "estates" or "orders" of church, government, and family.[63]

The differentiation of secular authority within the order of government was a momentous event, but it was not the only new thing that was taking shape in Luther's time. Other aspects of life were being organized in new and more specialized ways, and increased clarity about the nature of secular authority was matched by a sharper delineation of other vocations and the institutions in which they were lived. Although it is true that without law and government, no one could "support wife and children, feed himself, and serve God,"[64] secular authority alone is not sufficient to secure those goods. They depend on a variety of different social spheres, and the goods that make physical and spiritual life possible must be sought in each order or estate on its own terms. Each creates and maintains its distinctive goods according to its own pattern, developing its own discourse and its own rules to govern the process. The goods that human life requires are created in the multiplicity of these institutional contexts, so that what happens in the ruler's councils, courts, tax offices, and armories is only part of what a political realist should be watching.

Nor should we suppose that government, family, and church are privileged estates which make a difference to the human good, while there might be other areas of life that are morally indifferent. Luther intended the estates to be comprehensive, covering between them all the ways of life available to Christian people. Luther's "family" is an extended community

---

[62] Augustine, *City of God*, p. 948. See earlier pp. 49–50.

[63] Although Luther thought his teaching on civil authority was a return to the New Testament, the three estates have more immediate antecedents in medieval theology and ethics. See Ulrik Nissen, "Between Identity and Differentiation: On the Identity of Lutheran Social Ethics," *The Sources of Public Morality – On the Ethics and Religion Debate*, Proceedings of the Annual Conference of the Societas Ethica, August 2001 (Münster, LIT Verlag, 2003), pp. 152–57.

[64] Luther, "Secular Authority," p. 10. See earlier, p. 53.

that includes servants and workers and encompasses almost all economic activities of trade and production. Much of what we would think of as distinct spheres of education and culture were in Luther's time still part of the church. Later enumerations of the orders almost always include more than just Luther's three, and it seems that what is important is not their number, but the fact that together they provide what is needed to make a good life possible.

Those who developed this practical wisdom about the requirements of life did not, in most cases, think of what they were doing as politics. Many of them, indeed, questioned the new, modern politics or rejected its secular authority as unchristian. But the sharp differences that separated the magisterial reformation of Luther and Calvin from the radical reformation of the sectarians were softened by developments that followed outside the sphere of government. To understand the possibilities for contemporary Christian realism, we need to recall these post-Reformation developments in some detail, lest the well publicized arguments between today's realist Witness and today's Antiutopian Realist mislead us into thinking that subsequent history has been nothing more than a recapitulation of the sixteenth century. The questions that Christians faced as European society developed were more complex than whether to accept or to reject secular authority, nor should we let our field of vision shrink to the point that this seems like the only question we have to answer.

By the beginning of the eighteenth century, European society was much more complex than it had been at the time of the Reformation, and the developments that most affected people's lives had shifted from church and government to other areas of business and culture. Those who withdrew from secular politics now had a different set of options from those that confronted the early Anabaptists. Some continued to migrate to unsettled parts of Central Europe, Russia, or North America, but others were drawn to growing cities. There, they found themselves among many others who stood on the margins of modern politics. Calvinists, whose theology made more place than the sectarians allowed for secular authority, often found that the prevailing secular authorities wanted no part of their Calvinist theology. Baptists and Independents created small congregations that stayed clear of both Catholic and established Protestant connections. Religious refugees and migrants of all sorts brought their faiths with them.

All of these were politically marginalized, but they made a place for themselves in social and economic life nonetheless. Merchants, bankers, and traders found new ways to organize themselves to share risks and make money. Those who prospered in trade turned around and created new schools, cultural centers, and social institutions. The modern world was creating a multiplicity of new ways to create human goods and ways to live the good life that did not exist in the medieval world and the age of Reformation. Those who had withdrawn or who were excluded from the recognized forms of religious organization were perhaps the most effective participants and the greatest beneficiaries of these changes. English dissenters, French Protestants, politically marginalized Scots, working people made sober and industrious by evangelical preachers, and disenfranchised North American colonists of all religious persuasions not only found a place for themselves in the midst of these changes. They reshaped the institutional landscape available to themselves and others. During the two centuries from 1600 to 1800, these politically marginal people on both sides of the Atlantic found ways to make themselves more wealthy, better educated, and more effective in their philanthropy than the political and religious elites who initially regarded them with such suspicion. The American Revolution marked the beginning of a long struggle for political standing to match their social achievements, but by that time, they had their own ideas about what made a good society. Where Luther and Augustine had emphasized the importance of order in times of dissolution and conflict, John Wesley and Adam Smith emphasized practical collaboration on shared goods that helped people be virtuous, as well as orderly.[65]

It would be hard to overestimate the importance of these developments for the future shape of religion and politics, especially in Britain and North America. The marginal groups eventually became the mainstream, but they retained the commitments to voluntary associations, mutual aid, and private philanthropy that their traditions developed during their years of political isolation.

Perhaps most important, although the people who developed the marginal model became the mainstream, their way of thinking about faith and life continued to provide others on the margins with a way to understand their situation, exercise some control over their lives, and even influence the direction of the wider society. Quite beyond the intentions of the mainstream, and in some cases against their active resistance, the

---

[65] Gertrude Himmelfarb, *The Idea of Poverty: England in the Early Industrial Age* (New York: Alfred A. Knopf, 1983); Herbert Schlossberg, *The Silent Revolution and the Making of Victorian England* (Columbus: Ohio State University Press, 2000).

institutional models they had created became available to the very groups that they thought they needed to exclude, expel, or control. In the United States, African Americans after the Civil War, European immigrants in the late nineteenth century, and women in the early twentieth century all found the model of free congregations, voluntary organizations, and a commitment to mutual assistance to be the key to a better life, and ultimately, the key to political empowerment. African American churches, colleges, and businesses replicated, with a distinctly American accent, the successes of the middle-class Nonconformists in England a century or two before. None of these groups wanted to be excluded from political power, and all of them eventually found ways of acquiring it. But by the time they did acquire it, they had learned that there were ways of shaping society that did not depend solely on success in modern politics.

Or perhaps we should say that these politically marginalized people reshaped politics, along with the other institutions they remade. Here, instead of modern politics, narrowly focused on the requirements of order and public reason, we have Aristotle's politics, continued by other means. From this point of view, it is not quite true that modern politics no longer concerns itself with the full reality of human good. There is no single deliberative body and no single system of rules that governs all discussions, but there are many different social spheres, each creating a discourse appropriate to its own goods and goals – religion and government, but also education, commerce, and culture. The variety of shared human goods that are possible in the modern state creates a pluralistic politics, in place of the dualisms of secular and spiritual, or public and private.

PLURALIST REALISM

Luther, as we have seen, was a political realist who rejected the tradition of virtuous rulers governing their kingdoms according to a Christian ideal. But he was also, like Augustine, a moral realist who recognized peace and order as genuine human goods and concentrated his political thinking on the kind of authority that would be required to create and maintain them. We have traced the developments that take that kind of political and moral realism from Luther's secular authority to recent versions of political liberalism and Christian realism. As the modern world grew more differentiated and its institutions became more complex, similar ways of thinking emerged in each of the spheres of human life where less than ideal authorities nonetheless recognized and mastered the requirements of real human goods. The result has been several modern versions of the doctrine of orders and estates.[66]

What this pluralist realism seeks is not some ideal configuration of the orders, but recognition of the genuine variety of human goods. Orders or spheres are ways of coping with this variety. The relatively simple structures of late medieval or early modern society might be understood in terms of fewer orders than we need today, but given the genuine diversity of human needs, it is unlikely that any society could provide all of them without some differentiation of its activities and authorities. As the level of knowledge and social organization required to produce and maintain any good increases, more and more goods will require distinct institutions with their own ways of working, and the number of recognized orders or estates will increase.

The political realist also emphasizes that diversity of existing institutions is not to be brought too quickly into harmony under some single idea of the good. Different values which are at home in different institutional settings and different goods that exist in some tension and competition with one another are part of the conditions of life, especially in modern times. Work, family, church, and culture are so different from one another that we cannot think about them as they really are and still think about all of them in the same terms.

This point is made in various ways in various traditions. Reformed theologians have developed it most extensively, which is not surprising, given the role of Calvinists and other Reformed Christians in shaping the social and economic institutions that developed rapidly after the Reformation. Emil Brunner's theology of the "orders of creation" is an important example. Brunner finds parallels in other areas of life to the ordering and preserving role of the state. It is not just the state which secures order in a world of conflict, and the order it preserves is not just its own. State, church, family, labor, and culture are "orders of creation,"[67] by which God sustains human life against the destructive forces unleashed by human sin. Against a simplification of Luther's thought that made the ruler's law alone responsible for the restraint of evil, Brunner argues that each of the structures of social life has its own law-like authority, derived from its role in preserving the essential order of God's creation. "This means that we have to acknowledge

---

[66] James W. Skillen and Rockne M. McCarthy (eds.), *Political Order and the Plural Structure of Society* (Atlanta, GA: Scholars Press, 1991).

[67] *Schöpfungsordnungen.* See Emil Brunner, *The Divine Imperative*, Olive Wyon (trans.) (Philadelphia: Westminster Press, 1947), p. 208.

divinely appointed objective limits to our freedom and objective guides to the ordering of our society. That is the only way out of this chaos – the way which gives to the Reformers' ethics on the one hand their assurance and on the other hand their realism."[68]

Dietrich Bonhoeffer developed a similar conception of the orders in his early lectures on Genesis 1–3, in which he speaks of "orders of preservation."[69] He returned to the idea in his unfinished *Ethics*, where he describes the "divine mandates" of work, marriage, government, and church.[70] Bonhoeffer's development of this idea cannot be separated from his role in the church's resistance to Hitler. In the context of a totalitarian state which sought to impose a common political order on all social institutions, Bonhoeffer insisted not only on the diversity of the mandates, but also on their interdependence and even their potential for conflict with one another. The mandates do not exist in splendid isolation. They are oriented toward one another, and Bonhoeffer recognizes this means they will sometimes oppose one another. A social environment free of conflict and opposition is a sure sign that an artificial order has displaced the complex interaction between the mandates that Christian realism studies. "Where *being-over-against-one-another* is no longer present, God's mandate no longer exists."[71]

The pluralist perspective, however, is not found only among theologians who explicitly develop the Reformation idea of estates or orders. John Neville Figgis developed an Anglo-Catholic pluralism that relied more heavily on traditions of natural law and connected pluralism more directly to the medieval institutions of church and university, which developed according to their own laws, undefined and relatively unconstrained by the laws and courts of kings and princes. For Figgis, the tendency in modern politics to treat every institution as though it existed only by legislative fiat marks law's abandonment of moral realism. The result may have power, but it lacks plausibility. "Does the Church exist by some inward living force, with powers of self-development like a person," he asked; "or is she a mere

---

[68] Emil Brunner, "Nature and Grace," in Emil Brunner and Karl Barth, *Natural Theology*, Peter Fraenkel (trans.) (Eugene, OR: Wipf and Stock, 2002), p. 52. See also Brunner, *Divine Imperative*, pp. 262–3. A similar idea is expressed by Abraham Kuyper (1837–1920), who ascribed to each of the spheres of social life the same kind of independence that modern sovereign states claimed for themselves. See Abraham Kuyper, *Lectures on Calvinism* (Grand Rapids, MI: Eerdmans, 2000), pp. 90–1.

[69] Dietrich Bonhoeffer, *Creation and Fall: A Theological Exposition of Genesis 1–3*, Dietrich Bonhoeffer Works, vol. III. (Minneapolis, MN: Fortress Press, 1997), p. 140. We will explore Bonhoeffer's relation to Brunner in more detail in the next chapter.

[70] Dietrich Bonhoeffer, *Ethics*, Dietrich Bonhoeffer Works, vol. VI. (Minneapolis, MN: Fortress Press, 2005), p. 68. The list of the mandates differs slightly at different points in *Ethics*.

[71] Bonhoeffer, *Ethics*, p. 394.

aggregate, a fortuitous concourse of ecclesiastical atoms, treated it may be as one for purposes of convenience, but with no real mind or will of her own, except so far as the civil power sees good to invest her for the nonce with a fiction of unity?"[72]

Figgis's question was first addressed to clergy, but it encouraged the development in British political thought of a pluralism represented in the work of G. D. H. Cole and Harold Laski.[73] More recently, William Galston has developed these political ideas in relation to the "value pluralism" of Isaiah Berlin. By this path, Galston makes a case for liberalism based on political pluralism and moral realism, in contrast to Rawls's theory of justice, which focuses narrowly on the requirements of public reason and confines itself to the "public, political forum." Michael Walzer has also offered a pluralistic account of the "spheres of justice," though he seeks to remain altogether within the political realm, without philosophical or theological commitments to moral realism. In effect, Walzer accepts liberal theory's priority of the right over the good, but he provides a pluralistic account of the right.[74]

In a quite different way, unrelated to the Reformed and Anglican theologies we have just surveyed, Catholic social teaching developed a version of pluralism that provided a way to adapt the Christian idealism of the medieval church to the changing institutional environment of the modern world. Leo XIII's encyclical *Rerum Novarum* (1891) reasserted the inviolability of an ordering of society required by natural law, but rejected the conservative conclusions about the new claims for the rights of labor that natural law had previously been seen to require. The fact that human beings are social creatures who meet their needs in communities does not lock them into a permanent place in an unchanging social hierarchy. New forms of worker organization at the local level can claim recognition and respect both from the property owners who run the businesses and from the state. For *Rerum Novarum*, the moral realism of Catholic doctrine is not a permanent commitment to the structures of a medieval economy. A

---

[72] John Neville Figgis, *Churches in the Modern State* (London: Longmans, Green and Co., 1913), p. 40. This book began as four lectures delivered to Anglican clergy in the Diocese of Gloucester in 1911.

[73] Henry M. Magid, *English Political Pluralism: The Problem of Freedom and Organization* (New York: Columbia University Press, 1941); Paul Q. Hirst, (ed.), *The Pluralist Theory of the State: Selected writings of G. D. H. Cole, J. N. Figgis, and H. J. Laski* (London: Routledge, 1989).

[74] See William A. Galston, *Liberal Pluralism: The Implications of Value Pluralism for Political Theory and Practice* (Cambridge: Cambridge University Press, 2002); Isaiah Berlin, *Liberty*, Henry Hardy (ed.) (Oxford: Oxford University Press, 2002), pp. 212–17; Michael Walzer, *Spheres of Justice* (New York: Basic Books, 1983), pp. 8–19. For a very useful typology of political theories in relation to the questions of pluralism and realism, see Galston, *Liberal Pluralism*, pp. 3–11.

cautious measure of political realism recognizes that new institutions can form and differentiate themselves from existing structures.

By the fortieth anniversary of *Rerum Novarum*, papal social teaching had moved a long way in the direction of accepting institutions created in modern times as a way to organize work, education, and welfare. Pius XI's encyclical *Quadragesimo Anno* (1931) gave a name to the developing concept of "subsidiarity," which held that social problems should be solved when possible by people organizing themselves at the local level.[75] The implicit pluralism of Catholic social teaching became more explicit as the popes confronted totalitarian regimes in Italy and Germany that proposed a sweeping reorganization of social life under the leadership of a central, state authority.

Both the course of events and the internal logic of the papal social teaching have required further development of this pluralism. Concern for peace and global economic development, the conflict with communist regimes in Eastern Europe, and the new set of economic questions posed after the collapse of the Soviet Union have elicited further developments in relation to the diversity of modern institutions.[76] Papal teaching continues a strong commitment to an ideal ordering of these various institutions and their relationships, but increasing attention to the details of specific problems and increasing recognition of the diversity required by local conditions allows the combination of a kind of political pluralism and moral realism within the framework of Catholic social teaching.

David Hollenbach explores this possibility in his study of the common good.[77] Full participation by Catholics in public life requires not only an ideal, but historical and social categories which can guide action in nonideal situations.[78] These categories come from the interaction between a theological unity of human good and an understanding of the variety of social and institutional forms that societies develop to maintain the goods they share. In the reality of historical existence, Hollenbach says,

---

[75] Michael Pakaluk, "Natural Law and Civil Society," in Simone Chambers and Will Kymlicka (eds.), *Alternative Conceptions of Civil Society*, Ethikon Series in Comparative Ethics (Princeton, NJ: Princeton University Press, 2002), pp. 131–48.

[76] Primary documents of this development include *Pacem in Terris* (1963), *Populorum Progressio* (1967), *Laborem Exercens* (1981), and *Centesimus Annus* (1991). For texts, see David O'Brien and Thomas Shannon (eds.), *Catholic Social Thought: The Documentary Heritage* (Maryknoll, NY: Orbis Books, 1992).

[77] David Hollenbach, *The Common Good and Christian Ethics* (Cambridge: Cambridge University Press, 2002).

[78] David Hollenbach, "Human Work and the Story of Creation: Theology and Ethics in *Laborem Exercens*," in John Houck and Oliver Williams (eds.), *Co-Creation and Capitalism: John Paul II's Laborem Exercens* (Washington, DC: University Press of America, 1983), p. 75.

Christian theology ". . . demands full respect for the many different forms of interrelationship and community in which human beings achieve their good in history. None of these forms of community may be absolutized or allowed to dominate all the others. Each of them has a place within the framework of social existence, but none of them can be granted absolute status."[79]

In a variety of ways, then, both theologians and political theorists have recognized that the diversity of estates, orders, spheres, or subsidiary institutions provides the starting point for a Pluralist Realism that recognizes the variety of human goods and the historical development of the institutions and conditions required to create and maintain them. Max Stackhouse summarizes the idea in these terms:

The brilliant idea of spheres implies, as can be seen in the older 'orders theory,' that quite stable functional requirements of human living demand the participation in and maintenance of some viable institutions that are logically prior to the state and cannot be fully controlled by it. This stability only in part derives from forms built into creation to which we must adhere. The spheres also change in number and contours in history; they expand or contract in role and importance depending on the total dynamics of a society.[80]

VARIETIES OF CHRISTIAN REALISM

We have now completed a brief history of Christian realism that complements the study of today's contending versions in the previous chapter. By showing especially how Witness, Antiutopian, and Counterapocalyptic realists argue within the limited space marked out by the modern idea of secular authority, we see more clearly that these are disagreements within a closely related family of Christian realisms that share much common history and many presuppositions. At the same time, post-Reformation social and theological development alerts us to other ways of thinking that share the Christian realist's political pluralism and moral realism, although perhaps without such deep entanglement in the arguments about liberal democracy and public reason.

Not all of modern Christianity can be located in the framework of this historical survey, but a very large number of thoughtful Christians in the modern world have tried to be Christian realists in the ways that we

---

[79] Hollenbach, *The Common Good and Christian Ethics*, p. 136.
[80] Max Stackhouse, "Public Theology and Political Economy in a Globalizing Era," *Studies in Christian Ethics* 14 (2001), 70–1.

have sketched in this chapter. They have attempted to live with faith and hope in the modern state and among the institutions that the successful modern state makes possible. They have made common cause with various forms of liberal democracy, sometimes incautiously equating their faith with their politics, but accurately identifying the commitments to justice and pluralism that make liberal democracy a favorable setting for realistic Christianity.

Christian realists in this broad sense have been a large, loosely connected, and sometimes argumentative family, whose members nonetheless get on well enough together for most outsiders to recognize their similarities. For most of the twentieth century, they were at least united by common enemies, antirealist movements of nationalism, revolution, or totalitarianism that sought to resolve the tensions of modern life by bringing private choices under public control and obliterating the distinctions between the various spheres of life that make up modern society.

In recent years, the family has become more fractious, and more susceptible to persuasion by those who insist that some members of the family do not really belong to it at all. Old aunts whisper in the corners that Niebuhrian realists are really secular liberals, or that a theology of spheres and orders is nothing but theocracy under another name. Some of the cousins seem inclined to believe the rumors.

Possibly this increase in internal conflict is a result of the loss of the common enemies outside. If democracy as a whole is not at risk, the question of what kind of democracy becomes more important, and we might expect more vigorous arguments between the advocates of different versions. But history will not end here, any more than it ended when Rome became Christian and, as Eusebius put it, "Old troubles were forgotten, and all irreligion passed into oblivion"[81] Prudent realists will anticipate different troubles, and will keep a sharp eye out for the return of old problems that had been consigned to oblivion. The modern state, which has provided the context for Christian political realism, is now challenged in ways that it has not been since its beginnings. Failed or failing states make it possible for private individuals and groups to threaten order and security in ways that they have not done since sovereign princes disarmed their barons and mustered the local knights into national armies. Even the successes of the modern state now pose challenges to its authority, as business corporations, cultural movements, and scientific inquiries cross borders in ways that render laws governing employment and wages, education, intellectual property, and biomedical experimentation largely ineffective.

[81] Eusebius, *History of the Church*, p. 332. See p. 45 earlier.

These new realities will challenge all previous versions of Christian realism, simply because they change the conditions under which we understand what it means to be realistic. And Christians, as always, will not settle for realism without hope. Without a dialectic between love and justice in relation to these new realities, realism might become merely an apology for order. Without a dialectic between the diversity of human goods and the unity of the human person, realism might accept general prosperity as a reasonable substitute for the common good. Those are mistakes that modern societies have made locally in the past. It may now be possible to repeat them on a global scale.

A Christian realism adequate to these political and theological challenges will have to do more than the Niebuhrian realism that related Christianity to liberal democracy in the struggle against democracy's twentieth-century rivals. Niebuhr's focus on the human capacity for justice and the political necessity of democracy will have to be integrated with a pluralism that makes a more complete statement about the human good and thus provides broader guidance in relation to the broader questions of our time.

Niebuhr wrote for a generation that at the beginning of his career still thought its energetic, utopian, social Christianity might create a "Christian" economic or political system. Realism required that they learn to put up with the ambiguities of history and accept the limited choices that a difficult century actually offered them. Those who now have opportunity to remake politics, economics, ecology, and possibly even biology must learn to accept limits of a different sort, imposed not by material circumstances and political opposition, but by our moral aspirations themselves. The human good in its variety and complexity is itself a limit on otherwise indeterminate possibilities. A Niebuhrian realism adequate to the new realities thus begins where Niebuhr himself was most skeptical, with a consideration of the reality of the orders, spheres, and laws of nature through which the more pluralist versions of Christian realism have sought to find some stable requirements of human living among the changing dynamics of human society.

CHAPTER 3

Contexts of Responsibility

POLITICS AND "VALUES"

Modern politics, as we have seen, begins with a sphere of secular authority whose concerns are distinct from the search for religious truth and moral virtue. For those who accepted this modern politics, it seemed axiomatic that increased diversity would require a progressively more rigorous distinction between the goals of politics and the human good. Under what John Rawls called "conditions of reasonable pluralism," public political discussions cannot be directed toward agreement on the good.[1] The possibilities of agreement are too remote, and there are many urgent questions that need to be answered first. Disagreements between reasonable people about the human good are a fact around which politics must be structured, not a problem that modern politics can resolve.

Nevertheless, it seems that one result of the growing diversity in contemporary society is an unanticipated public interest in "values." The more people see that their neighbors shape their lives in unfamiliar ways and follow different religious and cultural traditions, the more they want to know exactly what these neighbors think a good life would be. How do they think about their families? How do they see work in relation to the rest of their lives? What role does religion play in their choices?[2]

When new immigrants flow into a community, the old residents and the new alike become amateur anthropologists, trying to understand the world as others see it in relation to the world of their own experience. As economic pressures, mobility, and expanded choices create new lifestyles, family patterns, and work roles, people have to make new choices, not only about how they will live, but how they will live with the choices their

[1] John Rawls, *Justice as Fairness: A Reconsideration* (Cambridge, MA: Harvard University Press, 2001), pp. 33–4.
[2] David Hollenbach, *The Global Face of Public Faith: Politics, Human Rights, and Christian Ethics* (Washington, DC: Georgetown University Press, 2003), p. 3.

neighbors make. Even those who lead relatively stable, conventional lives find themselves living in a new social environment, and media and mass communications make them aware that there are many more possibilities than they might see in their own neighborhoods.

Those who aspire to political leadership in an electorate of amateur anthropologists intuitively grasp that they have to project an image of what life should be, as much as they have to articulate workable foreign and domestic policies. Our theories about ethics and politics would not lead us to expect this connection between growing social diversity and increased political salience of values and moral commitments. Indeed, the theories may have kept analysts from noticing what was happening until the changes were well underway. Political leaders have, until quite recently, focused on building coalitions that made interest groups more secure, rather than communicating a vision or embodying virtue. Values might be invoked, but only after interests had been tended. Bill Clinton's successful campaign for the American presidency in 1992 is said to have kept the staff focused with the slogan, "It's the economy, stupid!" Prosperity is an instrumental good that serves a wide range of interests.

Clinton's coalition of economic interests and Tony Blair's "New Labour" may, however, have marked the end of that era in Anglo-American democracy. Faced with growing ethnic and religious differences at home and greater awareness of cultural diversity around the world, electorates seem increasingly to demand explicit reassurances about their leaders' basic values. On both sides of the Atlantic, those who have mastered the politics of interests sometimes seem particularly inept at the politics of values. Little in their experience, or in recent theoretical accounts of politics, has prepared them for this.

This new connection between politics and "values" is not, however, a return to the Aristotelian or Augustinian idea that politics is the pursuit of human goods in common. The contemporary politics of "values" is not public deliberation about the human good, but a contest between different understandings of it. In extreme cases, it is about using the political process to impose a set of values on society generally. Movements to organize voters around "values" issues often reject the pluralism of modern society and seek to restore to public life the Christian presuppositions they believe were part of it at the beginning. Public deliberation about what these Christian presuppositions are or what they require is neither anticipated nor wanted. From this point of view, pluralism has introduced a variety of lifestyles and choices that are unsupported by our traditions and unsustainable in our polity, so the political task is to narrow the field of possible goods and values to the few that have historical legitimacy, and to do this as quickly as possible.[3]

It would be a mistake, however, to credit the current "politics of values" entirely to this sort of conservative traditionalism. For some, it points toward a more genuine openness in public discussion, eliminating privileged forms of secularism and relativism that have kept absolute moral claims, especially religious ones, from receiving a hearing in the public forum.[4] Although these critics do not reject the pluralism of civil society in principle, they suggest that some choices that are in fact rationally indefensible are sustained by the individualist, relativist terms to which public discourse is now constricted. A genuinely open discussion, in which religion and morality could make their case, would from this perspective probably reduce the number of plausible ideas about the human good and hold cultural change within more reasonable limits, even though no one would be coerced to surrender other choices and no one tradition would be normative.

Of greater practical importance, perhaps, is the widespread demand for a clearer statement of values in public life as a way to understand the choices that contemporary pluralism offers. Although they may not have thought about it systematically, many people no longer believe that there is a public consensus around which the diversity of religious and moral convictions cohere, and they are not convinced that political leaders, judges, or citizens generally can reliably follow neutral rules of public reason, uninfluenced by the variety of ideas about the good that they hold. We want to know how people see the human good in order to predict what sort of decisions they are likely to make if we put them in positions of authority.

This cautious, practical concern suggests that separation of political choices from ideas about the good may not be possible, or that it may not be useful, even if it could be achieved. Political theorists have given system to this intuition. Michael Sandel first pointed to the limitations of

---

[3] Accounts of this legitimacy differ, of course. In the United States, interest centers on Christian principles supposedly accepted by the eighteenth-century Founders as presuppositions of the Constitution. In Britain, the history reaches farther back, but also extends forward to the formation of conservative doctrine in the nineteenth century. For the United States, see Barry Alan Shain, "Revolutionary Era Americans: Were They Enlightened or Protestant? Does It Matter?" in Daniel Dreisbach, Mark Hall, and Jeffrey Morrison (eds.), *The Founders on God and Government* (Lanham, MD: Rowman and Littlefield, 2004), pp. 291–2. For Britain, see Maurice Cowling, *Religion and Public Doctrine in Modern England* (Cambridge: Cambridge University Press, 1980).

[4] See, for example, Stephen Carter, *The Culture of Disbelief: How American Law and Politics Trivialize Religious Devotion* (New York: Basic Books, 1993); "The Religiously Devout Judge," *Notre Dame Law Review*, 64 (1989) 932–44.

liberalism's "unencumbered self." It simply is not clear that we could make the choices required to come up with principles of justice at all if we did not have a more "thick" understanding of the human good than liberal theorists claim we need. This criticism of liberalism necessarily launches a search for a more adequate public philosophy, as it did for Sandel,[5] and the search has inspired a variety of civic republicans, common good theorists, and political pluralists to claim that they have found it.

Meanwhile, the practical interest of citizens is less to identify the correct public philosophy than to understand how the relationship between human good and political principles works for each of the contenders for political leadership. A revised Rawlsian theory of justice may assure us that there are a variety of moral conceptions, from which liberal principles of justice may be drawn. A political philosopher will understandably be concerned with the details of the derivation, to be sure that the principles are indeed the same, or at least that they "vary within a more or less narrow range."[6] But the practical participant in political life may instead say, "Explain to me the kind of life that you think a good person would lead. It seems that your principles of justice are the same as those to which I have consented, or that their differences from mine vary within that more or less narrow range; but it is difficult to be sure, and I will be more confident of the justice I will receive from you if I know how you think a good person ought to live, even if we have agreed at the outset that you are not going to try to make me live that way."

Social diversity was supposed to make us more concerned about principles of justice and less interested in the confusing multiplicity of ideas about the human good, but unless we are absolutely convinced that there is a public consensus on principles of justice that we can be quite certain are neutral with respect to those ideas of the good, prudent people will also want to know something about how their neighbors, their political leaders, and powerful figures in other areas of business, religious, and cultural life understand the human good. They want to know what other people think about the human good, just in case they have to seek justice from those others under less than ideal conditions.

The relevance of this point to political life is clear. The politics of values will be increasingly important as diversity in our social life increases.

---

[5] Michael J. Sandel, *Liberalism and the Limits of Justice* (Cambridge: Cambridge University Press, 1982), See also Michael Sandel, *Democracy's Discontent: America in Search of a Public Philosophy* (Cambridge, MA: Harvard University Press, 1996).

[6] John Rawls, *Political Liberalism* (New York: Columbia University Press, 1993), p. 164.

Questions about values, goals, and the human good are important in politics, not only for those who want to reduce diversity, but also for those who intend to live with it. We can imagine a race of philosopher-kings who could define principles of justice so precise and so obviously independent of ideas about the good that their neutrality would never be in doubt. But the realities of social life and the search for justice in a liberal democracy give us at best a family of political conceptions that yield principles of justice that "vary within a more or less narrow range." Under those conditions, a statement about the goods, goals, and virtues that make for a good human life is an important amplification and clarification of more specific policy proposals and claims to justice that are made in the public political forum. Those who seek to shape our common life under conditions of diversity will have to tell us not only what interests we share and what justice requires, but also how they think a good life ought to be lived.

RESPONSIBILITY

Can Christian realists participate in this public discussion of the human good? The history of Christian realism certainly provides some resources for that purpose. Even the limits of human possibility on which Christian moral realism dwells presuppose a definite human nature that can flourish within those limits, be frustrated when held below them, or fail disastrously when trying to live above them. Niebuhr, Bonhoeffer, and others who described the failures of judgment and misplaced commitments that marked the twentieth century were not pessimists or cynics. They did not see war, revolution, and class conflict as tragic necessities imposed by contradictions at the heart of the moral life, however attractive a tragic interpretation might have seemed to their contemporaries who were wearied by the struggle against the same evils.[7] For Christian realism, it is the willful defiance of the limits of human nature, and not human finitude itself, that produces the catastrophes that mark history and personal life.

It should be an easy task for those who have discerned the evils which follow when the limits of human life are ignored to describe the good that is possible within those limits. However, that sort of definitive, universal statement about the human good is precisely what Christian realism tried to avoid during the middle of the twentieth century. Indeed, Christian ethics across a spectrum of theological positions hesitated before the task. Catholic

---

[7] See Reinhold Niebuhr, *Beyond Tragedy* (New York: Charles Scribner's Sons, 1937), pp. 155–69; Dietrich Bonhoeffer, *Ethics*, Clifford J. Green (ed.), Dietrich Bonhoeffer Works, vol. VI (Minneapolis: Fortress Press, 2005), pp. 264–5.

natural law theory gave new attention to the historical setting of natural law ideas, to their development through history, and to the diversity of uses to which natural law ideas had been put. Protestant theology emphasized "responsibility" in specific choices in contrast to general formulations of the moral law.

The reason for the hesitation can be traced to the events of the time. By the end of the nineteenth century, bold generalizations about human nature and universal history which had once been the province of Christian theology were in the hands of new ideologies. Nationalism and colonialism generated theories about cultures and races that suggested a fixed human nature which conferred an imperial destiny on some peoples and imposed subordination on others. Socialist materialism, by contrast, saw human nature as the product of social relations, so that a political and economic revolution could remake human nature itself. In either case, the people – *das Volk* or the proletariat – had to be freed from the inherited constraints of religion, monarchy, and property so that the possibilities of human nature could be realized.

When these ideas were translated into political movements and the movements acquired political power, the ideas became powerful instruments of social change. The transfer of power to the new order proceeded with unprecedented swiftness and thoroughness, whether the new order was Lenin's dictatorship of the proletariat or the nationalism of Franco, Mussolini, and Hitler. Churches and other institutions, including universities and corporations, that had functioned with some independence from political power now had to be subordinated to the new system or destroyed.

Catholic theology and philosophy protested that these new theories about human nature were false, drawing their ideas from individualistic and rationalistic errors that the church had already rejected at the beginning of the modern era. In the twentieth century, however, making that case required new attention to historical transformations of the concepts of "nature," "good," and "reason." The idea of natural law keeps coming back to correct errors that are in fact distortions of its own more permanent truth,[8] but that narrative of natural law's eternal return involves the story of its own development. Even timeless truths have a history.

---

[8] Heinrich Rommen, *The Natural Law: A Study in Legal and Social History and Philosophy*, Thomas R. Hanley (trans.) (St. Louis: B. Herder Book Co., 1947). Rommen was a Catholic jurist and philosopher who fled Nazi Germany in 1938. His book was written, as his American translator explained, "as a protest against the widespread abuse of the idea of natural law in contemporary legal and political philosophy generally, but in particular in those circles most influenced by the Nazi *Weltanschauung*" (p. iv).

For Protestant theology, Reinhold Niebuhr's distinction between love and justice now took on more urgency. It was no longer Social Gospel optimism that offered the moral ideal as an immediate, historical possibility, but totalitarian ideologies that threatened to replace the universal Christian hope with the triumph of a particular race or class. Under the circumstances, even the dialectical relationship between love and justice could seem too easily subverted, and Karl Barth insisted on relying solely on the immediacy of divine command.[9]

Immediate dependence on the commandment of God does not, however, provide much structure for moral reflection, as Barth himself later acknowledged. There had to be some way to discuss the recurring questions of ethics without succumbing to answers that might either put the church at the service of some new political program, or set it in unyielding opposition to all modern developments. For Protestant theology, the concept of responsibility provided a way to ask the necessary questions of ethics.[10] "The idea of responsibility," Barth wrote, "shows us what is meant by moral reflection, the examination of what we are and will and do and do not do, of the mutual relationship between the command of God and our existence."[11]

The concept of responsibility in theological ethics draws meanings from moral, theological, and political contexts, and these multiple sources and settings are not always clearly distinguished. As William Schweiker points out, responsibility includes accountability, answerability, and representative action.[12] To act responsibly is to be accountable for what we do, to resist the temptation to say that we had no choice or that someone else commanded or compelled our actions. Responsible actions also take responsibility for someone, for whom one acts as an agent, guardian, or representative. Responsible action cannot be entirely self-interested. Responsibility obliges us to render that account of ourselves and our actions when we are questioned, and, especially, to be answerable for our being, willing, and doing before God.

The transcendent claim of responsibility or answerability before God rules out a more limited understanding of responsibility in which only the nation, the party, or the revolution may demand an answer. Because

---

Karl Barth, "No! Answer to Emil Brunner," in Emil Brunner and Karl Barth, *Natural Theology*, Peter Fraenkel (trans.) (Eugene, OR: Wipf and Stock, 2002), pp. 65–128.

[10] See Albert Jonsen, *Responsibility in Modern Religious Ethics* (Washington, DC: Corpus Books, 1968).

[11] Karl Barth, *Church Dogmatics*, G. W. Bromiley (trans.) (Edinburgh: T. & T. Clark, 1957), II/2, 643.

[12] William Schweiker, *Responsibility and Christian Ethics* (Cambridge: Cambridge University Press, 1995), p. 74.

God confronts us in every aspect of reality, it is impossible to say that the bourgeoisie, the capitalists, the communists, or the non-Aryans do not count, that we have no responsibility to them or for them. Likewise, the multiple, specific, competing demands of daily life cannot be set aside in order that we may bring about the revolution – or prevent it, as the case may be. The comprehensive and unlimited character of our accountability before God makes it impossible to select the persons and situations to whom we will be responsive, either by choosing in terms of our own self-interest or by allowing a political movement or ideology to make the choices for us. Paradoxically, it is precisely because we are always and everywhere account-able before God that we cannot formulate the sort of universal claims about nature, reason, or history that political movements and ideologies use to justify their unlimited demands.

... God seems hardly to be interested at all in general and universally valid rules, but properly only in certain particular actions and achievements and attitudes, and this in the extremely simple and direct way of desiring from man (as a father from his child or as a master from his servant) that this or that must or must not happen. Nothing can be made of these commands if we try to generalise and transform them into universally valid principles (unless, of course, we artificially distort them).[13]

When confronted by governments and ideologies that demand conformity to their ideas of absolute good and evil, responsible opposition is not a matter of resisting with an alternative vision of good and evil, although that might be a very courageous thing to do in the situation. Responsibility refuses to view existing reality in those absolute terms.[14]

Responsibility before God thus rules out a kind of ideological politics that draws its imperatives directly from history or from nature. Instead, it seems to require a politics that bears a strong resemblance to Max Weber's "ethic of responsibility." According to Weber, a political leader must take responsibility for specific choices and foreseeable consequences. A leader is responsible to real people and their interests, pays attention to the forces at work in particular situations, and makes compromises that enable govern-ment to make effective use of its power. These compromises may appear to sacrifice ultimate good to prevailing interests, but in fact, it is the uncom-promising pursuit of the good – what Weber called the "ethic of ultimate

---

[13] Barth, *Church Dogmatics*, II/2, 672.

[14] Douglas John Hall makes an important distinction between "resistance" and "responsibility" as strategies for Christian political participation. See Douglas John Hall, *Confessing the Faith: Christian Theology in a North American Context* (Minneapolis: Fortress Press, 1986), pp. 332–40.

ends" – that is apt to wreck the government and discredit the good in the process.[15]

Weber himself was uncertain whether religious commitment and political responsibility could be reconciled. He outlined his "ethics of responsibility" in 1918, as Germany faced political collapse at the end of the First World War. Under the circumstances, he was most worried that a Marxist revolution similar to the one that had just occurred in Russia would irresponsibly sacrifice order and political effectiveness to the aspiration for a new society. His illustrative example of an ethics that rejects responsibility is, however, a religious one: "The Christian does rightly and leaves the results with the Lord."[16]

No doubt the example seemed apt to many in Weber's audience. People had become accustomed to seeing Christianity used to bolster the sagging authority of established churches, monarchies, and governments, and the two decades that followed Weber's lecture witnessed a new alliance between the emerging Nazi movement and theologians who identified its program with Christian goals for church, family, and social life.[17] History and current events seemed often to contradict Christian claims to political responsibility. Weber's evocation of the irresponsible Christian may be a mistake, or even a slander, but theologians needed to provide some answer to it.

Barth himself took little interest in the task. Responsibility before God reduces self-understanding and being understood by others to insignificance and thus renders any form of apologetic theology inappropriate. Trying to answer Weber's suggestion that Christian politics is unable to focus on concrete responsibilities merely suggests that the theologian is more worried about Weber's judgment than about the judgment of God. Apparently it is another Barthian paradox that in claiming to be responsible, we deny our most important responsibility.

Reinhold Niebuhr and Dietrich Bonhoeffer, in different ways, suggest a different response. Each of them found collaboration with others who took a responsible approach to politics a necessary implication of his own theological understanding of events, and that collaboration required accountability to those who were also engaged in politics. For Niebuhr, this meant interpreting the biblical understanding of politics to those who shared in the defense of liberal democracy. For Bonhoeffer, it meant explaining how

---

[15] Max Weber, "Politics as a Vocation," in H. H. Gerth and C. Wright Mills (eds.), *From Max Weber* (New York: Oxford University Press, 1946), p. 120.
[16] *Ibid.*
[17] Robert P. Ericksen, *Theologians under Hitler* (New Haven, CT: Yale University Press, 1985), pp. 98–109.

a Christian could take the moral risks involved in the conspiracy against Hitler.

Niebuhr adopted the language of political responsibility rather late in his career, perhaps as a result of new attention to the idea in ecumenical Protestant social ethics. The First Assembly of the World Council of Churches, held in Amsterdam in 1948 as Europe was rebuilding from the Second World War, adopted a statement on "The Responsible Society." Barth may have introduced the idea into theological discussion, but Niebuhr was quick to insist that responsibility in the emerging peacetime society required a more complex relationship of political engagement and critical distance than Barth's theology provided.[18]

If Niebuhr thought that Barth gave too little attention to actual political choices, he also believed that ecumenical Protestant social ethics at Amsterdam was still too preoccupied with finding a Christian social program. A decade later, he was more confident that the consensus had settled on Christian realism:

We have now come to the fairly general conclusion that there is no "Christian" economic or political system. But there is a Christian attitude toward all systems and schemes of justice. It consists on the one hand of a critical attitude toward the claims of all systems and schemes, expressed in the question whether they will contribute to justice in the concrete situation; and on the other hand a responsible attitude, which will not pretend to be God nor refuse to make a decision between political answers to a problem because each answer is discovered to contain a moral ambiguity in God's sight. We are men, not God; we are responsible for making choices between greater and lesser evils, even when our Christian faith, illuminating the human scene, makes it quite apparent that there is no pure good in history; and probably no pure evil, either. The fate of civilizations may depend upon these choices of which some are more, other less, just.[19]

Although Christian realists must be both critical and responsible in making political choices, Niebuhr suggested that their theological understanding of human nature primarily shapes the "critical" attitude. Once we

[18] See Jonsen, *Responsibility in Modern Religious Ethics*, pp. 79–86. For Niebuhr's response to Barth, see Reinhold Niebuhr, *Essays in Applied Christianity*, D. B. Robertson (ed.) (New York: Meridian Books, 1959), pp. 168–82. Niebuhr's earlier discussions of responsibility focused on theological questions of how individuals become responsible for their choices and actions. See Reinhold Niebuhr, *The Nature and Destiny of Man* (Louisville, KY: Westminster John Knox Press, 1996), vol. I, 241–64.

[19] Reinhold Niebuhr, "Theology and Political Thought in the Western World," *The Ecumenical Review* 9 (1957), 253–4. This essay is reprinted in Reinhold Niebuhr, *Faith and Politics*, Ronald Stone (ed.) (New York: George Braziller, 1968), pp. 55–66.

appreciate the complexity and ambiguity of the human person created in the image of God and yet given to sinful self-aggrandizement, we will be less likely to make absolute claims about right and wrong and more open to asking what is responsible. The biblical understanding of human nature proves more effective at the critical task than its ancient or modern rivals, but it does not dictate the responsible choice. For that, Niebuhr's Christian realism seems to leave us largely to knowledge drawn from secular sources and to ordinary good judgment, with neither a determinate rule of nature nor a specific divine command for guidance.

For Niebuhr, the complexities of the biblical understanding of human nature defy formulation into rational principles, and the demands of Jesus's teaching both affirm and then transcend the most rigorous moral requirements. Biblical understanding does not provide the certainty that an ethic of ultimate ends requires, so that we might refer the question to scripture and then say, "The Christian does rightly and leaves the results with the Lord." Biblical understanding dissolves premature certainties and calls settled conclusions into question. That is the starting point for the critical attitude with which the Christian realist approaches all systems and schemes, whether they are revolutionary proposals or established social practices.

The Christian realist's critical attitude thus rejects moral absolutes drawn from human experience, but it also differs from Barth's theological ethics, which declares common experience theologically irrelevant and relies solely on the command of God as the starting point for ethics. Niebuhr is less certain than Barth that we can purge our theology of human experience. In any case, Niebuhr expects that the ordinary events of social and political life will draw us into discussion of human goods and human nature. He reads Barth as requiring the Christian to denounce that discussion and refuse to participate in it, but that is not how Niebuhr understands the critical task. Refusal to participate would hardly be responsible, even if we had the critical resources to make the case that society's idea of the human good was pervasively corrupt, self-interested, and false. The critical task is to expose the limits of every conception of human good and to show the ways in which each of them is partly true and partly false.

Every effort to formulate the requirements of human nature includes both an apprehension of permanent truths about human life and a projection of the self-interest of those who make the formulation. Every social ethics will mistake some of the existing patterns of power for necessary structures of social life. The limitations that apply to all of our ideas of human good do not keep us from identifying some of these ideas as better than others, nor do they prevent us from using our critical skills to improve our moral systems and our moral lives, but we should not suppose that we can transcend the limitations entirely and arrive by careful stages at a determinate truth about the human good.

The reason for this is that human nature itself is indeterminate. Human nature is the result both of physical and biological requirements and the cultural systems human beings have created partly to survive and partly to master those realities.

Man requires freedom in his social organization because he is "essentially" free, which is to say that he has the capacity for indeterminate transcendence over the processes and limitations of nature. This freedom enables him to make history and to elaborate communal organizations in boundless variety and in endless breadth and extent. But he also requires community because he is by nature social. He cannot fulfill his life within himself but only in responsible and mutual relations with his fellows.[20]

A critical attitude drawn from biblical sources thus exposes the inevitable distortions of self-interest and at the same time puts before us the full range of possibilities inherent in human freedom. Responsible choices emerge as possibilities after this criticism, if only because once the critical process is complete, there are no pretenses to ultimate ends left to distract our attention. The critical attitude makes it possible for us to take responsibility before one another for our ideas about human good, because it keeps us from taking a particular account of the human good as an ultimate end and confusing this with our responsibility before God.

Niebuhr's Christian realism thus establishes both a critical distance and an enduring relationship between theological understanding and political responsibility. It is not the case, as Weber and Barth suggest in their different ways, that we must choose *either* theological understanding *or* responsible politics. Rather, a theological understanding of the human good drawn from biblical sources demonstrates that all the choices about human good available to us are matters of more and less in relation to other competing goods and to the particular circumstances in which we make the choice. Theological understanding shows us that responsible politics is the only possible politics and at the same time reminds us that politics needs a certain kind of theological understanding to keep it responsible.

---

[20] Reinhold Niebuhr, *The Children of Light and the Children of Darkness* (New York: Charles Scribner's Sons, 1960), p. 3.

BONHOEFFER ON RESPONSIBILITY

Dietrich Bonhoeffer offers a different understanding of the relationship between theology and political responsibility. Bonhoeffer thought that the American style of social ethics he observed as a visiting student at Union Theological Seminary in 1930–1931 had abandoned real theology for the study of economic and political problems.[21] His own work in ethics shows a consistent determination to maintain a direct connection between theology and ethics.

The sayings of Jesus Christ . . . are the divine commandment for responsible action in history insofar as they are the reality of history that has been fulfilled in Christ, that is, insofar as they are the responsibility for human beings that has been fulfilled in Christ alone. Therefore they are valid not [within] an abstract ethic – indeed, there they are completely incomprehensible and lead to insoluble conflicts. Rather, they are valid within the reality of history, because this is their source. Any attempt to disconnect them from this origin distorts them into a weak ideology. Only when rooted in their origin do they possess the power to gain control of reality.[22]

In contrast to Niebuhr's insistence that the sayings of Jesus do not connect directly to ordinary moral choices, Bonhoeffer here seems to make obedience to the divine commandment the sole measure of responsible action.[23] The passage illustrates the strong influence of Barth on Bonhoeffer's thinking about ethics generally and, in particular, his admiration for Barth's treatment of the idea of Christian responsibility.[24]

What Bonhoeffer wants to avoid, however, is any implication that this command imposes a responsibility that is external to the historical situation, as though our responsibility before God were in principle different from and possibly in conflict with responsibilities we have to other people in particular situations. Bonhoeffer's theological ethics centers on the command of God, immediate and specific, in contrast to abstract moral principles or general

---

[21] Dietrich Bonhoeffer, "Studienbericht für das Kirchenbundesamt," in *Barcelona, Berlin, Amerika, 1928–1931*, Dietrich Bonhoeffer Werke, vol. X (Munich: Christian Kaiser Verlag, 1991), pp. 265–6; See also Bonhoeffer, *Ethics*, p. 51.

[22] Bonhoeffer, *Ethics*, pp. 263–4. The interpolated "within" was supplied by the editors of the German text.

[23] Cf. Bonhoeffer, *Ethics*, p. 378: "We are thus led beyond the 'ethical' to the only possible subject matter of a 'Christian ethic,' namely the '*commandment of God*.'"

[24] While working on his own *Ethics*, Bonhoeffer made three wartime visits to Barth in Switzerland, read galley proofs of the section on "The Command of God" in *Church Dogmatics* II/2, and proposed that Barth write an essay on "Christian responsibility." See Bonhoeffer, *Ethics*, pp. 455–61.

human goods, but he emphasizes that the God who commands is also fully present in history in Jesus Christ. "The commandment of God revealed in Jesus Christ embraces life as a whole. It does not merely guard, like the ethical, the boundaries of life that must not be crossed, but it is at the same time the center and fullness of life. It is not only ought, but also allowed. It not only prohibits, but also liberates us for authentic life and for unreflective doing."[25]

What is apparent in the Gospel narratives themselves is that these sayings of Jesus which become the divine commandment are addressed to people who are already in relationships of responsibility – as husbands and wives, masters and servants, debtors and lenders, buyers and sellers, tax collectors and tax payers. These responsibilities set the context in which Jesus's words show them how to understand life. Obedience to the commandment and acceptance of responsibility give life unity and possibilities that escape those who seek to justify themselves, to provide for their own security, or to assert their own importance. In this way, the commandment has power to gain control of reality – although not, perhaps, the kind of control that the hearers at first thought they wanted. Life is no longer lived at cross-purposes, where every move must be calculated. Responsibility becomes a matter of "unreflective doing." By gaining control of reality through responsible action, those who follow the sayings of Jesus lose the need to seize control of it for their own purposes, and they also lose the need to flee this multiplicity of conflicting demands and risks for some wilderness in which responsibility before God would be the only responsibility. As Brian Brock puts it, the command of God ". . . is meant to create a unity in *lived* life."[26]

The sayings of Jesus cannot, of course, be turned into a literal set of commandments that could be set up in the public square for instruction, as though Christians have some reference manual, independent of the real situations in which they live, which they must consult for directions regarding what to do next. The sayings of Jesus remain relevant for us today because we, too, are already immersed in responsibilities which we need to interpret and accept in order to unify our lives and gain control of reality. The sayings of Jesus are not addressed to an abstract individual who surveys life from a distance, but to a real person facing particular questions and difficulties that arise out of responsibilities that are already present in some way in that

[25] Bonhoeffer, *Ethics*, p. 381.
[26] Brian Brock, "Bonhoeffer and the Bible in Christian Ethics," *Studies in Christian Ethics*, 18 (2005), 21.

person's own experience, even if that presence in experience for the moment takes the form of confusion, fear, or resentment.

Bonhoeffer explains the specificity of our responsibilities in relation to the realities of our situation by saying that the commandment of God is addressed to us in the "divine mandates" of work, family, government, and church.[27] The commandment that we receive in these settings is not a message from God that these particular goods shall be created according to this specific pattern, so that the sayings of Jesus or the scripture as a whole provide a blueprint for the ideal family, government, church, or workplace. What we can say about the commandment in general terms is only that it requires us to take this family, this church, or this job as a place of responsibility. In being responsive to others and to the realities of the situation, in taking responsibility for them and for their well-being, and in accepting responsibility before God for the choices we make, we gain a kind of control over the situation that includes understanding it and knowing what to do next. But it is not easy to do this. It is easier, more "natural" to us, to give in to the situation and let it carry us along passively from one demand to the next, or to try to impose a control on it shaped only by our own interests and what we think we can get from the employer, the state, the church, or the family.

Responsible action is possible only in a real situation where we already live and act, but it seems at first an alien demand that goes against all of our usual ways of dealing with the familiar reality. When we hear the commandment of God for responsible action, the scripture that tells us that those who seek to save their own lives will lose them, or warns us against worrying about what will happen tomorrow, or commands us to step out of the boat onto the stormy water begins to make sense, or rather – Bonhoeffer would put it – the sayings of Jesus interpret reality for us.[28]

All this contrasts with what happens when the commandment is taken out of its concrete setting and turned into an abstract ethic. Then, indeed, it becomes incomprehensible. As a general precept addressed to no one in particular, "take no thought for tomorrow," is incomprehensible. We are apt to praise it because Jesus said it, while reducing it to a prudent warning against undue anxiety that is perfectly consistent with ordinary self-interest.[29] Or we may take it literally as an invitation to irresponsible actions

---

[27] Bonhoeffer, *Ethics*, p. 68, 380. See earlier, page 78.   [28] Bonhoeffer, *Ethics*, p. 263.

[29] Reinhold Niebuhr also recognizes the tendency of an abstract, liberal Christian ethics to reduce the demands of the Gospel to ordinary prudence. See Niebuhr, *An Interpretation of Christian Ethics*, p. 63.

that jeopardize the future for ourselves and others. We have no idea what it means.

Taken from its place in the context of family, work, government, or church, the commandment loses its power to gain control of reality and becomes, as Bonhoeffer puts, it "a weak ideology." The sayings of Jesus start to function like the other versions of the ethics of ultimate ends that were on offer in Bonhoeffer's world, whether fascist, socialist, imperialist, or populist. To call any of these a "weak ideology" was a remarkable statement in the midst of the Second World War, but Bonhoeffer did not mean that ideologies and abstract ethics lacked power. Dictators and demagogues could back up an ideology with plenty of power. What they lacked was "power to gain control of reality." They could not provide real solutions to the problems faced by people in historical situations, so they were obliged to make more and more demanding promises, sacrificing the real people on whose concrete aspirations their power had been built. Bonhoeffer's claim that ideology is weak because it cannot gain control of reality would have seemed laughable to Hitler, had he known about it in 1942, but in the end Bonhoeffer had it exactly right.

CONTEXTS

Niebuhr and Bonhoeffer thus agree in a general way that responsible action requires specific choices that are neither prescribed by general rules nor justified after the fact by ethical principles. The commandment of God may be quite direct, but Bonhoeffer insisted that obedience in difficult situations involves readiness to accept guilt, not the self-assurance of those who know they have done exactly the right thing.[30] Niebuhr likewise identified gratitude and contrition as "the dominant attitudes of prophetic faith," because to live responsibly at all, we must embrace the circumstances in which we find ourselves and acknowledge the limitations of our moral achievements. "In such a faith," he observed, "both sentimentality and despair are avoided."[31]

Especially for Bonhoeffer, the ambiguities of moral choice and the inevitability of guilt are connected to the diversity of human goods and the impossibility of maintaining any unity among them strictly on our own terms.[32] The goods people seek are multiple: art, music, poetry, stories, and other sources of aesthetic satisfaction; good food, secure homes,

---

[30] Bonhoeffer, *Ethics*, pp. 274–6.   [31] Niebuhr, *An Interpretation of Christian Ethics*, p. 64.
[32] Bonhoeffer, *Ethics*, pp. 277–80.

comfortable surroundings; good health, a positive outlook on life, and good prospects for the future; love shared with friends and family, respect among associates, and also a secure sense that we ourselves are people capable of giving love and respect and worthy of receiving them. These goods are not only numerous. They are quite different kinds of good. Some are personal experiences or dispositions, including what we might call virtues and what we might call piety – knowing ourselves to be a certain kind of person and knowing ourselves in relationship, not just to certain other people, but to God and to the world as a whole. Some goods involve material conditions – adequate food and shelter, appropriate care for our injuries and illnesses, a sense of security from danger, injury, and overwork. Some are relationships of love, friendship, social cooperation, leading and following, teaching and learning, or sharing in worship and creativity. Nearly all of these goods involve other people in some way, but some goods are distinctively social. Security, order, and peace must be generally shared to exist at all, while justice allows us to feel that the various goods we enjoy are distributed widely and fairly, rather than held by those who happen to have them by accident or who have managed to seize them by force.

This diversity of goods gives rise to multiple contexts which make it possible for us to enjoy different kinds of goods. Human experience, even in a fairly narrowly defined space of geography and history, sets us in the midst of a multiplicity of different goods and different kinds of good. To wait for the commandment of God is not to abandon these goods as irrelevant to the Christian life. It provides a way of organizing and understanding human goods by focusing on the specific places in our lives where they are created and maintained. That is the most general idea behind the accounts of "spheres," "subsidiary institutions," "orders," "estates," or Bonhoeffer's mandates, where various kinds of human activity are organized by laws intrinsic to their own purposes and cannot be subsumed under any other authority.

To speak in more general terms of these spheres or orders, without adopting any one of the sometimes conflicting theological accounts of them, let us call them "contexts." The important point for our purposes is that they are what Robert Benne calls "places of responsibility."[33] They are settings in which from a theological point of view responsible action is possible because the command of God can be received in its immediacy and directness and specific goods, understood in specific social and historical settings,

---

[33] Robert Benne, *Ordinary Saints: An Introduction to the Christian Life*, 2nd ed. (Minneapolis, MN: Fortress Press, 2003), p. 63.

can be created and maintained. Contexts organize our thinking about goods because we learn from experience what kinds of good they can create and what general patterns and structures enable a context to create the goods which are proper to it.

That is not to say that the contexts are themselves the human good. Families, governments, jobs, and churches can all be horrible evils, which do great harm to the people involved in them and to others. Human goods are more specific experiences of intimacy, leadership, creativity, or aesthetic enjoyment that are possible in the contexts of family, politics, or culture. They may be dispositions that are best cultivated in a particular context, as politics can elicit courage or the church can nurture piety. The human goods may be material conditions that require a highly structured context to bring them into being, like the varieties of food, clothing, and shelter that modern agricultural and industrial production make possible, or they may be the material conditions of nature, which increasingly require protection and preservation to keep them from being overwhelmed by the organized human world.[34]

There is at least some connection with the tradition of natural law in all of these theological discussions of contexts, though both Niebuhr and Bonhoeffer are skeptical of efforts to derive universal moral rules from the functional requirements of social contexts. Bonhoeffer often appears to be following Karl Barth in rejecting any formulation of the ethical problem that focuses human goods known in human terms.[35] Barth, in turn, assures us that this is what Bonhoeffer meant and that it is only on this basis that the idea of "orders" or "spheres" can have meaning for Christian ethics. Bonhoeffer's mandates are preferable to Brunner's orders of creation, Barth argues, because Bonhoeffer more clearly distinguishes his position from the tradition of natural law. "Bonhoeffer's 'mandates' are not laws somehow immanent in created reality and to be established at random by the moralist and proclaimed in a form which he himself discovers."[36]

That, at least, is how Barth read Bonhoeffer, and that is how many other readers have understood the idea of the "mandates" ever since. But we should perhaps not be so quick to accept Barth's sharp distinction between

---

[34] William Schweiker, *Theological Ethics and Global Dynamics* (Oxford: Blackwell Publishing, 2004), p. 12.

[35] See, for example, Bonhoeffer, *Ethics*, p. 47: "Those who wish even to focus on the problem of a Christian ethic are faced with an outrageous demand – from the outset, they must give up, as inappropriate to this topic, the very two questions that led them to deal with the ethical problem: 'How can I be good?' and 'How can I do something good?' Instead, they must ask the wholly other, completely different question: What is the will of God?"

[36] Barth, *Church Dogmatics* III/4, p. 22.

Bonhoeffer's divine mandates and the broader tradition of natural law. About the time that he was formulating his ideas for *Ethics*, Bonhoeffer wrote to his brother-in-law, Gerhard Leibholz, that he was still thinking about natural law, and he notes that Brunner has some very wise things to say about the subject – "especially in the footnotes."[37] Although he understood the importance of Barth's criticisms of natural theology, Bonhoeffer was unwilling to render the command of God completely unavailable in the experience of social life. The concrete, specific requirements of the mandates become evident in the experienced failure of schemes that ignore them, quite as vividly as in the church's proclamation of the divine command.[38] Longer experience with the Confessing Church convinced Bonhoeffer that a resistance based entirely on the Word of God was not necessarily a more effective source of courage or political wisdom than the secular virtues of the civil servants and military officers whom he met after he became part of the conspiracy against Hitler late in 1940. Reflecting on the experience of those who were bound together in that venture of responsibility, he wrote: "It is one of the most surprising experiences, but at the same time one of the most incontrovertible, that evil – often in a surprisingly short time – proves its own folly and defeats its own object... We learn this from our own experience, and we can interpret it in various ways. At least it seems possible to infer with certainty that in social life there are laws more powerful than anything that may claim to dominate them, and that it is therefore not only wrong but unwise to disregard them. We can understand from this why Aristotelian – Thomist ethics made wisdom one of the cardinal virtues."[39]

Bonhoeffer thus ends up closer to Brunner and the tradition of natural law than Barth would have us believe.[40] What separates the divine mandates in *Ethics* from the orders of creation as Brunner understood them are matters of emphasis and detail, not a complete difference in kind, notwithstanding the polemical accentuation of the differences by various interpreters,

---

[37] Dietrich Bonhoeffer, *Illegale Theologen-Ausbildung: Sammelvikariate, 1937–1940*, Dirk Schulz (ed.), Dietrich Bonhoeffer Werke, vol. XIV (Munich: Christian Kaiser Verlag, 1998), p. 297.

[38] Compare Emil Brunner's statement that "all attempts to operate with the concepts of love or with those of 'law' or 'commandments' without the help of the concept of the ordinances, lead either to rationalistic social constructions (liberalistic doctrines of the State and matrimony) or to an uncertain attitude towards the ordinances of society as given factors, vacillating between acknowledgement and rejection." Brunner, *Natural Theology*, p. 52.

[39] From the essay "After Ten Years," in Dietrich Bonhoeffer, *Letters and Papers from Prison*, Eberhard Bethge (ed.) (New York: Macmillan, 1972), p. 10.

[40] Jordan J. Ballor, "Christ in Creation: Bonhoeffer's Orders of Preservation and Natural Theology," *Journal of Religion* 86 (2006), 1–22.

and occasionally by Bonhoeffer himself. Bonhoeffer was concerned to avoid any use of "orders" that could be confused with racist or nationalist uses of the term by pro-Nazi "German Christian" theologians. "Orders of creation" had therefore to be rejected as a vocabulary for speaking about the contexts for making human goods. "Orders of preservation" suggested a more humble task of maintaining, under fallen human conditions, those resources that God had provided to keep humanity from destroying itself before the work of redemption is complete.[41] When even that language proved susceptible to manipulation by the "German Christian" theologians, Bonhoeffer abandoned the terminology and the idea completely for a few years, until preliminary work on his *Ethics* convinced him that this pluralism was an essential part of the moral life. So in *Ethics*, what were "orders of creation" or "orders of preservation" become the "divine mandates."[42] Bonhoeffer was not altogether happy with that choice, but after running through other options with more tradition behind them, he concluded that this new formulation was the best he could do. "Lacking a better word we thus stay, for the time being, with the concept of mandate. Nevertheless, our goal, through clarifying the issue itself, is to contribute to renewing and reclaiming the old concepts of order, estate, and office."[43]

Does this, however, make Bonhoeffer too much like Brunner for Niebuhr to be fully satisfied with his alternative to Barth? Niebuhr thought that any effort to locate the requirements of human nature in existing social structures, including Brunner's orders of creation, runs the risk of mistaking contingent arrangements constructed by power and self-interest for permanently valid moral constraints. The connections between power and principle are just too strong and the possibilities for self-deception are too subtle for us to trust anything but a thoroughgoing social explanation of the arrangements that our society happens to have made around what we are here calling a "context." In a brief review of Bonhoeffer's *Ethics*, published when it first appeared in English translation, Niebuhr commends Bonhoeffer's "shrewd common sense in dealing with the stuff of life" and for that reason claims him as a Christian realist, but he expresses some skepticism about whether Bonhoeffer's theological formulation of the mandates helps

---

[41] Dietrich Bonhoeffer, *Creation and Fall*, John W. DeGruchy (ed.) Dietrich Bonhoeffer Works, vol. III (Minneapolis, MN: Fortress Press, 1997), pp. 139–40.

[42] See the summary of Bonhoeffer's use of these terms in Clifford Green's introduction to Bonhoeffer, *Ethics*, pp. 17–22.

[43] Bonhoeffer, *Ethics*, p. 390.

us understand the structural and institutional realities that shape ethical questions.[44]

It is important not to give too permanent an ontological or theological status to the four mandates that Bonhoeffer mentions. As Niebuhr observes, that mistake allows historically created patterns of authority and power to go unquestioned. It also loses the connection with historical reality that is, for Bonhoeffer, essential to the way that Jesus Christ gives the commandment of God to us. Clearly, contexts change over time and in number. In Luther's time, the context of work was only beginning to be separated from the family or household, which was an economic unit as much as it was a generative and nurturing one. The household context encompassed the whole of productive economic life, as distinguished from the church, which cared for religion, education, and culture, and from government, which at that time was itself only beginning to take the form of a sovereign state administered by agents who could be distinguished from the royal household. The descriptive value of just three "estates" was questionable already in Luther's time. To understand Bonhoeffer's world requires additionally a separate context for work as well as a very different understanding of the family. It might also require a separate context for culture,[45] and maybe even a context for education distinguishable from both work and culture (although education obviously prepares people for both of those contexts).

The increasing differentiation of new contexts also changes the identity and purpose of those that have been previously recognized. The church has less to do with education and only with difficulty retains some role as a center of cultural creativity. The family becomes increasingly distinct from economic, educational, and religious institutions and has more to do with nurture, intimacy, and personal formation. Historical changes in contexts do not pass without controversy, as we can see in the conflicts over child labor beginning in the nineteenth century or in more recent debates about how to contextualize intimate relationships that are different from traditional marriage.

However we understand the spheres, orders, or contexts that structure pursuit of human goods, it is evident that they change over the course

---

[44] Niebuhr perhaps failed to explore Bonhoeffer's idea in detail, since his review identifies Bonhoeffer's mandates as "labor, marriage, the church, and the world." See Reinhold Niebuhr, "*Ethics*, by Dietrich Bonhoeffer," *Union Seminary Quarterly Review* 11 (May 1956), 57–8.

[45] Bonhoeffer sometimes speaks of the mandate of "culture" and in other places of "work." See Bonhoeffer, *Ethics*, p. 388, n. 2. It is not clear whether he is just naming the same thing in different ways or thinking of different contexts.

of history.[46] We should not, therefore, take Bonhoeffer's statement that the four mandates are drawn from the Bible as a literalist's claim that the authoritative list can be found somewhere in scripture.[47] His theological point is that "[t]he commandment of God revealed in Jesus Christ embraces in its unity all of human life."[48] This unity of life contrasts to a certain Lutheran understanding of the "orders" that made one responsible before God for a specific vocation, so that the householder had nothing to do with the work of the ruler, who had nothing to do with the ministry of the pastor. To sustain Bonhoeffer's theological point about the claim of God on all of life, we should, in fact, regularly reexamine the way we think about contexts, to be sure that we have not allowed some new area of life to differentiate itself from others in a way that escapes the call to responsibility.

The question of how to describe and differentiate contexts is primarily a question of whether technological possibilities and forms of social organization have developed in ways that pose fundamentally different challenges to responsible action. Responsible parenting has become so different from responsible governing that no abstract principle can provide meaningful guidance in both contexts.[49] A university or a symphony orchestra is, among other things, a business operation, but increasing questions about the use of business models in cultural institutions suggest that work and culture are different contexts, with different standards of responsibility that apply to their leadership. What might a century ago have seemed a fairly homogeneous world in which responsible gentlemen engaged in activities outside of the home and apart from government and the church is now divided into quite different spheres of activity in which competitiveness, for example, is sometimes a virtue of responsible leadership and sometimes a betrayal of institutional purposes. Indeed, one problem with efforts to understand free societies in terms of the development of institutions of civil society between government and the individual is that these institutions are today so diverse in their organization and mission that "civil society" can hardly be more than a generic term for a variety of contexts in which quite different standards of responsibility apply.

We need a plurality of contexts in which to meet the requirements of responsibility with the specificity and directness that the command of God

---

[46] Max Stackhouse, "Public Theology and Political Economy in a Globalizing Era," *Studies in Christian Ethics* 14 (2001), 70–1.

[47] See Brock, "Bonhoeffer and the Bible in Christian Ethics," 24.

[48] Bonhoeffer, *Ethics*, p. 388.

[49] See the idea of "complex justice" in Michael Walzer, *Spheres of Justice: A Defense of Pluralism and Equality* (New York: Basic Books, 1983), pp. 17–19.

demands. Otherwise, the command is stretched into an abstract principle that elicits confusion or submission, rather than responsibility. But we also want to avoid an endless fragmentation of responsibilities, as though the university, the symphony, and the museum had nothing in common that distinguishes them from an airline and a department store chain. There is no magic number above which there are too many contexts and below which there are too few. There is no mechanical rule to determine exactly when responsibilities become so different that a new context comes into being. For most purposes, it seems that the full set of contexts that Bonhoeffer names as mandates works well enough for our purposes, too, although we might want to rename them more inclusively for a more diverse society and economy: family, government, religion, business, and culture. The important thing is not the list, but the claim that it is in the diversity of these places that we hear the command of God.

CRITICAL AND RESPONSIBLE

Despite their differences, both Niebuhr and Bonhoeffer are reluctant to describe the human good in general terms that could provide goals for a political movement or organize the life of a whole society. Instead, they emphasize responsibility in the pursuit of a variety of goods in specific settings where those goods are created and maintained. These two theologians who spoke so clearly to their own generation may thus seem somewhat out of place in a time that increasingly demands a general account of the human good as an act of political responsibility. Our contemporaries assume that political movements and leaders have an idea of the good by which they think everyone should live, and they increasingly mistrust those who are not forthcoming with it.

The reticence of Niebuhr and Bonhoeffer on this point makes each of them appear to different observers as conservative or radical, reactionary or revolutionary, an apologist for prevailing social powers or an advocate for the oppressed. In Niebuhr's case, the length of his career and the sheer number of issues he addressed may account for some of the differing views, but the variety of interpretations of Bonhoeffer's brief, focused theological career suggests that any effort to identify Christian realism with a political program may be missing the point.

For Niebuhr and Bonhoeffer alike, the Christian faith cannot be identified with an ideology that brings all of life under a unified set of purposes and a common authority. The only possible unity is the ultimate unity in Christ, which preserves for the duration of history the diversity of the mandates. In the historical competition between political systems, Christianity makes no endorsements among the rival claimants, and it does not enter the competition as a contender in its own right.

In the twentieth-century world in which political life was often understood as a competition between ideologies and systems, one might suppose that those who shared Niebuhr's and Bonhoeffer's insistence that Christianity has no part in that contest would withdraw from public life altogether, as sectarian Protestants withdrew from the world of secular authority at the beginning of modern politics. That is the way that Witness Realism understands this legacy,[50] and there is some initial plausibility to the interpretation. Maintaining a distinctive Christian community with its own virtues has never been an easy task. Perhaps it is the best we can hope to do under the conditions of modern life.

For Bonhoeffer and Niebuhr, however, the difficulties of modern political life have quite different implications. Multiple loyalties, conflicting obligations, and competing demands from different institutions and groups all serve as barriers to the premature unity that ideologies and political programs seek to impose. Rather than suggesting that these differences would go away if everyone sought the true good or allowing that differences should be suppressed if people do not recognize what the true good is, Christian realism emphasizes the persistent disagreements and perhaps even encourages the conflicts. The results create a space for responsible action that might well be lost in a public life dominated by competing absolute claims of rival ideologies.

Pluralist Christian Realism dispels the notion that the life of society must be structured by these ideologies and refuses to withdraw from politics in the face of them. A biblical perspective, as Reinhold Niebuhr recognized, provides a critical attitude in which the relative validity of all systems and schemes of justice can be recognized, because they identify injustices – often long-standing and systemic injustices – that are part of existing social structures. At the same time, the claims of the new system can always be criticized from a more inclusive perspective that reveals the abstractions and oversimplifications behind its promises of perfect justice. The critical attitude relativizes the differences between ideologies, rather than taking sides between them. Criticism from a biblical perspective, however, is not political nihilism, as though ideological claims about justice had no element of truth in them, or as though there were no meaningful differences between them. The point is rather that those truths will never be as complete and

---

[50] See pp. 23–27 earlier.

the differences will never be as absolute as the claims each ideology makes for itself.

What the critical attitude provides is the freedom to take a "responsible attitude," rather than its own distinctive set of imperatives. To know that we are human beings and not God empowers us to make human choices between limited goods, at the same time that it reveals the ambiguity in every choice. Less adequate accounts of human nature confer on human beings the godlike power to make unambiguous choices, or cast them as tragic heroes who nobly defy a fate they cannot control, or reduce them to the pursuit of self-interest in a world in which ideals and values have no meaning beyond individual satisfaction.

In a world structured by competing systems and ideologies, Niebuhr and Bonhoeffer focused instead on responsible choices in specific contexts. Neither the promise of a new order nor the security of existing institutions receives uncritical endorsement from Christian realism, but the contexts where people actually live their lives provide settings in which all promises and securities can be tested. Whatever human good the systems offer will have to connect to the goods that people know in the lives they already have, to support them and not to replace them.[51]

For those who draw more immediate connections between religious commitment and political programs, this has appeared to be either dangerous radicalism or reactionary legitimation of the status quo. When ideological divisions separated blocs of nations capable of suppressing internal dissent and waging war on one another, the Christian realists' insistence on responsible choice and examination of one's own goals and motives seemed to undermine the unity and certainty that the decisive struggle for the world's future required. Even Reinhold Niebuhr, at the end of *Moral Man and Immoral Society*, suggested that more could be accomplished by fanatics who believe in perfect justice than by realists who know that perfect justice is impossible.[52] When pursuit of the absolute begins to take control of politics, realism seems dangerously ill-equipped for the conflicts that it so perceptively analyzes.

Two decades later, when the contenders in the global struggle had been reduced to the Cold War blocs led by the United States and the Soviet

---

[51] Michael Rustin observes that "if a socialist view of the world is to be the least bit plausible, it must be grounded in good aspects of the lives that people have now." The same point might be made about more conservative worldviews that seek the stability of existing institutions. See Michael Rustin, "Equality in Post-Modern Times," in David Miller and Michael Walzer (eds.), *Pluralism, Justice, and Equality* (Oxford: Oxford University Press, 1995), p. 18.

[52] Niebuhr, *Moral Man and Immoral Society*, p. 277.

Union, Niebuhr saw the matter differently. The task was to support liberal democracy's resistance to totalitarianism without evoking democracy's own self-righteousness and religious certainty. For that purpose, it was important to keep the critical attitude focused on America's own achievements, as well as on the rival ideology. The most hopeful aspect of liberal democracy was its openness to this sort of criticism. A democratic society "provides for checks and balances upon the pretensions of men as well as upon their lust for power; it thereby prevents truth from turning into falsehood when the modicum of error in truth is not challenged and the modicum of truth in a falsehood is not rescued and cherished."[53]

Recognition of the pluralism of competing interests and a readiness to compromise ideological purity for the sake of political cooperation gave democracy the flexibility and responsiveness to new conditions that it needed to prevail over the long run. Although it might be impossible to articulate the values of democracy with the unanimity and certainty possessed by its ideological rivals, that diversity proved to be its decisive strength, while unanimity and certainty proved in the end to be fatal weaknesses. As Dietrich Bonhoeffer suggested, abstraction from the discrete, diverse historical settings where responsible choices are made distorts religion or politics into a "weak ideology" that cannot gain control of reality.

If this point was obscure at the beginning of the ideological conflicts of the twentieth century and difficult to maintain in the midst of them, it remains a very important lesson now, when liberal democracy has emerged as the sole survivor of those ideological struggles. Responsible decisions about the human good must be made in specific contexts, because the good is known in parables that connect to the places where we have already tried to grasp it. To project political power without regard for these contexts shatters the "mandates" by which God sustains limited, weak, and divided human life for God's own purposes and takes on the apocalyptic role of bringing about the final unity beyond present differences.

Bonhoeffer insisted that success invites a form of idolatry that dulls human capacities for judgment and ends by denying divine judgment itself. "Ethical and intellectual capacity for judgment grow dull before the sheen of success and before the desire somehow to share in it."[54] The successes he had in mind were the successes of Adolf Hitler, but there can be no doubt that he intended the theological point to apply to any other ideology that might view its achievements as though they were the last word of divine

---

[53] Niebuhr, *Christian Realism and Political Problems*, p. 14. [54] Bonhoeffer, *Ethics*, p. 89.

judgment, rendering criticism from a human point of view irrelevant, even blasphemous.

Bonhoeffer and Niebuhr remind us of the weakness of every effort to resolve all questions about the human good by an ideology separated from the contexts in which specific goods are experienced and responsible choices have to be made. On that point, their warnings about the weakness of ideology and the idolization of success remain immediately relevant to our situation, even though the ideological conflicts that structured global politics for much of the twentieth century have largely disappeared. The discussion of human goods, goals, and values in public life should be approached with some caution, even in a pluralistic society where it may seem to be an appropriate way of clarifying the aims and interests of political leaders. Every discussion of human good that gets tied to a political program runs the risk of imposing premature unity on the goods that people create and share in the multiple contexts of everyday life. What starts as a question about the relationship between family life and a political program becomes an ideology of "family values." Asking a legislator to pay attention to the effects of a tax policy or an educational program on family life may be a legitimate demand for political responsibility, but it is easy to pose the question in a way that defines the goods of family life too narrowly, and the resulting political program may make that limited set of family goods the only criteria for decisions about economics and culture. Whether the resulting ideology of "family values" is created by the leaders or by their constituents, the substitution of ideology for responsibility is a perennial problem in political life. It does not happen only when politics is structured by ideological choices on a grand scale.

DIVERSITY OF GOODS

Another aspect of the contemporary concern with human goods in politics poses quite different problems for Christian realism. Alongside those for whom "values" invite the creation of new ideologies that impose an artificial unity on human goods, there are others for whom a public conversation about goods and values serves chiefly to remind us of the diversity of opinion on these matters. When they question political leaders about values, what they seek is reassurance, beyond abstract affirmations of freedom and rights, that what these leaders value will not impinge on choices about the human good that individuals make for themselves. What they seek more than anything else in politics is their freedom to pursue the good on their own terms. They rejoice in the disappearance of the restrictive ideologies that demanded everyone's commitment to a single system of values, and they are vigilant against any program that might return us to that kind of politics. The one point of agreement they share with those whose interest in values is more ideological is that values must become more open objects of public discussion in order for us to see what is at stake.

This anti-ideological perspective, with its emphasis on freedom and the diversity of values, sees public discussion as an ongoing conversation in which few decisions should be made that limit individuals in the pursuit of their own understanding of human good. The articulation of a variety of values, goals, and goods serves important public purposes, since it gives people clearer ideas about the choices they have available, and when the conversation is genuinely open, it exposes such a range of possibilities that the idea of arriving at unity while still retaining freedom quickly becomes incredible. This conversation cannot, however, be understood as moral deliberation in the usual sense, that is, a collective limitation of the available choices on moral grounds. It might more accurately be characterized as a survey of moral possibilities, in which the full range of understandings of human good which are actually in play becomes available to everyone, so that necessary democratic decisions can be made in light of that set, rather than some more restricted list of socially approved options or a new ideology that promises future unity at the price of present freedom. If the conversation eliminates any possibilities, it does so only on the assumption that most people want freedom, so that they will reject any leader or program exposed by the conversation as harboring more restrictive intentions.

This understanding of the diversity of human goods poses quite a different challenge to Christian realism from the ideological politics that preceded it. If ideology threatens the diversity of real life with an imposed unity, this unrestricted conversation about goods and goals raises questions about the limits of diversity. How far can a real political community go without agreement about the human good? How "thin" can the good be that all share before they share nothing but their disagreements about the good? How much conflict over these questions can a community handle, not in the occasional crisis, but as an ongoing part of ordinary public life?[55]

Neither Niebuhr nor Bonhoeffer contemplated a democracy that would outlast its ideological rivals only to find itself uncertain about the terms of its own conversation. However, the same realistic attention to the specific

---

[55] For a detailed examination of this question that compares recent philosophical and theological answers, see Raymond Plant, *Politics, Theology, and History* (Cambridge: Cambridge University Press, 2001), pp. 330–59.

contexts of choice and action that limits premature unification of human goods also provides an alternative to their endless diversification. We are not simply engaged in a general conversation about human goods. We are joined with one another in specific contexts where we create and maintain them. The ongoing conversation happens someplace in particular, among people who already have purposes in common, or they would not be in the conversation in the first place. In that sense, the goods themselves structure the discussion about them.

The basic political problem about human goods is that there appear to be so many of them. People want quite different things, and under conditions of scarcity, they cannot each have all of them. Securing agreement on what the real goods are and how they relate to one another does not appear likely, especially on the scale of a large modern state. The strategy of modern politics has been to regulate the conflict, rather than to resolve the question.

Nevertheless, agreements do begin to develop. The goods people seek are not infinitely varied. Goods conflict, but they also converge. The convergences begin along the natural boundaries of human life – needs for food and shelter, our dependence on one another for physical care and emotional well-being, awareness of our own mortality and of the limits of our intellectual and technical powers. Because all human beings share these limits, the anxieties they provoke, and the aspirations to control or transcend them, the goods people seek tend to have a great deal in common, even if they are rarely exactly the same. As Thomas Ogletree observes, "Although societies can provide for these functions in an amazing variety of ways, the variety is not endless. It revolves around a relatively limited set of possibilities."[56]

Moreover, few goods are available just for the taking. The conditions of scarcity that make choices about the good more urgent also tend to make choices more alike. No human good can be completely idiosyncratic, because it requires a common effort to conceive goods and to create them. In the local settings where goods are created and enjoyed, people cooperate to bring a new product to market, support a symphony orchestra, or join in a liturgy without fully agreeing on the meaning of work, art, or religion. Certainly they will not all agree with each other on how this good on which they are working together relates to other goods. Much of the humor and hostility inherent in any cooperative activity relate to people who, we judge, take the task too seriously, or not seriously enough. What most of the participants will agree, however, is that this good is not the only good

---

[56] Thomas W. Ogletree, *The World Calling* (Louisville, KY: Westminster John Knox Press, 2004), p. 56.

there is, and that their shared efforts to create it fit into various ways of combining it with other goods into a sustainable and even happy life.

People not only seek a variety of goods. They seek particular goods for a variety of reasons. A young couple may enter into family life because they want to shape their lives according to an ideal they have been taught, or because they want deliberately to create an alternative to the families in which they grew up. A software designer may work on computer games because she is fascinated with the technology, because she thinks it is a position in which her skills will be challenged and rewarded, or because she has a moral conviction that computer games should be providing a different kind of entertainment, more like art and less like violence.[57] Some politicians run for office because they think that government can provide real solutions to problems, while the legislator across the aisle is in politics to restrain government from interfering with individual initiative. There is rarely any assurance that everyone involved in the organized activity that produces and maintains a good understands it in the same way or seeks it for the same reasons. The neighbors next door, the person in the next cubicle, or the people in the next pew may have quite different reasons for being there.

People often enter into contexts unaware of these differences, or perhaps they believe that they can transform the setting so that it conforms better to *their* sense of its purposes. The software designer expects to create a new line of games that will be commercially successful while promoting different values and aesthetics, and she might not begin at all if she lacked this confidence. A new administrator takes on the culture of a problem school system, expecting to make it both economically efficient and educationally effective. New parents envision a family unlike the harried homes of their overly busy friends and colleagues. Only gradually does it become apparent that the context imposes its own rules and ways of doing things. Everyone makes some adjustment to the context that exists. Some, indeed, surrender to it completely, exchanging their vision for its reality and becoming fervent supporters of the status quo. Others cease to see this context as a place where real goods can be created, so that their participation becomes merely instrumental to their responsibilities in other contexts where they think the important goods are really to be found. Nevertheless, despite the pressure of institutional demands and the disappointment of many aspirations, these visions of what is possible do change the context. A context never becomes

---

[57] Michel Marriott, "Counterpoint: Artistry, Not Uzis, in the 'Hood," *New York Times*, sec. G, August 12, 2004, 7.

exactly what people envision it should be, but neither does it remain what it was.

One of the striking characteristics of modern life is that it allows for the development of institutions and systems in which people pursue goods about which they do not completely agree. We work for our candidate's election at the same time that we want to change the party's program. We can be both convinced that our university's priorities are misplaced and committed to the effectiveness of its teaching and the importance of its place in society. We can be convinced that our nation's policies are unjust and still work to maintain the political system in the hope that it can become an instrument of change. We are so accustomed to this range of commitments and opinions in our corporations, universities, and political parties that we pay little attention to the complexity of the agreements it requires.

We seek the good in contexts that are not as good as we wish, or not good in exactly the way we wish. For those whose principal concern is not to compromise their own commitments, this may seem mere hypocrisy, but it is part of the structure of responsible life. In a complex, modern society, important human goods require large institutions and highly struc-tured human practices. As a practical matter, obtaining most goods requires engagement with the aspirations of those who want something similar, even if it is not exactly the same thing we want. It also requires engagement with existing institutions and established ways of doing things. The alternatives are to avoid compromise by foregoing this particular good in its present form altogether, or to become a mere consumer, accepting goods on the terms offered without challenging them.

KNOWLEDGE AND CONFLICT

Against the claims that we can have complete knowledge of the human good, Christian realism locates responsible action in contexts that provide only part of what a whole life requires. One reason why it is difficult for people to agree about the good as a whole is that the places where they work on it together encompass only a part of it. Even within these contexts, moreover, it is unlikely that the participants share complete agreement about the goods they create together. Participants in a context have their own ideas about the goods it provides. What they create together is only a partial realization of the good they seek, and given the differences among participants, it is most likely a partial realization of several different ideas about the good that is not completely shared. Responsible people work both to create the good that a context can provide now *and* to change the context so that the good it provides will be more like the good they envision. Because they do not all envision it the same way, even their cooperation involves them in occasional conflicts. Because their cooperation is always aimed at change, as well as preservation, contexts are neither unchanging nor as universal as some theological accounts of orders and preservation have made them seem. A realistic account sees these changes and conflicts as essential to the achievement of whatever human good is possible under the conditions of history, rather than as an obstacle to it. That is the key point of connection between a contemporary account of contexts and responsibility and the historic Christian idea of orders, spheres, and subsidiarity.[58]

Recognition that contexts give us knowledge of the human good that is always limited and incomplete should not, however, obscure the fact that every context does represent an important fund of shared knowledge of the goods with which it is concerned. When people come together as a family, a corporation, a church, or a university, they do create and maintain goods that they all recognize as valuable in a good human life. Despite disagreements, they think that they know what these goods are and how to produce them. Because they believe that what they accomplish together is good, they take responsibility for it, and they make claims for it in relation to other contexts, to ensure that they have the resources and the freedoms their context requires for its distinctive purposes. Together, we know that some things are good, and we know what we have to do to create and keep them. We cooperate, negotiate, compromise, and change in an effort not to deny the core of what we jointly know.

For contemporary Christian realism, responsible action in the contexts where human life is lived recognizes the diversity of human goods and the real, but limited knowledge we have of them. This engagement with specific, concrete choices extends beyond the political context in which Niebuhr and Bonhoeffer observed it most closely. It seems to be a general requirement of life in modern society. It is not as though we reluctantly accept the necessity of responsible action in politics, but refuse to compromise our principles at home or in church. Having any good involves a commitment to ongoing negotiations about its meaning, in which our idea of that good is tested both against the demands of a particular context and against the ideas of the other people who also participate in the context.

[58] See pp. 76–81 earlier.

Ideological unity and modern politics both promise, each in its own way, to bring an end to conflict about the good. Ideology offers a unified perspective that renders dissent unacceptable. Modern politics offers a secular authority to maintain order so that agreement on the good is unnecessary. Responsibility, however, expects conflict about the good to continue, both within contexts and between them.

CHAPTER 4

Unapologetic Politics

CHRISTIANITY AND DEMOCRACY

In previous chapters, we explored the history of Christian realism and ways of thinking about a society made up of differentiated contexts in which people create and maintain goods important for human living. Whether in Protestant language of "orders," "spheres," and "mandates," or in Catholic social teaching regarding "subsidiary" institutions, Christian theology has called attention to the concrete, local responsibilities that bind people to their neighbors in these contexts. Participation in contexts sets the terms in which much of the moral life is lived, and sustaining the more general social and political conditions under which all of the contexts of human life can flourish is an important standard by which the governments of modern states are judged.

Concern for these contexts and the human goods they provide brought Christianity and liberal democracy into close connection during the twentieth century. Against promises of new orders in which human life would be remade and human goods redefined, both Christianity and democracy rediscovered the value of goods already available in the institutions of work, family, faith, and culture, and they renewed the collaboration of religion and politics to sustain those goods and the pluralistic society that created them.

This collaboration did not make Christian realists into uncritical apologists for democracy, but it did make them important political allies and conversation partners in developing the intellectual framework for the renewed democracies which would emerge from this time of crisis. Already in 1937, the Oxford Conference on Church, Community, and State, which convened under the shadow of increasing international tensions, began to look toward a new European political order. Ecumenical social thought continued to develop through the war years, and religious leaders became important participants in public discussions when the work of postwar reconstruction actually began. Christian realists had a part in shaping the foreign policy of Western democracies at the beginning of the Cold War era, and church leaders led the campaign for the Universal Declaration of Human Rights.[1] Although Bonhoeffer was unable to participate directly in the early stages of this work and did not live to see its outcome, he followed it with interest, and his discussions with other conspirators in the plot against Hitler about the shape of government and society in post–Nazi Germany were a clandestine version of the same thinking about the future that his counterparts in democratic states could do more openly.[2]

After the war, a pragmatic, historical approach to politics, which welcomed Niebuhrian insights into human nature, converged with a Niebuhrian willingness to submit the claims of theology to a sort of preliminary evaluation by history. Together, they suggested a new way of thinking about theology and politics, which would give less attention to the purity of ideas at their point of origin and more attention to their long-term results in practice. Looking forward from the middle of the twentieth century, one might have expected a world in which both theology and political philosophy would be engaged in different ways in the critical thinking by which institutions are measured against human purposes and societies maintain the flexibility that allows them to respond to changing conditions. In such a world, political philosophers could hardly do without ideas about human good and human nature that are regularly discussed by theologians, and theologians might apply their ideas to politics without controversy – at least without controversy regarding their speaking as theologians. In some respects, the most important liberal political philosopher of the twentieth century anticipated just such a world when he wrote a senior thesis at Princeton on "A Brief Inquiry Into the Meaning of Sin and Faith," drawing heavily on the work of Emil Brunner.[3]

John Rawls subsequently changed his own thinking, and as we have seen, he changed the terms of the discussion.[4] The theoretical development of liberal political philosophy that began with Rawls's *A Theory of*

---

[1] Reinhold Niebuhr, "The Development of a Social Ethic in the Ecumenical Movement," in *Faith and Politics*, Ronald Stone (ed.) (New York: George Braziller, 1968), pp. 165–84; Heather Warren, *Theologians of a New World Order: Reinhold Niebuhr and the Christian Realists, 1920–1948* (New York: Oxford University Press, 1997); John S. Nurser, *For All Peoples and Nations: The Ecumenical Church and Human Rights* (Washington, DC: Georgetown University Press, 2005).

[2] See especially the political essays in Dietrich Bonhoeffer, *Conspiracy and Imprisonment, 1940–1945*, Dietrich Bonhoeffer Works, vol. XVI (Minneapolis, MN: Fortress Press, 2006), pp. 502–39. For a more complete account of the political thinking of the conspirators against Hitler, see Christoph Strom, *Theologische Ethik im Kampf Gegen den Nationalsozialismus* (Munich: Christian Kaiser Verlag, 1989).

[3] Eric Gregory, "Before the Original Position: The Neo-Orthodox Theology of the Young John Rawls," *Journal of Religious Ethics* 35 (2007), 179–206.

[4] See p. 63 earlier.

Justice focused new attention on the rules of democratic discourse. One result has been to make it more difficult for theologians to gain admittance to the conversation on their own terms. Christian realists who want to remain part of a broad public discussion now have to locate themselves in it with some care. From the point of view of an explicitly Christian politics, pluralist Christian realism appears to lack the distinctive Christian witness required in a time of moral decay and political disorder. For liberal political philosophers, by contrast, any truth stated in religious terms is politically suspect. As John Rawls put it, "The zeal to embody the whole truth in politics is incompatible with an idea of public reason that belongs with democratic citizenship."[5] Christian realists who want to remain a part of a broad public discussion must insist that their zeal for the truth does not extend to imposing it on those who do not see it, while at the same time maintaining, against the criticism of some other Christians, that their commitment to the truth of Christian faith is authentic.

It is perhaps understandable that some Christians faced with this problem have preferred Christian witness to public discourse, but Christian realists have found this withdrawal unacceptable, politically and theologically. For one thing, responsible participation in public life may strengthen a religious community's own understanding of its faith and tradition. Religious communities which refuse responsibility to or for the wider society may be freed to bear witness to their own identity, but they may also withdraw into a self-righteous consciousness of their distinctive virtues. More to the point, without the stimulus of the wider conversation, they are apt to lose the critical skills that enable them to distinguish identity from self-righteousness. The ongoing conversation of a modern, pluralistic democracy is good for Christianity, because Christianity, too, seeks reasons and not only authority. As Franklin Gamwell puts it at the conclusion of an extended argument for Christian commitment to political discourse, "... the truth of Christian faith depends on an understanding of God's nature that argument can validate. At least in this respect, Christians have no cause to resist and every reason to embrace full and free discourse as a form of political rule."[6]

The difference between full and free political discourse and a zeal to embody the whole truth in politics may, however, be more clear today than it was to a previous generation of religious and political thinkers. Gamwell

---

[5] John Rawls, *Collected Papers*, Samuel Freeman (ed.) (Cambridge, MA: Harvard University Press, 1999), p. 574.

[6] Franklin Gamwell, *Politics as a Christian Vocation* (Cambridge: Cambridge University Press, 2005), p. 78.

suggests that Reinhold Niebuhr and John Courtney Murray, for example, thought that the core convictions of American democracy also expressed the enduring meaning of the Christian confession.[7] Although Gamwell's assessment of Niebuhr and Murray may oversimplify their accounts of American history, he has identified a problem with one strategy of argument that they do sometimes employ. Part of what they were eager to show was the way that Christian ideas had shaped the presuppositions of American democracy. They did not consider the possibility that this might call the reasonableness of liberal democracy into question, rather than provide it with enhanced legitimacy.

PUBLIC REASON

Drawing on religious ideas to support political programs or systems in the way that Murray and Niebuhr connected their Christian traditions to American democracy was hardly an innovation in theology or politics. It had been a staple of American public discourse from the beginning. To be sure, Americans had learned a wariness of religious authority from the English Dissenters. They did not want churches to dictate law or use the state for purposes of religious discrimination. But they assumed that widely shared religious ideas could lend urgency and moral significance to political choices, and preachers and politicians alike built those connections into their arguments on public occasions.[8] A purely historical survey would suggest a connection between religious support and political legitimacy, and a study of American rhetoric could hardly ignore the place of religion in the public discourse of liberal democracy.

Developing a theory for liberal democracy challenged those practices and assumptions. Theory required moving from multiple systems of belief that were widely shared, although not universal, and mutually reinforcing, though not completely consistent, to fundamental principles which could win rational agreement from all citizens. Once the theoretical move is made, arguments based on other ideas, such as an appreciation of tradition or compatibility with religious doctrine, become irrelevant, and they distract from the required universality of rational consent. Because a government must include all people within its territory under its authority, government by the people cannot base that authority on ideas that only some of them accept.

[7] *Ibid.* p. 70n.
[8] John Meacham, *American Gospel: God, the Founding Fathers, and the Making of a Nation* (New York: Random House, 2006).

To the extent that contested or contestable beliefs are incorporated into the theory, they weaken the logic of liberal democracy, even though they might make some people more willing to support it. That is why Rawls says that zeal to embody the whole truth is incompatible with democratic politics. "Comprehensive doctrines," which offer a complete account of human goods and organize them into a whole way of life, cannot be a starting point for democratic politics.

Elegance and rationality are virtues in the making of theories, and Rawls begins with just two principles which appear to be requirements of reason for anyone forming a government to which rational people would consent.[9] Other theorists have been less certain that the principles of liberalism can be so concisely summarized. Michael Walzer's liberal pluralism holds that liberalism is a system of "complex equality" in which there is a different distributive principle for each sphere of primary goods with which a society must be concerned. It is, however, important for Walzer, as for Rawls, that these principles derive from the idea of a liberal society free of arbitrary power and domination, and not from some other system of beliefs that the citizens happen to hold.[10]

A completely rational liberal theory may be as difficult to achieve as an elegant one. Rawls proposes that in the absence of a complete, rational demonstration of the necessity of the principles of justice, we might rely on an "overlapping consensus" of comprehensive doctrines that support the same principles in different ways. Indeed, in later reconsiderations of his theory, he concluded that we probably do have to rely on such a consensus.[11] Walzer and other liberal pluralists were not surprised by that result, having begun their reflections on more local conditions in the first place.[12]

Even with an overlapping consensus, however, it is important for the rationality of the theory that democratic principles be framed strictly from the points of agreement within the overlap, without relying on other elements in a comprehensive doctrine to buttress their legitimacy. Too close an association between any one system of belief and the democratic political system raises the suspicion that the unanimity of its political principles has been compromised. Acknowledging that comprehensive doctrines are normal, necessary, and important contributors to the political consensus

---

[9] John Rawls, *A Theory of Justice* (Cambridge, MA: Harvard University Press, 1971), pp. 62–5.

[10] Michael Walzer, *Spheres of Justice* (New York: Basic Books, 1983), pp. 17–21.

[11] John Rawls, *Political Liberalism* (New York: Columbia University Press, 1993), pp. 133–72.

[12] Walzer, *Spheres of Justice*, p. xiv. See also William A. Galston, *Liberal Pluralism: The Implications of Value Pluralism for Political Theory and Practice* (Cambridge: Cambridge University Press, 2002), pp. 4–11.

on which a liberal democracy rests may thus have the paradoxical effect of intensifying the scrutiny of the most familiar religious traditions, lest their ideals slip undetected into a political consensus which, in the nature of the case, cannot answer questions with the finality that the religious believer or the political ideologue seeks. The problem, according to the liberal theorists, is not only that religions often become repressive or intolerant when they are given access to power. Their political questions are simply different from those that shape the ongoing conversations of a liberal democracy. They tend, Walzer says, to ask, "How would we organize civil society (if we had the chance)? Or what would civil society look like if everyone shared our faith or ideology?"[13]

The principles of liberal democracy, once established, largely determine what will count as a good reason when citizens or their representatives make decisions in the "public political forum."[14] There, the reasons that we give for taking an action cannot simply be *our* reasons. If they are intended to guide the policies of a democratic government, reasons must be based on accepted democratic principles and on matters that can be determined by investigation and reasoned argument. The argument that I make in support of a public policy must be more than a signal to other people who happen to share my comprehensive doctrine that they ought to support it too. The test of public reason thus becomes that any reasonable participant in the discussion might find it persuasive. That does not mean that everyone will be persuaded (or, indeed, that anyone will be persuaded). Other public reasons might be more persuasive. But a public reason will not appear arbitrary or incomprehensible, even to those who disagree with it.[15]

The theorization of liberal democracy thus significantly changes our ordinary understanding of the public forum and challenges some ideas held by Christian realists and other religious thinkers about how public discussion ought to work. In place of a discussion in which a political understanding of justice is subjected to testing and criticism by the prophetic tradition and the "impossible ideal" of love, we have a forum in which public reason tests the reasonableness of comprehensive doctrines. This means, in effect, that reasonable comprehensive doctrines are those which support the political principles of democracy, for whatever reasons those doctrines deem appropriate. They are reasonable insofar as they support the overlapping consensus.

[13] Michael Walzer, "Equality and Civil Society," in Simone Chambers and Will Kymlicka (eds.) *Alternative Conceptions of Civil Society* (Princeton, NJ: Princeton University Press, 2002), p. 44.
[14] Rawls, *Collected Papers*, p. 575.
[15] Rawls, *Political Liberalism*, pp. 212–54.

It would, of course, be implausible to suggest, even in theory, that the principles of democracy have been worked out so thoroughly that all the arguments in the public forum are merely questions of application. But it is essential to the theory that the major changes can be seen, at least in retrospect, as supported by democratic principles and public reason.[16] This holds true even for such dramatic changes as the end of racial segregation and the abolition of slavery, and it holds true despite the language of religious judgment in which Martin Luther King Jr. or Abraham Lincoln interpreted those struggles. Indeed, for liberal theory, it is especially important that public reason prevails in these dramatic cases. Otherwise, there is no democratic way to justify the demand that everyone accept the change as a matter of coercive law, and no way to distinguish between these changes and forms of discrimination, persecution, or even religious terrorism that some doctrine might succeed in enforcing as public policy in the future.

John Rawls's development of liberal democratic theory thus seems to require a substantial rethinking of our ideas about the historical influence of religion on the public pursuit of justice, and it calls into question aspects of what Niebuhr and his contemporaries thought of as the realistic application of religious ideals to the distinct sphere of public policy. The reaction of religious thinkers who protested that they had suddenly been excluded from what was now a "naked public square"[17] was understandable, as was the quite different approach to public discussions that they developed in response. We will turn to that momentarily.

However, we must first conclude the discussion of public reason in liberal theory by noting that hostility toward the public role of religion is neither the theoretical justification nor, in most cases, the motivation for insisting on a strict standard of public reason. The strict standard is made necessary by the narrow purpose of the public political forum, which is, in fact, a rather smaller space than the public square to which Rawls's critics now demand access.

It is imperative to realize that the idea of public reason does not apply to all political discussions of fundamental questions, but only to discussions of those questions in what I refer to as the public political forum. This forum may be divided into three parts: the discourse of judges in their decisions, and especially of the judges of a supreme court; the discourse of government officials, especially chief executives and legislators, and finally, the discourse of candidates for public office ... [18]

---

[16] See pp. 69–72 earlier.
[17] See, for example, Richard John Neuhaus, *The Naked Public Square: Religion and Democracy in America* (Grand Rapids: Eerdmans, 1984); Stephen L. Carter, *The Culture of Disbelief: How American Law and Politics Trivialize Religious Devotion* (New York: Basic Books, 1993).
[18] Rawls, *Collected Papers*, p. 575.

In other discussions, the rigorous constraints of public reason do not apply. This is what Rawls calls the "background culture," with its wide array of voluntary organizations, educational institutions, civic groups, and communications media.[19] It would appear that there are few general rules that govern the offering of reasons in the background culture, and Rawls in any case does not elaborate them.

The reason why liberal theory is so insistent about the application of public reason to the public political forum goes back to the basic idea of democratic government. Government exercises unique coercive powers that apply to everyone and which are brought to bear by courts, legislatures, and executive officials. The constraints of public reason ensure that these coercive powers are not arbitrarily deployed, but that their use serves the purposes of democratic government itself.

This is one reason why religious grounds alone are not properly considered a sufficient basis of coercion even if they happen to be shared by virtually all citizens. If fully rational citizens cannot be persuaded of the necessity of the coercion – as is common where that coercion is based on an injunction grounded in someone else's religious scripture or revelation – then from the point of view of liberal democracy, the coercion lacks an adequate basis. A liberal state exists in good part to accommodate a variety of people irrespective of their special preference for one kind of life over another; it thus allows coercion only where necessary to preserve civic order, and not simply on the basis of majority preference.[20]

Democracy limits not only the ways in which power may be used, but also the purposes for which it may be used. Democratic governments use their coercive powers, as William Galston puts it, to "serve the cause of ordered liberty."[21] Purposes not connected to democratic government cannot be arbitrarily substituted for those that are. The requirements of public reason are reminders of what democratic governments must do to remain democratic. To insist that those limits be observed identifies you as an advocate of democracy, not as an opponent of religion.

UNAPOLOGETIC THEOLOGY

Nevertheless, critics discern the effects of liberal theory behind what they see as limitations aimed specifically at the public role of religion. Stephen

---

[19] *Ibid.*, p. 576.
[20] Robert Audi, "Liberal Democracy and the Place of Religion in Politics," in Robert Audi and Nicholas Wolterstorff, *Religion in the Public Square: The Place of Religious Convictions in Political Debate* (Lanham, MD: Rowman and Littlefield, 1997), pp. 16–17.
[21] Galston, *Practice of Liberal Pluralism*, p. 26.

Carter has criticized the "culture of disbelief" that renders religion invisible in the media and public life and imposes a silence on religious convictions that does not apply to other moral commitments. Like Reinhold Niebuhr, Carter believes that religion has helped to keep the ongoing discussion of liberal democracy open and critical, and he expects that role to be even more important in the future.[22] For liberal democracy, a "culture of disbelief" is self-defeating. By repressing the independent religious voices that raise fundamental questions about society's prevailing values, the culture of disbelief invites the very rigidity in belief and practice that it fears religion will impose.

Carter's argument, however, is not primarily a case for the political usefulness of religion, to be offered as a reply to those who emphasize its political risks. To say no more than that would be to accept the premise that the political culture sets the terms for public expression of religious ideas, appealing to that culture for a larger place in the discussion on the basis of an argument that religion can serve the purposes of liberal democracy, after all. Carter's purpose is to challenge the terms, to insist that religious voices may enter into public discussion on their own terms.

What is needed is not a requirement that the religiously devout choose a form of dialogue that liberalism accepts, but that liberalism develop a politics that accepts whatever form of dialogue a member of the public offers. Epistemic diversity, like diversity of other kinds, should be cherished, not ignored, and certainly not abolished. What is needed, then, is a willingness to *listen*, not because the speaker has *the right voice*, but because the speaker has *the right to speak*. Moreover, the willingness to listen must hold out the possibility that the speaker is saying something worth listening to; to do less is to trivialize the forces that shape the moral convictions of tens of millions of Americans.[23]

Carter's argument for accepting religious voices into democratic discourse on their own terms coincides with theological developments that emphasize the coherence and integrity of religious traditions, casting doubt on the idea that they could restate their meaning in strictly secular terms, even if they wanted to do so. Where earlier theologians might have regarded modern scientific and social thought as a neutral framework in which specific religious insights could be restated for public purposes, this new theology questions whether religious ideas can be transferred from one setting to another without significant loss of meaning.

---

[22] Carter, *Culture of Disbelief,* pp. 271–4.
[23] Carter, *Culture of Disbelief,* pp. 230–1. [Emphasis in original.]

The result is what William Placher calls "unapologetic theology."[24] Unapologetic theology rejects the task assigned to "apologetics" in the conventional ordering of theological subdisciplines. It regards efforts to make a case for Christian beliefs in terms already accepted by some other audience as unlikely to persuade and far more likely to reduce the theological idea to a moral platitude with no critical power to call prevailing practices into question. Recast the "impossible ideal" in terms acceptable to public reason, and you lose the critical power Niebuhr expected it to exercise. It accomplishes no more than the nineteenth century theological liberalism which Niebuhr himself criticized for attempting to ". . . prove the relevance of the religious ideal by reducing it to conformity with the prudential rules of conduct which the common sense of many generations and the experience of the ages have elaborated."[25]

Today's unapologetic theology thus rejects the traditional role of theological apologetics. But unapologetic theology also rejects "apology" in a more colloquial sense: It expresses no regrets for presenting itself in its own terms and expecting to be understood.

INTEGRITY

Unapologetic theology may at first appear to be the antithesis of public reason, but this appearance is misleading. Although the arguments are made by different people, who see the problems of a pluralistic society in different ways, there are parallels between the case for public reason and the case for unapologetic theology. Democratic government, as we have seen, uses the criteria of public reason to rule out proposals that would use the powers of government for undemocratic purposes. Unapologetic theology uses theological language to preserve the distinctiveness of its metaphysical and moral claims, ensuring that its rigorous demands are not mistaken for other, easier ideas. Because the integrity of democracy or theology is the primary concern, it would seem that neither public reason nor unapologetic theology requires a rejection of the other. It should be possible, in principle, to affirm both.

In practice, however, the peaceable kingdom of public reason and unapologetic theology is disturbed by complaints from both sides. Some unapologetic theologians deny that modern democracy has any integrity

---

[24] William Placher, *Unapologetic Theology: A Christian Voice in a Pluralistic Conversation* (Louisville, KY: Westminster John Knox Press, 1989).

[25] Niebuhr, *An Interpretation of Christian Ethics*, p. 63.

that public reason might preserve.[26] Likewise, some philosophers committed to democracy as a continuing conversation about how we are to live together find religious ideas about how we ought to live so inhibiting to open discussion that they become a "conversation-stopper."[27] Even a cursory review of recent literature on religion and public life will provide many variations on this opposition between religion and reasoned democracy.

But commitment to unapologetic theology does not entail cultural pessimism, and commitment to democratic discussion does not entail the judgment that religious beliefs are conversation stoppers. There are many people who combine those commitments in practical ways, living their lives as believers and as citizens without contradiction, although not necessarily without conflict. The images of a secularized public square that excludes religion and militant religion that uses law to impose its values obscure the relationship between faith and politics that many people maintain in practice.

The difficulty for both theory and practice is that there is no neutral position from which rules of discourse might be formulated for every participant in every discussion. The public reason of the liberal theorist is not a general account of rationality. It concerns the kind of reasons we offer for certain legal and political choices, and its rules are derived from the requirements of democratic politics. Public reason justifies its constraints by showing that they maintain the balance between freedom and coercion on which democracy, properly understood, depends.[28] Likewise, "unapologetic theology" does not explain how its pronouncements are comprehensible in the world of politics, nor in business, education, or the arts, for that matter. It focuses on what must be said to make a statement meaningful in its own theological language, so that it will not be misunderstood theologically or mistaken for some other kind of statement.

This would not be a problem if discussions could simply proceed on their own terms. Indeed, that is how many of them do proceed, in the pages of the theological journal, in the legislative committee meeting, or in the corporate board room. The participants understand the rules of

---

[26] Stanley Hauerwas, *After Christendom? How the Church Is to Behave If Freedom, Justice, and a Christian Nation are Bad Ideas* (Nashville, TN: Abingdon Press, 1991).

[27] Richard Rorty, "Religion as Conversation-Stopper," *Common Knowledge* 3 (1994), 1–6.

[28] The criteria of public reason do not provide a general account of rationality, but one specific to the purposes of liberal democracy. Other political systems might, in fact, have different criteria for public reason. Public political discourse is probably most developed in modern democracy, but we could imagine, for example, a Puritan commonwealth or a colony planted by a trading company that would have vigorous public discussions. What would count as a public reason in those polities would, however, be quite different from what counts as such in a liberal democracy.

argument specific to the setting, and they make their cases in those terms. But these settings are part of those communities and institutions we called "contexts" in the previous chapter. Contexts interact with one another in very concrete ways, and when that happens, the people involved inevitably wind up in one another's discussions.

"The Body of Christ takes up physical space here on earth," Bonhoeffer warned in *Discipleship*. "By becoming human Christ claims a space among us human beings."[29] This means that the church requires some freedom and resources to organize its own life. Real churches in specific, local settings get that freedom and those resources from the contexts among which they live. A church has its own theological understanding of the place where it gathers its members for worship and learning. But if the space the church takes up is also a physical structure, the gathering of the community involves the church with laws concerning property and taxation. If its resources take the form of money and other tangible assets, the use it makes of them are business decisions as well as expressions of discipleship.

To say that the church "takes up physical space" means that it cannot avoid making some claims on the people and institutions around it. But to take up space also means maintaining its own understanding of its life and purpose in the world. The church cannot simply be absorbed into the space of government regulations, asset management, and cultural activities. Its claims about what God is doing through the church in history must "take up physical space" by resisting those who would deprive it of the resources needed for its own life. But the church must also resist those who would support it by saying how useful its ministries are to society and those who would make its message intelligible by reducing the Gospel to a compendium of sociological, psychological, or historical truths. The church's witness persists in its own integrity against the forces that would deprive it of space on earth and even against those who would demonstrate how important and necessary the church is when understood in some other terms.

If Bonhoeffer's argument from *Discipleship* that the Body of Christ "takes up physical space here on earth" is compelling, we should also remember his later warning, in *Ethics*, that theology must not falsely set the church apart from all other mandates, as though the church alone could make a claim for itself as the locus of God's activity and the place where God's commands can be heard.[30] Family, business, culture, and government also take up space.

---

[29] Dietrich Bonhoeffer, *Discipleship*, Dietrich Bonhoeffer Works, vol. IV (Minneapolis, MN: Fortress Press, 2001), pp. 225.
[30] Bonhoeffer, *Ethics*, p. 69.

To see them as contexts of responsibility is to treat them as distinct spheres of discussion and action that retain their integrity in concrete interactions with other contexts. One can never be entirely reduced to another, even as one cannot exist in history entirely apart from the others.

What we need is neither a single standard of public reason for all discussions, nor an indiscriminate pluralism that accepts whatever reasons people want to offer. What we need is a principle that preserves the integrity of different discussions when they interact.

Because this principle draws on the insights of unapologetic theology, let us call it the Unapologetic Principle: *No context is required to explain itself in terms that reduce it to an instrument of other purposes.* Because the Body of Christ takes up space, the church cannot be reduced to purposes that happen to fit into some other discussion. Religious activity may improve the mental health of those who participate in it. Churches sometimes preserve architectural monuments or provide unique settings for musical performances. The presence of a church may even increase safety and raise the level of economic activity in the community where it is located.[31] But government, the arts, or business may not act as though these effects, which are of interest to them in various ways, were the only reasons for churches to exist.

Note immediately, though, that other contexts may invoke the Unapologetic Principle as well as religion. A secure, orderly society probably makes people more industrious and encourages them to plan for the future. It may encourage benevolence and self-discipline, so that its laws are a school for virtue as well as a restraint on vice. However, churches, charities, and businesses may not act as though government exists to produce these effects. The requirements of ordered liberty make their own claims, whether or not any other purposes are served.

Each context has an integrity derived from the human goods it creates and maintains. That integrity allows each of them, unapologetically, to claim what it needs from other contexts to make those goods possible. Integrity also allows contexts to reject claims that explain their goods reductively, as though they were justified only by their usefulness for some other purposes. If the Unapologetic Principle allows a context to make its case in its own terms, the denial of that principle is, in effect, a demand for an apology.

---

[31] A recent study by the Quality Planning Corporation reports, "People who live within one mile of a church are 10 percent less likely to have an accident resulting in a property damage claim than if they lived more than one mile from the church." http://www.qualityplanning.com/qpc_resources_public/news/051206 QPC Locations_F.htm [July 20, 2006].

It insists that a context make its claims in terms that suit the purposes of some other context, usually the one represented by the party making the demand.

The more assertive forms of unapologetic theology emphasize the distinctiveness of the religious context in a way which suggests that different discussions need to be kept entirely separate. Indeed, unapologetic theology is often identified with narrative theology, which so closely identifies theological truth with the language in which it is expressed that it becomes difficult to see how theological ideas could figure in other discussions.[32] That, however, overstates the Unapologetic Principle, which is a practical guideline for maintaining integrity in different contexts, rather than a theory about language and meaning.

Most important, the Unapologetic Principle is protective, rather than restrictive. Although it says that groups and institutions will not be *required* to formulate their claims in a certain way, it does not say that they are not *allowed* to do so. A church that believes that its programs serve important social purposes or confer certain benefits on other institutions is free to say so, even though it cannot be required to justify its claims on society in those terms alone. In a pluralistic society, the church must make a place for itself among other institutions, and it probably will want to make such claims, if it can do so consistently with its own central purposes.

Judgments about the appropriateness of an argument are likely to be decided by a balance between persuasiveness, on the one hand, and consistency with the central beliefs and purposes of the religious community, on the other. Under conditions of pluralism, the successful arguments are likely to be those that identify points of contact between religious beliefs and other interests. Religious claims that make no sense to outsiders cannot be ruled out of order, but they are unlikely to be persuasive. Those who add practical arguments based on results or political arguments based on shared social values to their purely religious reasons may be more successful, even though unapologetic theology rejects efforts to require that they do so.[33]

Still, success is not the only consideration, especially when success is measured on a short timeline. It may be important for a religious community to witness to religious reasons for opposing war or ending racial discrimination, even when it is unlikely to be successful and no one is making the

---

[32] Raymond Plant, *Politics, Theology, and History* (Cambridge: Cambridge University Press, 2001), pp. 352–3.

[33] Wolterstorff, "The Role of Religion in Decision and Discussion of Religious Issues," in Audi and Wolterstorff, *Religion in the Public Square*, pp. 112–13.

case in nonreligious terms.[34] It might even be important for religious voices occasionally to assert the Unapologetic Principle gratuitously, reminding public audiences that it is appropriate for them to be "confessional" and "unintelligible" when drawing out the implications of central tenets of their faith.[35]

For Christian realists, these are matters of judgment. Both accommodation to prevailing social and political ideas and resolute adherence to religious terms can put important goods at risk. A rigorous religious ideal of identification with the poor can be diluted by culture to a self-satisfied benevolence that takes pleasure in small donations to socially acceptable charities and uses those organizations to insulate itself from real contact with people in need. But religious isolation can also divide energies and resources, with the result that needs go unmet, while Christian "humility" prides itself on having higher standards than those who actually get something done. Christian realists must find the equilibrium between distinctive witness and mutual recognition by resisting their own temptations, whether they incline to arrogant self-assertion or to meek conformity. Above all, however, they must know the real circumstances in which they find themselves – the values, goals, and fears that shape choices in their society, the concrete opportunities for social transformation that no Christian can ignore, and the persistent evils that will swallow up anyone foolish enough to join them in hopes of changing them.[36]

A discussion governed by the Unapologetic Principle will be less structured and less predictable than one governed strictly by criteria of public reason. All sorts of arguments will be admitted, with people making claims on society and proposing how it should be organized that further the purposes of a whole range of contexts and beliefs. The demands on public attention and understanding will be large, because ideas cannot be ruled out in advance because they are not sufficiently "public." At a practical level, discussion will tend to converge on a smaller range of proposals for immediate action, because participants seek reasons that can win general assent, even when that means collaborating on specific goods that fit into

---

[34] Christopher J. Eberle, "Religion, Pacifism, and the Doctrine of Restraint," *Journal of Religious Ethics* 34 (2006), 203–24.

[35] See, for example, Hauerwas, *With the Grain of the Universe*, p. 15. Hauerwas would likely reply that unintelligibility is not a rhetorical strategy that the theologian chooses, but an inherent feature of the incommensurability a narrated system of theological meanings. Contrariwise, a theological realist will have to admit larger possibilities for connecting theology to ways of speaking about reality, but might on particular occasions choose to emphasize the differences nonetheless.

[36] Cf. Bonhoeffer, *Ethics*, pp. 339–51.

quite different understandings of human good as a whole.[37] But there will always be a range of voices that keep the discussion open by witnessing to other possibilities that challenge understanding, even when they have no immediate prospects for success.

CONTEXTS AND FORUMS

Attentiveness to the Unapologetic Principle provides a broader understanding of the ways that modern democracies relate religion and government. A great deal is happening in the "background culture" that disputes about the rules of public reason do not address. By attempting to reformulate the issues in terms that apply generally to *all* contexts, we may also set today's contentiousness about the public role of religion in perspective.

The making and answering of claims between contexts is a general feature of life in modern society, a result of historical developments in which contexts have become at the same time more interdependent and more specialized. The tensions are not unique to religion and government. We see a similar, recurrent conflict between government and economics, which tend to differ over the degree of freedom which should be allowed to unrestricted market forces. Conflicts between religion and culture also have a long history that is intertwined with conflicts between religion and government, as religions have sought to impose public censorship on art, literature, or drama, and cultural organizations have sought legal protections for freedom of artistic expression. Similarly, the conflict between religion and scientific culture over intelligent design, evolution, and human origins has become so sharp that factions on both sides now turn to government for a resolution.

As contexts become both more specialized and more interdependent, they find it at once more necessary and more difficult to explain their claims to one another. No context can provide all that it needs to maintain its distinctive goods. It makes claims on other contexts to survive. A cultural institution, such as a university or a symphony orchestra, has to have a place in the economy, a way to obtain the resources required to pay professors, artists, and staff, maintain facilities, and prepare for the future. It also demands from government a certain freedom for its teachers and performers to go about their work, and it even requires that families loosen their grip on the cultural formation of their members so that they can participate in education or artistic activities in this wider context. The cultural context, likewise, fields claims from governments or families who want to make its

[37] See pp. 110–14 earlier.

goods more consistent with their own goals, or from businesses that want to calculate the economic value of the benefits it returns to the community.

Those who take responsibility within a context must negotiate its external relations as well, and large changes within any one context will inevitably lead to adjustments and reordering in all the rest. The rise of the corporation as a principal way of organizing economic life changed the ways that both governments and families relate to the world of work. But a great many ordinary, ongoing activities involve this same kind of negotiation across contextual boundaries. Fund-raising, appeals for tax relief or subsidies of various sorts, claims to academic, religious, or expressive freedom, and even the appeals that people in need make to charities and social welfare programs involve claims one context makes upon another for the resources and conditions that make it possible to provide the specific human goods associated with the context making the claims.

This exchange of claims and counterclaims across the boundaries of contexts is the primary way in which modern societies deliberate about human goods. Each context creates and maintains the goods associated with it by discussing them – organizing their productive activities, evaluating their work, envisioning new possibilities, setting directions for the future. In cultural contexts, this discussion is often precisely what defines the context. Philosophy in large measure just is the ongoing discussion of ideas and refinement of theories that goes on in philosophical discussion. But even more material goods require a great deal of talk to maintain their production and, especially, to shape their future in light of changing needs and changing circumstances. The institutions that make up a context discuss product development, or curriculum, or environmental policy. Scientific conferences refine the research questions that individual scientists and laboratories will pursue. Businesses establish accounting standards and financial reporting requirements, sometimes assisted by government regulators. Families join together in neighborhood associations that identify key issues for the quality of family life in the community as a whole, and by those deliberations, it becomes more clear to all of the participants what it means to be a family. Very little of this work proceeds simply by tradition or gets determined by force. We have the goods we do in the particular forms that we have them because people talk about them, constantly, at all levels, from the most particular discussions on the shop floor about whether the product coming off the line this hour meets standards of quality to the most abstract, conceptual discussions of the future of art in an age of electronic media.

Let us, then, summarize this complex system of discussions about human goods by saying that context, as it develops, creates a "forum." The term evokes an image of the ancient city-state, but this kind of forum is a distinctly modern development, as Charles Taylor's discussion of the "public sphere" has shown.[38] Forums are created as the flow of communication increases, contexts become differentiated from one another, and ways of doing things lose their purely local character. As a result, people begin to develop ways of thinking and acting that connect them to people in other places, and they require new media of communication to maintain that connection. They share common purposes, and they are involved in a common discussion, even though they may never meet. They occupy a sort of "non-local common space."[39] Taylor focuses his attention on the public sphere which becomes a forum for the discussion of government and politics, but similar developments take place in every area of life as the institutions of modern society become more differentiated from one another in their local settings and more connected to other, similar institutions in distant places.

A forum, like the idea of a context itself, transcends the specific events and locations in which discussions actually happen. A corporation holds many discussions about the details of its business. The content of these discussions is determined by the particularities of the business and shaped by a specific corporate culture, but the participants in those discussions are also recognizably involved in the business forum, which provides a larger framework of purposes and values that shape the discussions in all of the institutions that make up the context.

The integrity which is essential to a context both arises within and is maintained by these forums. Contexts generate their own traditions, rules of discourse, and standards of rationality. They sometimes do this consciously, when a professional association adopts a new code of ethics, or when parents set rules announcing new boundaries within which adolescent children may challenge the prevailing patterns of family life. Most often, they do it indirectly, in the very process of socialization by which persons learn and adapt their roles in the specific tasks by which they contribute to the goods the context creates and maintains. Knowing what to say and how to say it is an important part of personal participation, and even in intimate associations like the family, those who do not know or will not follow the rules will find themselves consigned to a minor role in the common life.

Many discussions in any context are governed by these expectations of the forum about who may speak and what they may say, so that the

---

[38] Charles Taylor, *Modern Social Imaginaries* (Durham, NC: Duke University Press, 2004), pp. 83–6.
[39] *Ibid.*, p. 86.

forum in practice imposes a fairly exacting set of rules. Such discussions are internal to the context or "private" in a sense that most people would recognize. Not everyone is qualified to participate in them, and the rules governing access to and activity in the forum are usually fairly well defined. A business organizes the flow of resources into its operations and the flow of products and services out to its customers. A university allocates resources among departments, makes appointments to its faculty, admits students, and decides what tuition to charge. Many people outside the institution may find themselves affected by the outcomes, and the decisions take place in an environment of law and regulation, but we generally assume that they will be made by people within the institutions, guided primarily by values, purposes, and procedures internal to it.[40] Indeed, we assume that something has gone badly wrong if a cultural discussion becomes dominated by business values, or if a business discussion starts to resemble a family argument.

Contexts, however, cannot participate in the larger process of claim and counterclaim by which they create their distinctive human goods solely by maintaining tight control on their forums and excluding those who might challenge their assumptions. The symphony that makes decisions about programming strictly by artistic criteria may believe that it is preserving the integrity of the cultural context, but if the wider public does not share the enthusiasm for artistic purity, next year's brochure is apt to emphasize new, "family-friendly" programs and popular works from the standard repertoire. It may also announce the appointment of a new artistic director.

The discussions that go on in any forum will include discussions in which other contexts make claims for their own needs or seek a voice in this forum on their own terms. Institutions that attempt to exclude these claims or fail to anticipate them risk their own marginalization in the interdependent forums in which society makes choices and sets directions for the future. Integrity, in a world of multiple and interdependent contexts, thus requires flexibility and openness, as well as attentiveness to the particular requirements of the goods that a context creates and maintains. An unexpected claim from an unfamiliar context almost always elicits initial responses that reassert the requirements of private discussion, limiting the impact of the new claim, if not excluding it from discussion altogether. Nonetheless,

---

[40] This statement would have to be qualified for institutions such as a state university or a county hospital, where the general public has a role in supporting the institution. Even in those cases, however, good practice supports leaving a substantial share of governance in the hands of the institution itself.

healthy institutions have strong incentives over the long run to encourage openness in their forums, both by finding ways to listen to unfamiliar voices and by incorporating that diversity into their own constituency of voters, clients, customers, students, or employees.

As institutions make and respond to these claims, each forum thus comes to include public discussions which are open to more people and operate under different rules from discussions which are internal to the context. Let us designate these discussions in which claims are made and answered across the boundaries of contexts as a "public forum," in contrast to the private or internal forum that we have previously described.

Highly developed public forums are characteristic of modern societies. Although we associate a public forum especially with the government of a free society, all contexts have them, and healthy institutions in each context make good use of them. In a pluralistic society, where no master plan dictates the allocation of tasks and resources, it is in the public forum that businesses, cultural institutions, and religious groups learn to make their claims in effective ways, and also establish the boundaries beyond which they will not go to accommodate the needs and goals of other institutions and contexts. The alternative for religious groups is a sectarian withdrawal that takes no part in defining social structures because it seeks no place among them. Even the family maintains a public forum under modern conditions. Its members all participate in other contexts and, unlike earlier patterns of subsistence farming, the modern family supplies very few of the goods it needs for the life its private choices have created.

These public forums are a primary way that persons in modern societies participate in shaping the full range of human goods that their lives require. Without public forums, social participation would be confined to a narrow vocational identity. We would have some hand in creating and maintaining the goods associated with a context in which we had mastered the requirements of the private forum, but for the rest, we would be consumers, taking the goods available on the terms that other contexts offered them. No doubt there are persons who choose to live that way, completely absorbed by their work. Persons who write books or create works of art tend to fall into this group. Others are forced into it, because the expectations of their work are so high or its rewards are so low that nothing is left for participation in other contexts. This group includes both those aspiring to the highest social status – medical students and associates in law firms, for example – and those confined to the lowest – the working poor, migrant workers, and unemployed single parents. Although these ways of life are familiar features of modern society, it is doubtful that they qualify as a good life, or, when undertaken as a matter of choice, a moral one. That is one reason why religious ethics has in recent years developed the idea that participation is an important criterion of social justice, alongside a fair distribution of society's goods.[41] The public forum is essential both to the justice of society as a whole and to the moral life of individuals.

A context in which human goods are created and maintained thus generates as part of its own activity something like the public forum for which, in liberal theory, the rules of public reason are formulated. The distinctions between public and private in this pluralist perspective are, however, drawn quite differently from the way they appear in liberal theory. First, we cannot speak of a single public forum, separate and apart from the public forum within each context. Public discussions about human goods necessarily relate to some particular context. Although we might imagine a different society, less differentiated and less interdependent than our own, in which all goods could be discussed at once by people who were equally knowledgeable about them and equally responsible for them, that is simply not how these discussions take place in the modern world. Goods are created and maintained in differentiated, interdependent contexts, and that is where they must be discussed, at least insofar as the discussions have any practical implications. Although theologians could conceivably discuss ethics and economics without any relation to the actual world of business and philosophers could discuss justice without any discernable connection to real political systems, such abstractions are the stuff of caricature, not ethics. The public forum is located within each of the forums that contexts create, not in some one place separate and apart from them.

Likewise, as we have noted, the public forum is not simply the forum associated with the context of government. Much of the confusion about the rules of public reason arises from the fact that what Rawls refers to in technical terms as the "public political forum" turns out to be public only in the equivocal sense by which we refer to anything connected with government as public. The discussions in the courts, legislatures, and administrative offices of a democratic government have all the characteristics of the private or internal discussions that take place in other contexts. There is a fairly exacting set of rules about who may speak and what they may say. The discussions must concern the specific goods that government creates and maintains, and they do so in specialized language and forms of argument that have been developed for those purposes. As in other

---

[41] David Hollenbach, *The Common Good and Christian Ethics* (Cambridge: Cambridge University Press, 2002), pp. 190–200.

contexts, it is highly troubling when decisions seem to have been made for inappropriate reasons or by unauthorized people. The attentiveness to rules and procedures in government is a measure of how seriously we take the idea that these decisions belong to the people who have been designated to make them.

What distinguishes the context of government in a democracy is not that it has no private discussions, but that the private discussions in this forum must be open to public scrutiny. Legislators conduct public hearings and listen to constituents. Citizens write letters and take out ads in newspapers. Those who personally lack the expertise to participate effectively hire lobbyists and lawyers to make their views known. When people are drawn unwillingly into these discussions, as defendants in criminal trials for example, we insist that competent counsel be provided. In contrast to the corporate boardroom or the scientific conference, the assumption is that everyone who wants access to these private discussions in the context of government should have some measure of it. That, in turn, requires that the discussions be accessible to public understanding. What makes a democratic government democratic is that its private forum is governed by the rules of public reason. If Rawls is correct, this private forum may be the only place where the rules of public reason strictly apply.[42]

PUBLIC FORUMS

In the forum of government, as in other contexts, what is genuinely public is small compared to the scope of the private discussions, but very important. What is public are those discussions in which contexts make and answer claims upon one another, and so set the boundaries within which private discussions are decisive and outside of which the results of those discussions will be open to question. The line between public and private does not separate one forum from the rest. It runs through all of them. Every context requires certain resources in order to survive and thrive, and so each context must make claims on the others in order to provide the goods it creates and maintains. Each context, likewise, fields a steady stream of claims against it. As institutions make and respond to these claims, each context creates within its ongoing discussions a public forum which operates under very

---

[42] I leave aside the complication that Rawls also includes campaigns for public office within the scope of the public, political forum. It is not immediately clear why those discussions are related to the coercive power of government in a way that distinguishes them from, say, editorials, public policy studies, or books on ethics.

different rules from the private discussions by which ordinary business in the forum is conducted.

What makes these forums public is that they are open to claims and counterclaims from any direction. Families may claim that the workplace is failing to provide a living wage, or that the terms of employment do not offer the security that is essential to stable family life. Business may respond that demands for wages and benefits leave it with insufficient resources to do its job of creating wealth and opportunity. Religion may suggest that the pursuit of wealth leads to a consumer mentality that undermines both familial intimacy and devotional piety. Education may argue that both business and government should provide larger resources for educational purposes, while rejecting claims from family and church that educational institutions should devote some of those resources to the supervision of morals and to education in virtue. And so it goes.

The political life of a modern, democratic society does not take place exclusively in government, nor in an idealized "public square" where everyone gathers to make all of the decisions about their common life. Politics is made up of discussion of goods within contexts and the negotiation and renegotiation of claims between contexts. The differentiation of a variety of interdependent contexts that shape important areas of life makes that inevitable.

If there is a public forum wherever contexts interact, then the rules of argument in a public forum must be rather more open than in the private forum where the work of the context is discussed by those who are more regularly involved in it. Within a context, people are expected to know how to participate in the discussion, or at least to obtain the services of an advocate who does. A church that requires a zoning variance is well advised to seek a good lawyer, rather than a good theologian. But in a public forum, where claims are made against a context and its boundaries are tested, the Unapologetic Principle applies: No context is required to explain itself solely in terms that belong to the discourse of other contexts. When a church finds its distinctive witness threatened or challenges the values around which government policy is organized, it may have to make its claims in religious terms.

Consider, for example, this statement about the meaning of "the nation" by Joan Lockwood O'Donovan:

What is this new meaning of the nation? It is a meaning that takes shape in the penumbra of the church's eschatological witness in a sinful world. The nation is a concrete territorial order, judgment, and tradition that sustains a space within the sinful human condition for the gathering of Christ's faithful people through the work of the Holy Spirit. In a sense, the nation remains what Israel revealed it to be – its constitutive elements have not changed: a government that gives judgments, laws, and protection from enemies, a population inhabiting a homeland, linked by historical, linguistic, and cultural ties, and bound authoritatively by customs, laws, and political judgments. But its theological significance has changed, its role in the divine economy *ad extra* has changed: it is no longer revealed to be the vehicle of salvation, but merely the guaranteed social space within which God's saving work proceeds. It is revealed to belong to the Father's sustaining governance of the world, rather than his transforming governance through the Spirit of Christ. The nation is a reality of the old age which is passing away, but whose continuing sway serves the proclamatory mission of the renewed Israel.[43]

The origin of this claim in religious discussion is obvious. The purpose of the nation is stated in terms of its place in God's action in history. God's action is understood in terms of Christian revelation. The power of the nation, contrary to appearances, actually serves the purposes of the church's mission, as this purpose is known in the church's witness. There is not even the suggestion that it could be known by looking at Israel, the church, and the nations in any other way. One needs a considerable background in Christian theology even to understand what is being claimed here.

Nevertheless, the argument in its implications for the church and its place in society belongs in the public forum. It announces the attitude that Christians who share this belief will take toward the nation in which they live. It enumerates the things that the nation should supply, in order for the church to fulfill the mission it has in God's plan. It suggests, with only a little further reflection, some things that the nation should not do or claim, if it expects the cooperation of Christians.

These are public claims that a Christian religious context makes on the other contexts, and especially on government. In making these claims, Christians do not ask for assent to their theological interpretation of history and politics. They do that in other ways, at other times. But they do make statements about how a Christian community will live and about what a government should be in order for the church and its distinctive goods to flourish. Without this unapologetic argument in the public forum, the church loses its distinctive identity and becomes a mere instrument of other purposes. That is precisely what Bonhoeffer's claim that the Body of Christ takes up physical space was intended to forestall. The church cannot exist

---

[43] Joan Lockwood O'Donovan, "Nation, State, and Civil Society in the Western Biblical Tradition," in Oliver O'Donovan and Joan Lockwood O'Donovan, *Bonds of Imperfection: Christian Politics, Past and Present* (Grand Rapids, MI: Eerdmans, 2004), pp. 285–6.

as a mere idea. It requires institutional form among the contexts where the goods that sustain human life are preserved. That was what brought Bonhoeffer's church into inevitable conflict with a regime that sought to define all institutional space in its own terms and prohibit any other claims made on other grounds.

If we are to move beyond a theology of Christian discipleship in a totalitarian state to an ethics of Christian participation in a pluralistic democracy, however, we must understand that the Unapologetic Principle is not the exclusive prerogative of the church. Family, culture, work, and even government may be unapologetic, too. The church should not surrender this sort of claim to a totalitarian government that forbids it. It should not abandon it to a secular culture that labels religious claims as "conversation-stoppers." But neither should the church be surprised that other contexts in a pluralistic society make their claims in similarly unapologetic ways.

A university, for example, makes its claims as part of a cultural context in which people pursue truth according to the methods of academic inquiry, without regard to the political acceptability or economic utility of what they find. People need not all believe what scholars tell them in order for the university to claim a place for scholarly inquiry. At the outset, the university simply explains the goods around which its activity is organized and claims the resources it needs to go about those purposes. If the university, or its development office, is in an apologetic frame of mind, it may take pains to explain the benefits that society generally obtains from having institutions of higher education in its midst. But it is in the nature of a modern, differentiated society that there is no one audience that has to be convinced. If one had to make a case for continuing a cultural activity in terms of public order or national security, or if – as seems increasingly the case in higher education – the benefits had to be justified in economic terms, that would itself be a sign that the differentiation of contexts that characterizes a successful modern society has been weakened. A public case for the university begins with an unapologetic statement of its self-understanding, not with accounts of how it serves the purposes of other contexts. At the same time, the modern university that knows how to explain its distinctive functions and the social arrangements that make them possible also knows that it must often seek support from business or government, even as it must be prepared to fend off the arguments of those who would reduce the university to its political or economic functions.

The public forum in every context thus ensures that successful institutions in a complex modern society cannot be completely absorbed in the private discussions that maintain their internal order and sustain their own purposes. The claims of other contexts are too insistent for preoccupation with internal matters to sustain itself for very long. Persons and institutions do live through phases focused on private concerns. A failing business has little time for the Chamber of Commerce and an educational institution in a leadership crisis is apt to neglect its role in the American Association of Colleges and Schools. Families with young children, tight budgets, and working parents are unlikely to show up at community forums and cultural events. But someone has to attend to the public forums, or businesses, schools, and families will find their position in relation to other contexts eroded, and the ones struggling with private problems will then find it even harder to meet their needs.

Taken together, these public forums create the pluralistic order that characterizes the successful modern state. People who have responsibility for an institution know roughly where they stand with respect to other institutions and contexts. They know who will supply the legal, cultural, and economic resources their institution needs to function, and they know what they will be expected to provide to this whole social structure in return. Business corporations provide specific human goods, but along with their products and services, they are supposed to be sources of stable employment and supporters of cultural activities, and they are increasingly expected to order their core economic activities in ways that at least do not damage the families of their workers or the natural environment. Churches, mosques, temples, and synagogues are centers of religious activity, but they are also important providers of social services, and their buildings, activities, and educational programs contribute to the culture of the wider community. Government provides law and order, but also education, employment, and social services.

This does not mean that the relationships between the contexts are universally agreed. They are in fact in continuous dispute. Churches argue with governments about tax exemptions and funding for faith-based programs. Schools argue with parents about educational goals and family values. Cultural preservationists argue with businesses and churches about maintaining historic buildings. Businesses resist government regulation and pressure schools and cultural institutions to do things that will improve the local business climate. The remarkable fact is that without any central authority to plan it or any single set of rules to guide it, a public forum develops within each context that allows these claims and counterclaims to continue. In that public forum, some working balance is struck in which the human goods around which one context is organized also serve the purposes of the other contexts, without becoming merely instrumental goods.

HUMAN GOODS AND PUBLIC REASON

These public forums are such a pervasive feature of life in successful modern states that few give them much thought, but they are a remarkable achievement, unpredicted by early modern political thought and not entirely accepted today by those who would prefer a society with more fixed rules of argument. Early modern political thought built on the differentiation of contexts by envisioning a state that would take responsibility for the goods of order and security while removing religious, cultural, and economic goods from political consideration. By providing a sovereign authority strong enough to ensure security, conflicts, especially conflicts about religion, could be prevented. The capacity of religious leaders, locally powerful landlords, or popular movements to make claims that might interfere with effective government would be greatly reduced, if not eliminated.[44]

What the theorists of this new political realism did not anticipate was that a durable framework of order and security provided by the government would make other centers of social activity stronger, not weaker. By the beginning of the twentieth century, business, culture, family, and church all were flourishing in the new, modern state, and they continued to press their claims against one another and against the sovereign authority, often more vigorously than anyone could have imagined in earlier times. For Reformation realists, the political task was creating a sovereign state strong enough to prevail over religious divisions and local centers of authority. A monopoly of coercive power seemed sufficient to elevate the prince's governmental authority above all its competitors, to a height from which it alone could set the terms of public life. But what prince in Reformation Europe could have foreseen the cultural power of the *philosophes* to subject government authority to reason and the rule of law? Or the way that mercantile and industrial corporations created a new kind of economic power that could operate independently of government and eventually reshape our understanding of what government is supposed to do? Or the transnational influence of religion on human rights law and policy?

---

[44] David Fergusson, *Church, State, and Civil Society* (Cambridge: Cambridge University Press, 2004), pp. 47–54; William A. Galston, *Liberal Pluralism: The Implications of Value Pluralism for Political Theory* (Cambridge: Cambridge University Press, 2002), pp. 24–7.

As the contexts in which our lives are lived have become more differentiated from one another and more complex internally, politics has become broader than the work of government, if we mean by politics the deliberations by which we order our lives with others to make human goods and good lives possible. Government remains unique because its order includes everyone and its deliberations result in legitimate uses of coercion against those who fail to comply. As we have seen, however, democratic governments achieve this scope and power only by severely limiting the influence of ideas about the good on their political principles and goals. If we want to reflect explicitly on what a good life is and how we might achieve it, we often begin in some other context, though when we turn to implementation, it usually crosses our mind that it would be nice to have the government's powers of coercion available for that purpose.

So we speak wryly of "office politics," and "church politics," and "academic politics," meaning usually that other people involved in the context have been acting like stereotypical politicians. The humor also conveys the deeper insight that a great deal of our good does depend on what happens in these places, and most of what we can do to determine the good for the people around us will be done there. Whether we call it "politics" or not, the ways that people at work shape products and services, the ways that parents, preachers, and teachers shape minds and lives, and the ways that artists, musicians, and writers shape thoughts and feelings are the forms that serious political activity takes for most of us. The politics associated with government is more remote, and we treat it often as a form of entertainment, rather than a moral deliberation in which we are ourselves involved.

This may be a problem. It is one of the odd characteristics of successful modern states that they often have low levels of interest and involvement in the politics of government. Their citizens seem to want consistency, predictability, and a government that requires little tending. They prefer a small number of major parties whose programs and candidates are not easily distinguished from one another, except when successfully "branded" by marketing strategies. Many who are eligible do not vote. Many who do vote are uncertain about who the candidates are, except for the highest-level offices. It is as though the people have heard about the theory of overlapping consensus and concluded that no matter what happens in the public political forum, their good is bound to be included in the result in some way.

We would not want to solve this problem, however, by dramatically increasing the range of available choices. One reason why politics in successful modern states is so predictable is that the number of real options proves to be small. You need parliamentary or presidential government, exercising limited control over a market economy, with at least minimum provisions for social welfare. You need strong protections for individual rights built into a written constitution or an independent judiciary, or both. Would-be leaders mounting serious campaigns for a system that differed from this paradigm in substantial ways would not be a sign of a healthy democracy. The example of Weimar Germany comes to mind.

What is needed is not a wider range of political options, but a new kind of political realism that would reconnect this familiar governmental politics to the framework of a larger politics that seeks human goods and seeks to make a good life possible. This realism would not neglect the factors of self-interest and power, but it would recognize that people sum up their long-term interests in comprehensive doctrines that influence how they act and what they hope for in every area of life, including the politics of government.

In a democracy that includes people from many different backgrounds, religions, and ways of life, political realism has to acknowledge this diversity in the principles which guide the work of government. If the political community is to be a place for serious, cooperative work that can engage the commitment of all its citizens, this acknowledgement has to be more than a grudging acceptance that there will regrettably be some people around who do not share my faith and my values.[45] If they are to be political coworkers, they must be persons whose freedom can be respected and whose judgments can be trusted, so I would want to know that they consent to the commitments we share, rather than to suspect that they have accepted them only because they had no other choice. In that way, the strategy of liberal theory to arrive at political principles that require minimal assumptions about human nature and that can be shared across a wide range of comprehensive doctrines is eminently realistic. Any approach that tries to establish democracy on a different basis would be relying on self-interest and power to accomplish more than they can.

At the same time, it is realistic to suppose that people will try to understand the results they negotiate in terms of the goods they seek, in government or in any other context. The more general the principles of government and the longer they remain in place, the more a political realist will expect to see their meanings transformed by the aspirations for life as a whole that people bring to their relationship to government. Expectations for transformation will grow, too, if the make-up of the people changes over time, particularly if new groups and classes of people become active

<hr />

[45] Plant, *Politics, Theology, and History*, p. 335.

participants in government. So the political realist will nod approvingly as a diverse, democratic people formulate neutral principles of justice and rules of public reason, and she will smile knowingly when those principles and rules turn out to mean quite different things after major economic changes, religious revivals, or large migrations of people entering or exiting the polity.

Among liberal theorists, William A. Galston has most clearly understood the requirements of this kind of political realism. Galston's own political theory is "comprehensive," rather than "freestanding," to use two terms by which Galston organizes a very helpful typology of political theories.[46] His liberal pluralism establishes a relationship between political principles and comprehensive doctrines without collapsing the distinction between them.[47]

In a comprehensive political theory, political principles need not be formulated in the language of comprehensive doctrines, but they depend on these more complete accounts of human nature and the human good for their legitimacy. A principle that requires equality before the law or the consent of the governed may be stated in strictly political terms that reveal no religious commitments or metaphysical presuppositions. To that limited extent, the claim that liberal political principles can be freestanding is correct. Nothing requires that political principles be formulated in terms of any particular comprehensive doctrine, and among people who hold a wide variety of religious and moral beliefs, there may be practical advantages to this apparent neutrality. If the political system works well, the legitimacy of its principles may come to be taken for granted. But this appearance that political principles are freestanding is as Galston says, "an illusion, quickly dispelled in times of internal or external crisis."[48]

When the meaning of political principles comes into dispute in ways that cannot be resolved by established political procedures, we turn to comprehensive doctrine for clarification of what the principles mean and why they are important. Thus, Galston has a rather different view from Rawls of the arguments surrounding the abolition of slavery or the Civil

---

[46] Galston, *Liberal Pluralism*, p. 8–9.

[47] To avoid confusion about what Galston means, it is important to note that a comprehensive *political theory* is not the same thing as a comprehensive *doctrine*. A comprehensive doctrine presents a full account of the human good. A comprehensive political theory is one which gives comprehensive doctrine (or doctrines) a role in political discussions and the shaping of political institutions. The complete account of a comprehensive doctrine would, presumably, include a political theory, but a comprehensive political theory need not itself be a comprehensive doctrine.

[48] Galston, *Liberal Pluralism*, p. 41.

Rights movement. The Constitution of the United States was the product of political compromise, framed with an eye to assuring broad acceptance of its political principles, but the understanding of human equality and freedom shared by its framers and apologists was a comprehensive doctrine by any measure.

It is doubtful that the constitutional values Rawls presents as freestanding public reasons can be adequately understood as detached from comprehensive views. After all, the Preamble begins and ends by asserting the right of the people (and, by implication, *only* the people) to ordain and establish the Constitution. This was a revolutionary assertion of the basic republican principle, not at that time generally accepted in the West. This principle drew support from the kinds of premises Jefferson summarized in the Declaration of Independence – premises that, taken together, sketch what Rawls would have to call a comprehensive view. Human beings are equal because they are created equal; they are free because they are endowed with certain rights that cannot be taken away; and because they are free and equal, governments only derive their just powers from the consent of the governed.[49]

In crises over slavery, segregation, environmental degradation, or international human rights, public discussions outside the halls of government turn quickly to comprehensive doctrines. People attempt to understand their greatest problems in terms of the most complete account they know of how the world really is. That is part of how they distinguish what is truly morally compelling from personal crises and matters of local urgency.[50] So when today's religious leaders speak of climate change, AIDS, and the humanitarian crises sparked by genocide, they speak a language of divine judgment. Previous generations did the same regarding the abolition of slavery, the rights of labor, and racial equality. They are not addressing the questions in terms of public reason, but asking whether public reason is capable of grasping what is at stake.

To pronounce retrospectively that arguments that changed history did indeed conform to the requirements of public reason obscures the way in which comprehensive doctrines give urgency and moral importance to concrete political choices.[51] What is reasonable depends in part on whether we think that the choice before us is a routine political problem to be solved by compromise between the interested parties, or whether we think it is

---

[49] *Ibid.*, pp. 40–1.

[50] Michael Sandel, *Public Philosophy: Essays on Morality and Politics* (Cambridge, MA: Harvard University Press, 2005), pp. 224–30.

[51] Troy Dostert, *Beyond Political Liberalism: Toward a Post-Secular Ethics of Public Life* (Notre Dame, IN: University of Notre Dame Press, 2006), pp. 157–60.

a defining moment for our individual lives and the life of society. Public reason has a variety of frameworks in which such defining moments can be accommodated. Reinhold Niebuhr identified the equilibrium between liberty and equality as one of the most important, historically speaking.[52] More recently, Jean Elshtain has focused on the idea of sovereignty, which both legitimates the use of governmental power and at the same time raises the question of its limits.[53] In recent years, religious and philosophical ethics in several different cultural traditions have turned to human dignity as an important concept through which comprehensive ideas about human good can be taken into public reason.[54]

COMPREHENSIVE DOCTRINES AND PUBLIC REASON

It is by the unapologetic assertion of these comprehensive ideas in the public forum associated with law and government that religious traditions, and other comprehensive doctrines, too, have their impact on the private discussions of legislators, judges, and government officials, who do their work following the rules of public reason. The interaction between religion and politics, as it is understood in Galston's comprehensive political theory, becomes a paradigm for understanding the relationship between comprehensive doctrines and specific decisions about human goods taken in particular contexts of responsibility. It is important, however, to understand that this takes place across all contexts, not only in the context of law and government. Thus we come to see the role of comprehensive doctrine itself in a more comprehensive way.

Comprehensive doctrine requires unapologetic politics and an open public forum. We see this most clearly in the case of religious traditions, because they form communities of people who are shaped by an understanding of the human good and bear witness in the wider society to what that human good requires of all contexts in order to maintain its own integrity. Comprehensive doctrines are in this way the most public statements in the public forum. They make an unapologetic statement in their own terms of what

---

[52] Niebuhr, *Faith and Politics*, pp. 183–98.

[53] Jean Bethke Elshtain, *Sovereignty: God, State, and Self* (New York: Basic Books, 2008); Jean Bethke Elshtain, "Against the New Utopianism," *Studies in Christian Ethics* 20 (2007), 50.

[54] Charles E. Curran, *Catholic Social Teaching 1891-Present: A Historical, Theological, and Ethical Analysis* (Washington, DC: Georgetown University Press, 2002), pp. 131–6; Doron Shultziner, "A Jewish Conception of Human Dignity: Philosophy and Its Ethical Implications for Israeli Supreme Court Decisions," *Journal of Religious Ethics* 34 (2006), 663–83; Qianfang Zhang, "The Idea of Human Dignity in Classical Chinese Philosophy: A Reconstruction of Confucianism," *Journal of Chinese Philosophy* 27 (2000), 299–330.

the human good requires, rather than tailoring their claims to the prevailing language of the context. We saw this in the case of Joan Lockwood O'Donovan's theological understanding of the meaning of the "nation,"[55] which is more complete and less equivocal than a statement by the church cast in the language of government and politics. The same would be true of a theological statement about the meaning of wealth addressed to the context of business, or about the meaning of truth addressed to the context of culture, or about the meaning of love addressed to the context of family. Each of these would be more clearly public than an attempt to show that the claims of comprehensive doctrine could still squeeze into public discourse through the narrowing window offered by contemporary liberal theory. But these unapologetic statements require in each context a public forum open to all arguments, because in the private forum of profit and loss or the private forum of "public reason," the claims are either unacceptable or incomprehensible.

Unapologetic politics nonetheless requires the private forum, because it is in the nature of a public forum that though any claim can be made there, not all of them can be accepted. Private forums allow a context to reassert what its own integrity requires when it is under pressure from other contexts to offer more support for the goods that they create and maintain.

This is especially important when the context of government deals with claims made on the basis of comprehensive doctrines in the public forum. Democratic government is designed, by constitutional theory and practice, to maintain a legal order that constrains all citizens, but also rests on their consent. Its purposes are the purposes of "ordered liberty," as we have seen.[56] Although democratic government may be obliged to accommodate the religious practices of its citizens and to allow their religious understandings of the human good to play a role in their political lives, government should not allow religious arguments to defeat the democratic purposes on which its own goods depend. When a religion uses the power of a majority to pass laws that require everyone to follow its moral precepts, the relation between the power of law and the purposes of democratic government is ignored. The distinctive goods – order, security, and equal opportunity – that democratic government creates and maintains become casualties of the democratic process itself, because the process has become a mere instrument of other purposes. The rules of public reason are designed to prevent that from happening, and their articulation is itself an unapologetic statement of what the goods secured by democratic government require.

---

[55] See p. 139 earlier.   [56] See p. 124 earlier.

THE UNAPOLOGETIC MOMENT

The end of this lengthy exploration thus brings us back to a point that we noted much earlier: Although the concepts of public reason and of unapologetic theology have been developed in some opposition to one another, they are not necessarily incompatible. Some people consistently hold versions of both ideas, and both seem concerned with maintaining the integrity of contexts. We see now that in a larger, pluralistic understanding of the forums in which human goods are discussed, these two ideas are doing the same thing, although of course, the two different ideas do not usually serve the same people, in the same way, at the same time.

That is how unapologetic politics works. People with different responsibilities and different ideas about the human good make claims on one another in different contexts, and without any one set of rules to guide them, they manage to sustain a social order that produces all the many different goods that modern life has made possible, and that it now requires.

Modern politics needs the example of unapologetic theology, because all institutions share the need of theology and the church to assert the claims they make *in their own terms.* But unapologetic theology should be the starting point for unapologetic politics. Unapologetic theologians often seem uncertain about how to follow up a confessional statement of their theological self-understanding, or perhaps they are nervous about how this straightforward proclamation will be received. As a result, they emphasize the possibility of rejection and the likelihood that they will be misunderstood, as if no other group in society were making claims anything like theirs.

Today, however, an unapologetic moment is necessary for every context – for universities, theaters, and art museums, no less than for churches; among philosophers, physicians, and social workers, no less than among theologians. Otherwise, pluralism is vulnerable to political parties, economic schemes, and cultural ideologies that claim to represent the one context to which all other goods must be subordinated. Modern societies saw this clearly in the totalitarian regimes of the twentieth century, which were often at the outset embraced with popular enthusiasm, but resisted by religious groups that held to some version of the realistic theological pluralism that we have been detailing in this chapter.

That resistance is no less important at the beginning of a new century, as totalitarianism recedes and pluralism of various sorts prevails in successful modern states. Pluralism itself opens possibilities for exploitation and excessive demands that may not be present in less developed or more authoritarian societies. Where the state and the party make no universal claims to absolute loyalty, the employer, the family, the cultural community, and the teacher are free to make them in their own contexts. These may not have the reach of a totalitarian state, but they can be as destructive of other goods in their own orbits.

Unless each context in a pluralistic society makes its own claims unapologetically, people who live in what appear to be pluralistic democracies may find themselves living in what we may, with some irony, call "pluralistic totalitarianism." No one ideology claims all of life from everyone, but everyone ends up owing his or her whole life to some one context. An unapologetic church alone might delay that outcome, or at least maintain a reminder that it need not have happened, but the church will be even more clear in its own witness if it becomes more articulate about how a society would have to be organized to make unapologetic theology possible.

CHAPTER 5

A Global Order

QUESTIONS

Reinhold Niebuhr and Dietrich Bonhoeffer saw the problem of political order in global terms. No doubt this was partly the result of personal experience, for both of them traveled widely for young men of their day, and both came to maturity in a society that was having its expectations reshaped by the shock of global war and worldwide economic depression. Personal experience was reinforced for both men by participation in Protestant ecumenism, which before, during, and after the Second World War sought to make a united witness to the theological conditions for lasting world peace.[1] Bonhoeffer, in the secrecy of a resistance group, thought about what the world might be like after the war. Niebuhr and the political realists whom he influenced lived to help shape it.

A decade after the end of the Second World War, Niebuhr thought that the world was still in the beginning stages of global integration. Order on a global scale was needed to repair the disorder left after two world wars, organize the rapid growth of postwar trade and communication, and control the new threat posed by nuclear weapons. The necessary institutions and practices, however, were only slowly taking shape in the United Nations and regional security organizations, such as the North Atlantic Treaty Organization (NATO).[2]

One problem, as Niebuhr saw it, was that democracy, which provided the best reconciliation of freedom with the requirements of community, had arrived at its solution to this problem gradually, over time and by experiment. As a result, democracies have typically had little grasp of the principles that made their institutions work. This was particularly true in

---

[1] John Nurser, *For All Peoples and Nations: The Ecumenical Church and Human Rights* (Washington, DC: Georgetown University Press, 2005).

[2] Reinhold Niebuhr, *The Self and the Dramas of History* (New York: Charles Scribner's Sons, 1955), pp. 219–24.

American history, in which favorable circumstances of nature and history gave time to "arrive at a tolerable solution for these problems in actual experience without penetrating to the heart of the mystery of community."[3] Matters had worked out to place this fortunate nation at the center of world affairs, equipped with much useful experience but hampered by a lack of understanding.

Nonetheless, the postwar decade had made some progress toward a "tolerable solution" at the global level, and more would follow. Niebuhr's own political realism contributed a great deal to this emerging order, at least insofar as the order was shaped by American leadership and American ideas.[4] His realism also determined the scope of the problem. The aim could not be a utopian world order guided by a world government. The need was for an order adequate to the world's present problems. It would have to find stable arrangements that could include two nuclear-armed superpowers.[5] In retrospect, we can see that on his realistic and limited definition of the problem, Niebuhr got his tolerable solution. Strategies of containment and deterrence and institutions of diplomacy and regional security kept the peace until the end of the Cold War.

The conflict between the United States and the Soviet Union that was the background for Niebuhr's solution has now vanished. If his realism is still relevant, it must prove itself in relation to a new set of questions about global order. The end of the Cold War eliminated a large part of the "tolerable solution," and the world has returned to something like the uncertainties of the early postwar years. As in 1955, the role of the United Nations in relation to this new situation is still in formation. Regional security organizations have multiplied, often without notable increases in security. The Korean peninsula remains a flash point, even though the external powers that once supported the North Korean regime have changed almost beyond recognition. There are more successful modern states that have solved the problem of order and freedom in their own experience, but we are still not sure what the principles behind those solutions are, and we do not know whether they can work on a global scale. Does Niebuhr's realism still apply to these new realities? Political theorists, policy analysts, and commentators tell us that we could do worse than return to Reinhold Niebuhr's ideas about global order and try to apply his realism to the world that has emerged after

---

[3] *Ibid.*, p. 217.

[4] Campbell Craig, *Glimmer of a New Leviathan: Total War in the Realism of Niebuhr, Morgenthau, and Waltz* (New York: Columbia University Press, 2003).

[5] Reinhold Niebuhr, *Christian Realism and Political Problems* (New York: Charles Scribner's Sons, 1953), pp. 15–31.

1991 and 9/11.[6] What we have seen already in these pages, however, is that there is no unanimity among those who claim Niebuhr's legacy.

MORE QUESTIONS

The end of the Cold War marked a transition unlike the end of the Second World War. The superiority of American military power and industrial potential was indisputable in 1945, but American political principles were at the center of contention. The Soviet Union and, soon afterward, China continued the pattern of conflict between the Western democracies and a totalitarian system that could sustain a coordinated military, political, and economic opposition. Indisputable American power meant only that American leadership against this threat was unavoidable, not that the threat itself could be dismissed.

In 1991, by contrast, the world was full of powers poised to compete against the United States and Europe in a global economy. The command economies of the Soviet bloc had dramatically failed to match the last two decades of capitalist growth, but they had an industrial infrastructure and vast natural resources, along with a formidable nuclear arsenal loosely under Russian control. What was indisputable was not American power, but the principles of liberal democracy and market economics. No other system of ideas and institutions could make a comparable claim to provide guidance for a global future. The end of the Second World War marked a new phase in the struggle between democracy and the totalitarian challengers who had risen up against it at the beginning of the twentieth century. The end of the Cold War ended that struggle. There would continue to be authoritarian regimes and revolutionary theories, but none of the many contenders who had taken the stage since 1917 could claim to represent the future.

In 1991, therefore, the search for guiding principles in the unstructured, evolving democratic experience was far more important than it had been in 1955. As long as the democratic example was under threat from clearly iden-tified alternatives, democracy could define itself by contrast. Democracy is the opposite of what the authoritarian regimes and revolutionary ideologies believe and practice. Niebuhr's own defense of democracy, *The Children of Light and the Children of Darkness*, interpreted democracy through his the-ological understanding of human nature, but his formulations of political

---

[6] Anatol Lieven and John Hulsman, *Ethical Realism* (New York: Pantheon Books, 2006), pp. 55–83; David Brooks, "A Man on a Gray Horse," *Atlantic Monthly*, 290 (September 2002), 24–5; Peter Beinart, *The Good Fight* (San Francisco: Harper Collins, 2006), p. 16.

principle were notoriously ambiguous, strong on historical generalization and weak on normative specificity.[7] Or perhaps we should say that the weakness and ambiguity of Niebuhr's formulations became evident by comparison to the work that political philosophers began to do, once it was clear that democracy was the only viable alternative, and it became more important to figure out what it meant on its own terms.

The development of liberal political theory that we have traced in previous chapters thus arrived in a timely fashion to greet the slow decline of the Soviet Union, the economic liberalization of China, and the end of the Cold War with a clearer statement of what triumphant liberal democracy was really all about. But it is just at that point that we have to ask whether liberal democracy can be the answer to this historical question. The question posed by the end of the Cold War was above all a question about global order, or "global integration," to put it in Niebuhr's terms. When the barriers between two rival political and economic systems came down, the technological possibilities of global commerce and the efficiency of global markets inevitably led to a rapid globalization of the economy, and to cultural, communications, and scientific globalization as well. The end of the Cold War also triggered a realignment of regional security and economic arrangements, and it created an unanticipated – and as yet unfilled – need for internationally acceptable ways of dealing with failed and rogue states which in the good old days might have been kept in line by their superpower sponsors. The questions posed by the end of the Cold War were above all questions about global order. The answers available in the experience of the liberal democracies were about how to organize a successful modern state.

The realists who created a global order for the Cold War world had needed a different answer to an old question. Their question was about what kind of global order is possible when the world is divided into blocs of competing, hostile states, and the answer they needed was one that would not terminate in nuclear war between the superpowers. The end of the Cold War raises the quite different question of what kind of global order is possible when superpower competition no longer sets the boundaries. Nearly two decades later, we have not found that answer, and we begin to suspect that we do not understand the question. At the end of the Second World War, political realists knew they were still in the middle of an historic

---

[7] Reinhold Niebuhr, *The Children of Light and the Children of Darkness* (New York: Charles Scribner's Sons, 1960). See also the discussion of Niebuhr's idea of justice in Robin Lovin, *Reinhold Niebuhr and Christian Realism* (Cambridge: Cambridge University Press, 1995), pp. 191–8.

confrontation between democracy and totalitarianism. We are not quite sure where the end of that confrontation leaves us in the course of history.

Francis Fukuyama proposed an answer in *The End of History* that was, or was widely interpreted to be, that no answer is needed. In the absence of ideological conflicts, people will just organize themselves into successful democracies and market economies and repeat in their own settings the experiences that fortunate circumstances allowed America to anticipate by a couple of centuries. The global order will then consist of these democracies, holding regular elections and buying and selling things amongst themselves. This proves to be not quite sufficient, and as Fukuyama himself points out, that oversimplified way of putting it has the disorderly consequence that it encourages political leaders in successful, established democracies to intervene in states where the inevitable progress of democracy seems to be inhibited by bad leadership.[8] But if an answer to the question of global order is needed, is there *any* theoretical account of the experience of democratic states that can provide it?

It has been a complaint against contemporary liberalism since shortly after the publication of Rawls's *A Theory of Justice* that liberal theory provides no account of how justice works between societies or across the boundaries of states.[9] Liberal theory begins with an explanation of how free and equal people could bind themselves to live in a political order with one another. Both the experience of liberal democracy and most formulations of liberal theory suppose that these societies will relate to each other as distinct, independent states, unperturbed by how people live in other places and relatively unaffected by their choices.

It is increasingly clear that this is not the way that liberal democracies relate to other states in an age of globalization. Their economies are interdependent with those of other states. Even a successful, established democracy can find its prosperity and security at risk when things start to go badly in the politics of other states. Perhaps most interesting, successful, established democracies find that their citizens now expect their governments to intervene when other governments fail and humanitarian crises ensue. Genocide, famine, and pandemic disease seem to require some response, and in the absence of another superpower to warn them off, the Western democracies have to explain inaction rather than to justify intervention.

---

[8] Francis Fukuyama, *The End of History and the Last Man* (New York: Free Press, 1992). His own restatement of his position can be found in Francis Fukuyama, *America at the Crossroads* (New Haven, CT: Yale University Press, 2006), pp. 53–5.

[9] Brian R. Barry, *The Liberal Theory of Justice* (Oxford: Clarendon Press, 1973), pp. 128–33; Charles R. Beitz, *Political Theory and International Relations* (Princeton, NJ: Princeton University Press, 1979).

Some effort must be made to relate liberal democratic theory to the emerging global reality.[10] If what states have to do in this emerging global order cannot be explained by liberal democratic theory, that might be a sign that liberal democracy is obsolete.

Rawls provided a partial answer to this challenge in *The Law of Peoples*, which suggests a minimal set of human rights that govern the relationships of liberal societies to others that do not share their liberal commitments.[11] This seems, however, to be a statement of what a liberal society will not do, regardless of provocation, and not an account of human rights that describes what citizens of any state should expect from their government, or from the world community, if their own government fails them. Perhaps in Rawls's liberal theory, such an account of human rights is not possible. If the theory is political, and not metaphysical, some level of understanding and consent must be implied for any obligation to be imposed. That raises the question whether a global understanding of human rights is possible without a metaphysical or theological ground.[12] A substantive account of the human good which confers on all persons certain rights and obligations is difficult to achieve, and liberal theory has been built on the premise that if this difficult achievement can be omitted from the political agreements necessary to form a liberal society, it would be expedient to do so. But if such an account is required for a global order that includes human rights sufficiently robust that all governments must respect them, then many will argue that we should be developing theories that provide it. If it becomes clear that liberal theories cannot do that job, that might be an indication that the era of liberal democracy ends when a global order based on human rights begins. Instead of telling us what kind of global order we may and may not have, the limits of liberal theory may instead tell us when we are done with liberal theory.

THE END OF AN ERA?

Are we, then, at that end of an era Reinhold Niebuhr anticipated in 1934?[13] Perhaps liberal democracy and the modern state more generally are at the

---

[10] William A. Galston, *The Practice of Liberal Pluralism* (Cambridge: Cambridge University Press, 2005), pp. 197–9.

[11] John Rawls, *The Law of Peoples* (Cambridge, MA: Harvard University Press, 1999), pp. 78–81.

[12] Michael Perry, *Toward a Theory of Human Rights* (Cambridge: Cambridge University Press, 2007), pp. 7–29.

[13] Reinhold Niebuhr, *Reflections on the End of an Era* (New York: Charles Scribner's Sons, 1934). See the discussion of this work and its place in Niebuhr's thought at the beginning of Chapter 1.

end of their historical run, not because they have been defeated and replaced by something else, as Niebuhr thought they might be, but because they can no longer organize the world their own successes have created. If this era is at an end, it lasted nearly four hundred years, dating it conveniently from the Peace of Westphalia (1648). The distance from 1934 to 1991 might be small enough to put Reinhold Niebuhr within the margin of error for such predictions.

Certainly, that is how the Counterapocalyptic Realists would see it.[14] Global political and economic changes have produced such widespread dislocations that for a large part of humanity, ordinary historical frameworks no longer enable them to understand their situation or face their future with any hope. Add to that the recognition that these political and economic changes are now producing global climate change, and it begins to appear that the whole natural and social order of human life is changing, a shift of worlds and not just of regimes or economic systems. Under these circumstances, the apocalyptic literature of early Christianity has surprising relevance to a secular society.[15] But the Counterapocalyptic Realist is not a millenarian fleeing from the wrath to come and waiting for the age to end. The Counterapocalyptic Realist takes on the urgent political and theological task of keeping the existing political powers from seizing apocalyptic rhetoric and using it to validate their own promises of deliverance. If we find ourselves at the end of an era, it is important to face that fact squarely. If we find ourselves at the end of an era, the leaders of successful modern states, who are almost by definition part of the era that is coming to an end, are unlikely guides to the future. Better to listen to the poor, who, in the words of Sindiswe Mamputo, a South African AIDS worker, "have hope for some things that we are sure to receive, but we do not know when."[16]

There is no reason to expect the urgency of these challenges to diminish or to suppose that the number of people whose basic needs are unmet by existing political and economic systems will decline. But even if the requirements of global order begin to prove technically and politically manageable, it is not clear that liberal political theory provides much guidance. The next few generations may be left to work things out by experiment at the global level, as their ancestors invented the modern state and sent it on the way

---

[14] See pp. 32–37 earlier.

[15] Duncan B. Forrester, *Apocalypse Now?* (Aldershot, UK: Ashgate Publishing, 2005), pp. 49–64. See also Jeffrey Stout, "The Spirit of Democracy and the Rhetoric of Excess," *Journal of Religious Ethics* 35 (2007), 5–7.

[16] *Bambelela: (Never Give Up)*, Mairi Munro and Martine Stemerick(tr.) (Chicago: GIA Publications, 2002), p. 4.

toward liberal democracy during the seventeenth and eighteenth centuries. If that happens, enlightened citizens of the twenty-third century will no doubt regard themselves as living in the era of Jefferson and Voltaire. They will see us as having lived in the Middle Ages.

At this point, however, the Antiutopian Realist interrupts these apocalyptic meditations with a reminder that our need for the modern state is not measured by the quality of our theories about it, but by what it does that no other institution can do. We lack institutions with global scope that are capable of providing order, including provision for the enforcement of whatever human rights our substantive theories of the human good tell us people ought to have. Jean Bethke Elshtain again articulates this political realism that we can trace from Augustine through Luther to Niebuhr:

Absent such a structure, culminating in some form of political sovereignty – another name for "responsibility" of collective bodies in the world as we know it – the likelihood of what we now routinely call "humanitarian catastrophes" is magnified many-fold. A paradigm example of the ills attendant upon political instability absent a central, legitimate focus of power and authority is the disaster of so-called "failed states". It is, of course, the case that states themselves, whose very reason to exist is to maintain stability and a measure of internal civic peace, may become disturbers of the peace. But because sovereignty is the way we "name" responsibility, such states can and should be held to account.[17]

Other than states, we have no institutions that can take this responsibility, nor are we likely to have them in the foreseeable future. That is one reason why our political theories appear to presuppose an international system of sovereign states. Our political theories embody what we know about creating systems that can be held responsible in the way that Elshtain describes, and we simply do not know how to create anything else that we could turn into the basis for a global order. That is not to say that we cannot create useful systems and institutions for cooperation between states, even institutions that reach across borders to coordinate, regulate, and provide assistance. The growth of such institutions has, in fact, been part of the globalization of recent decades.[18] But these institutions do not mark the end of the modern state. They are a further stage in its development.

Elshtain reminds us that for a Niebuhrian realist, political solutions must be responsible in another sense, besides the fixing of accountability

[17] Jean Bethke Elshtain, "Against the New Utopianism," *Studies in Christian Ethics* 20 (2007), 50.
[18] Anne-Marie Slaughter, *A New World Order* (Princeton, NJ: Princeton University Press, 2004), pp. 1–35.

that sovereignty provides. Solutions must be formulated in a framework of predictable outcomes, involving known people and problems. Half a millennium is perhaps too wide a horizon for responsible action, and one of the problems with an apocalyptic perspective is that it is difficult to know what we should do in response to the changes it describes. Like the logical "Both X and not-X" from which *any* conclusion follows, an apocalyptic change of circumstances may appear to recommend almost any response.

Still, it is noteworthy that the responsibilities Elshtain imposes on sovereign states do not seem to be limited to those established by the political agreements that founded them, nor is the responsibility only to their own people. The international community holds states accountable for humanitarian catastrophes they cause, whether or not their own citizens are able or even willing to do so. Treating states as responsible in this sense may involve intervening to strengthen the elements of participation and accountability in their political systems, as well as relieving the suffering of their victims.[19] Presumably there is an idea of human good not derived from the political arrangements of the accountable state which allows the world community to identify a humanitarian catastrophe, and perhaps also an idea of political participation that would allow the world community to measure a state's response by some standard other than conformity to its own political arrangements.

A TOLERABLE SOLUTION

Half a century after Niebuhr probed the resources in experience and theory for a tolerable solution, the problem of global order remains before us, although it seems rather different from any of the forms in which Niebuhr himself saw it. The problems of global order today seem at once to lie outside the reach of state power, as the Counterapocalyptic Realists argue, and at the same time to require states to be responsible, as the Antiutopian Realists insist. What would a tolerable solution to that dilemma look like, and where would it leave us in relation to the long history that has given us the successful modern state?

Niebuhr's tolerable solution to the conflict between the United States and the Soviet Union was based on a balance of power. This equilibrium between opposing forces, which is part of all organized social life, makes its appearance in international relations when states seek their objectives of security and stability by making sure that no one of them is in a position to

---

[19] Elshtain, "Against the New Utopianism," pp. 50–2.

dominate the rest.[20] This concept had been part of European diplomacy at least since the Peace of Westphalia, and it became central after the Congress of Vienna, which settled arrangements between the European powers after the Napoleonic Wars. In the European balance of power among France, Germany, Britain, and Russia, diplomacy was active and alliances and loyalties were shifting, as each power tried to align itself with the others in ways that would prevent yet another power from gaining the dominant role. A bipolar balance of power between two superpowers, like the United States and the Soviet Union, works on somewhat different terms.[21] The two opposing parties acquire a mutual interest in preventing the rise of other contenders who might upset the bipolar balance. Calculations of relative strength become quite precise and may remain stable for decades as each side acts to prevent the other from acquiring a decisive military, diplomatic, or economic advantage. Niebuhr saw this equilibrium as a possible basis for global order early in postwar relations with the Soviet Union, and he continued to urge maintaining the balance of power as the goal of American policy, despite his growing hostility toward communism as a political and economic system.[22]

In the Cold War, balance of power began as a conscious decision by the United States after the Second World War not to pursue its military and economic advantages against the Soviet Union, but to rely on policies of containment and deterrence to prevent open warfare. Once the Soviet Union acquired its own nuclear weapons, the choice became irrevocable, since neither side believed it could win a nuclear war and each devoted its military and economic resources to ensuring that the other side would continue to calculate the odds that way. By the 1970s, an explicit strategic doctrine of "mutual assured destruction" prevailed. Each side maintained an arsenal of nuclear weapons many times that required to destroy the other, so that neither could count on a first-strike success that would eliminate the other's capacity for devastating retaliation.[23]

By the end of the Cold War, moral problems with this strategy had become apparent. The cost of an apparently endless arms race limited the resources available for other pressing problems, within each of the

---

[20] Hans J. Morgenthau, *Politics Among Nations: The Struggle for Power and Peace*, Fourth Edition (New York: Alfred A. Knopf, 1967), pp. 161–6.

[21] *Ibid.*, pp. 345–9.

[22] Reinhold Niebuhr, "The Hydrogen Bomb," in *Love and Justice: Selections from the Shorter Writings of Reinhold Niebuhr*, D. B. Robertson (ed.) (Louisville, KY: Westminster John Knox Press, 1992), pp. 235–7.

[23] John Lewis Gaddis, *The Cold War* (London: Penguin Books, 2007), pp. 119–203.

superpowers and in the wider world. Effective deterrence was based on a threat to inflict death and destruction on whole populations on a catastrophic scale. Can it be right to secure peace, moral thinkers asked, by threatening what it would clearly be wrong to do?[24] The balance of power left little room for human error, accident, or momentary lapses of judgment, with permanent consequences of planetary scope to follow from any failure. The system held until it was no longer needed, but as the Duke of Wellington said of the Battle of Waterloo, which inaugurated the great age of balanced power between nations, "It was the nearest run thing you ever saw in your life."[25]

A CLASH OF CIVILIZATIONS?

The creation of order in this realist perspective turns on identifying the powers that must be brought into balance to secure future stability. After the Second World War, the answer to that question was obvious. The balance of power between nations had been reduced to the two powers that resources and history had placed in positions to have imperial ambitions of global scope.[26]

One way to understand superpower conflict sees it as a contest from which one party emerges as the sole superpower – the United States, in the case of the Cold War that ended in 1991. A purely political realism expects that the sole superpower will be in position to set the terms of global order, at least until some new contender emerges, or until the sole superpower forfeits the position through failure to pursue the advantage or weakness of will.[27] For Niebuhr's combination of moral and political realism, however, balance of power is central to an ordered community. Where power is not balanced, there is no community, and no one can set the terms for what does not exist. In this more complicated arithmetic, the removal of one of two superpowers leaves not one superpower, but none. The two superpowers set the terms for world order for almost five decades because each was opposed by another superpower with similar imperial ambitions. States were forced onto one of the two sides or "tilted" toward one or the other in a tricky

---

[24] National Conference of Catholic Bishops, *The Challenge of Peace: God's Promise and Our Response* (Washington, DC: National Conference of Catholic Bishops, 1983), pp. 52–62.

[25] Arthur Bryant, *The Great Duke or the Invincible General* (New York: William Morrow and Company, 1972), p. 453.

[26] Reinhold Niebuhr, *The Structure of Nations and Empires* (New York: Charles Scribner's Sons, 1959).

[27] See, for example, the position of Kaplan and Kristol, *The War over Iraq*, discussed on pp. 31–32 earlier.

effort at neutrality.[28] Either way, less powerful states tried to keep political and economic forces within their borders under tight control, lest they lose the ability to manage their relationships with the superpowers. Take that superpower opposition away, and the system of opposing blocs devolves into multiple states, each pursuing its own interests. At a time when economic and technical developments make possible the rapid expansion of global commerce, these national interests are increasingly defined in economic terms. Ideologies, repressed nationalisms, ethnic animosities, and religious conflicts become threats to a domestic security that now depends heavily on providing a stable business environment. Global corporations, rather than superpower states, become the allies to be courted in the daily work of diplomacy.

So the end of the Cold War leaves us a world without superpower states, and the global economic and cultural developments that have accompanied those political changes make it unlikely that the pattern of competing superpowers will be repeated anytime soon. Certainly the risks of that version of global order were such that we should not seek a return to it, nor should we expect that the players in another Cuban missile crisis, whoever they might be, would be as skillful or as lucky as the participants in the original.

In the absence of superpowers, it might be possible to think instead of a global order composed more along the lines of the original vision of balance of power. A number of powerful states would maintain an order based on shifting alliances and changing assessments of relative strengths, ensuring precisely that the superpower role remains vacant for the foreseeable future. The powers, of course, would be different from those that emerged from the Congress of Vienna. Europe, in fact, probably would best be seen as a single power in this model, and the empires would be built on commercial, rather than colonial, relationships.[29] The historical record of this sort of balance of power at preserving peace is mixed, at best, but one could argue that it worked tolerably well until the imperial systems that it allowed to develop proved unable to contain their internal ethnic and religious conflicts.[30] That history lends some urgency to the Antiutopian Realists' call to develop systems that hold states responsible for the humanitarian

---

[28] Wilhelm G. Grewe, *The Epochs of International Law*, Michael Byers (trans.) (Berlin: Walter de Gruyter, 2000), pp. 638–43.

[29] Joerg Rieger, *Christ and Empire: From Paul to Postcolonial Times* (Minneapolis, MN: Fortress Press, 2007).

[30] See Niall Ferguson, *The War of the World: Twentieth-Century Conflict and the Descent of the West* (New York: Penguin Press, 2006), pp. 10–19.

crises that develop within their borders, because these are often caused
or exacerbated by the kinds of conflict that undermined the great powers
who were balanced against one another at the beginning of the twentieth
century.

For other observers, conflict between nations has been replaced by an
even more fundamental "clash of civilizations," in which the differences
are, at their roots, religious and irreconcilable.[31] Two different views of the
human good and the human future are at stake, and strategies of balance
that have maintained order between rival states will not work when the
contenders are civilizations and their representatives in the conflict may
be terrorist networks, radical clerics, and religious believers whose fundamental loyalties are not demarcated by national boundaries. The democratic, market-oriented, and – some would add – Christian West has been
challenged by a traditionalist, authoritarian, and – some would add –
Islamist vision of the world. There is no way to construct a balance of power
between forces so different. The two civilizations are destined to struggle
with each other for control of the planet.

The sense that something new and important is happening here is right,
but it seems that the "clash of civilizations" explanation does not quite get
what it is. These two civilizations have not suddenly just discovered one
another, the way Europeans blundered into the Aztecs and the Inca in the
sixteenth century. Each of them has been aware of the other for a long
time, and at least since the end of the Second World War, both the West
and Islam have lived fully in the modern world. They have, in fact, jointly
created a single modern, global civilization that runs on cheap, abundant
fossil fuel. That civilization may now be threatened by its own appetite for
energy, but what is threatened is the one civilization that we all inhabit.

What we have is not a clash of civilizations, but a new kind of competition of forces within the one modern world. What is new is the idea that
something other than the power of states might set the terms for global
order. Business and religion, in particular, seem poised to take this new
role. Business insists that the market can most efficiently allocate resources
to provide the largest sum of the goods we all seek, so that we should all
agree, whatever our system of law or our individual preferences, to live by
the judgments of the market. Religion counters that it has a way of life that

---

[31] The idea is clearly articulated in Samuel P. Huntington, *The Clash of Civilizations and the Remaking of World Order* (New York: Simon and Schuster, 1996). What I have in mind here, however,
is the more widespread and less well-defined use of that terminology that has recently become
popular.

transcends cultural differences and moral uncertainty, so that we should all agree, whatever our political theory or our individual preferences, to live by the judgments of God. Both Islamic and Western religious movements, usually characterized as "fundamentalist," insist that neither the laws of secular governments nor market forces and the desires they create should touch the lives of the faithful. Economic theorists and corporate leaders insist that neither government nor religion should interfere with freedom, meaning especially the freedom of people to desire what the market has to sell and the freedom of the market to sell it.

The successful modern state has hardly been reduced to a bystander in this competition, but it is now facing something that is quite different from the vicissitudes of state power since 1945, or 1917, or even 1815. States no longer have the unique capacity collectively to set the terms for global order, and they are not likely to get it back. Multinational corporations can locate operations where they find the terms of commerce most favorable. That allows them to negotiate those terms with governments in the places where they do business, if not, in fact, to dictate them. Entrepreneurship and the exploitation of labor are both harder to control, because neither is effectively limited by distance. The Internet and satellite television allow ideas, cultures, and religious movements to sweep the world faster than police can control them.

GLOBALIZED CONTEXTS

This competition of religious and economic powers may be less dangerous than a clash of civilizations, but to a conventional political realist who sees the world order as a balanced system of sovereign states, these are troubling developments, nonetheless. These realists do not like power that is not firmly under the control of some government. Semi-independent economic, cultural, and religious powers make it hard to negotiate international agreements that will stick, because weak governments may prove unable to enforce the commitments they have made. Weak governments may not even be around, because they may be toppled by economic oligarchies or religious demagogues.

To a Pluralist Realist, however, the process of globalization presents a familiar picture of differentiated social contexts developing their own spheres of responsibility. Pluralism has long been global in the sense that wherever the conditions of modern life have prevailed, the differentiated contexts of business, government, culture, family, and religious life have tended to emerge within modernizing societies. The global reality of that kind of pluralism would have been recognizable to Reinhold Niebuhr, or to Leo XIII, for that matter. What is new is that these contexts and their forums are themselves becoming globalized. It is not just that the pluralist pattern is widely replicated in different societies. The contexts themselves are changing in ways that blur the boundaries between societies and nations. To participate in any of them is increasingly to be involved in relationships that cross borders and to have responsibilities that are defined by a global market, or a worldwide community of inquiry, or international standards of professional practice.

Most people experience this globalization first in the contexts where they work, whether this is in business or in one of the other contexts, such as culture or religion. A history professor in Mexico City or an engineer in Cologne becomes a part of global culture and business in such a way that their most important colleagues, adversaries, or competitors often live in distant places. As the Mexican historian and the German engineer become increasingly adjusted to the global context of their work, they measure their abilities and achievements by its standards, which have considerable normative power over them and which may be backed up by enforcement mechanisms that they cannot ignore, if they want to continue working in the context.

Contexts cover these distances in part by the rapid development of their forums,[32] especially what we have called the "private" forums, in which there are specialized rules and roles for participants in the discussion, and recognized publications and other channels of communication in which their ideas can be circulated and evaluated. People with skills and access to education find that the rules and expectations in these forums are increasingly specialized, and much time and effort goes into the learning of them, just as a large part of the work of a globalized university is devoted to teaching them.

At the other end of the economic spectrum, those without skills or education are often among the first to experience the globalization of work in negative ways. They provide cheap labor for a global market that may be poorly regulated in the countries where they live, so they work long hours for low pay under unsafe conditions, or they may be drawn into a pool of migrant laborers who find employment far from their homes and families. Either way, they have little or no access to the forums in which decisions about their work are made, and they are isolated from other identity-forming connections to family, religion, and culture.

---

[32] Here I use the terms "context" and "forum" in the specific sense developed in Chapter 4.

Globalization spreads across contexts as it becomes more pervasive within them. Because of the globalization of business, a Pakistani executive may relocate to Toronto without changing employers. There, he will find familiar religious and cultural communities alongside the exotic indigenous Canadian ones. If he marries or his children grow up in Toronto, he may find that his family context becomes an extended global network. In an increasing number of countries, including Canada, this global family will find that local law has been revised to accommodate diverse cultural and religious patterns of family life. As the patterns of globalization work their way through and between contexts, even those who stay put where they were born find that the contexts of their lives are changed in significant ways.

Globalization marks a new phase in the process of differentiation and specialization that has gone on in modern social contexts from the beginning. To coordinate actions globally in an era of instantaneous communication, uniform expectations and procedures develop that are distinct to the context and unrelated to the particular place where the work happens to be done.[33] Each context becomes more differentiated from the others, and all of them are less connected to local settings. Because local communities and national communities are themselves comprised of these increasingly global contexts, local ties become weaker and established local ways of relating contexts to one another become less effective.

The weakening of local norms affects local and national governments, especially. If Mexican historians and German engineers are forced to choose, they may decide to be good scholars and good engineers, rather than good citizens. If it comes to that, they will be backed up by global communities of professionals who support their choices. In this way, the normative power of laws passed by the Congress or the Bundestag is correspondingly reduced. In relatively free societies like Mexico or Germany, this weakening of the state's sovereign authority might be barely perceptible, but it makes a difference in states like China or Cuba, where governments may have to choose between the costs of trying to maintain a closed society or opening themselves to global influences that may undermine a way of life that they have tried to legislate.

This relative independence of local law and practice is most obvious in large multinational corporations, which have increasingly "acted as if they were no longer bound by national loyalties and no longer eager to

---

[33] Thomas Friedman describes this "flattening" of the world of business in Thomas Friedman, *The World Is Flat: A Brief History of the Twenty-first Century* (New York: Farrar, Straus and Giroux, 2005).

promote specific national interests."[34] Cultural institutions display some of the same globalized characteristics. Top universities seek a global faculty and student body; leading museums, orchestras, and opera companies develop international reputations, and as they lead the globalization of the cultural context, lesser institutions emulate them, even though they remain more dependent on a local constituency. The museum director in Peoria, Illinois, explaining to the board the practices required to be a first-class museum, becomes in that modest way an agent of globalization in all of the other contexts in which the board members are themselves involved. They have all become that much less Peorians and more participants in a global museum culture. Religions, of course, maintained global interactions which gave them considerable independence from local control long before modern states began. For them, globalization marks a return to patterns that were limited by their ties to modern states after the Peace of Westphalia, and especially by the way that twentieth century totalitarian states demanded the incorporation of all institutions and loyalties into their own visions of national and global order. Contemporary globalization, however, makes these religious interactions across borders available to masses of people, not just to a clerical or monastic elite, and allows the pace of religious change to match the speed of global communication.[35]

The globalization of contexts proceeds in different ways and at different speeds, but in general, it leads to increased interaction within a context and across distance and to an attenuation of the ties that bind contexts to one another in local settings. The pace of these developments increased at the end of the twentieth century, but the results of the Internet and jet travel were anticipated in many ways by the steamship and telegraph. Niall Ferguson argues that the process we have come to call "globalization" was well under way in the nineteenth century and was interrupted by the First World War.[36] The resulting system of globalized contexts may not be inevitable or irreversible, but contexts generally are today more independent of the sovereign state than they were at any time during the twentieth century, and perhaps more independent than they have been since the modern state began.

As a result, individual citizens of successful modern states increasingly find themselves participating in multiple contexts with demands and expectations that may differ between them and without any clear, shared, locally

---

[34] Grewe, *Epochs of International Law*, p. 706.
[35] See, for example, Philip Jenkins, *The Next Christendom: The Coming of Global Christianity* (Oxford: Oxford University Press, 2002).
[36] Niall Ferguson, "Sinking Globalization," *Foreign Affairs* 84 (March–April 2005), 64–77.

authoritative guidelines for resolving the conflicts. In a world of strong contexts and widespread participation, an individual can look to several different sets of rules for guidance or for justification. Each of them is likely to be better developed than it was a generation or two ago, but local rules for settling which rules to follow – "the way we do things around here" – are likely to be less clear and less compelling than they were. The life of a modern citizen who is also fully engaged in culture, commerce, and religion begins to bear a certain resemblance to life in the medieval world, before the modern state.[37] A person is neither an autonomous individual nor the subject of a single system of sovereign law, but must navigate among multiple, overlapping jurisdictions, each claiming the right to decide disputed questions by its own rules.

For the individual, these developments have both benefits and risks. For the poor, the chief problem is not the jurisdictional overlap of contexts, but the risk of falling completely under the dominion of one or another of them. Repression by totalitarian government is well known, but in a global market, the poor face similar risks at the hands of business, even when the governments under which they live are relatively free. Enterprises that need cheap labor contrive to hold workers in conditions that approximate slavery, where they are not allowed to leave and have no recourse to other authorities in family, government, or community who might free them. In other places, religion becomes a repressive force, especially where it is closely associated with ethnic identity. Religious groups persecute members of other groups, drive them from their homes, and may even engage in genocide. All of these practices are, of course, in violation of national and international law, but as state power declines relative to other contexts, these forces are often able to violate the law on a large scale, and in a "failed state," they may operate completely outside the power of any government. The poorest members of a society are the most likely victims.

For those who are less vulnerable, living in globalized contexts with overlapping jurisdictions may offer real benefits. The global market can also offer pathways to success and prosperity that are not available in traditional cultures. Having relationships to other parts of the world through cultural, religious, and business connections provides multiple centers of authority and identity. This may give individuals new opportunities to choose the standards by which they measure their own worth, the rules that they will follow in situations of conflict, and the authorities to which they will appeal

---

[37] Hedley Bull, *The Anarchical Society: A Study of Order in World Politics*, 2nd ed. (New York: Columbia University Press, 1995), pp. 254–66.

when they are in need of protection. These are real increases in personal freedom that can result from globalization.

Living in multiple global contexts may also, however, lead to personal fragmentation. Lives are divided between work, family, religion, and culture, and each context seems to make increasingly distinct and specific demands. Even in developed Western societies where patterns of interaction between contexts have been worked out over time, there are fewer traditional, local ways of resolving the conflicts, and individuals feel overstretched and guilty for their failure to meet the demands of all their contexts completely. Where the tension between work, family, and religion is culturally a new experience, the disruption of lives and relationships can be severe. There is also evidence that the initial result of this diversity in local settings is not wider interaction, but increased social isolation. People respond to multiple possibilities by choosing the ones they can easily live with and insulating themselves from the rest. The resulting ways of life may actually be quite narrow, despite the expanded range of choices.[38]

ANARCHY AND IDOLATRY

Globalization thus leads us toward more differentiated contexts, with stronger internal organization and greater independence from local settings. If this suggests a pattern of global order, it will be quite different from the one that prevailed during the Cold War, the global wars of the twentieth century, and the long period of balanced power between states that preceded it. To arrive at those balances of power and to understand them, political leaders and political theorists alike assumed that states had control over all forces operating within their territory. Secular authorities claimed this power at the beginning of the modern period to create order and security, and where they were successful, they acquired a sovereignty that could not be effectively challenged in practice and which was unlimited in theory. What a sovereign power claimed for itself, it expected in others, so that agreements between states were necessary and sufficient to establish the terms on which transactions might be conducted across borders. International order was global order.[39]

The assumption of unlimited sovereignty continued, despite rapid developments of culture and commerce within these sovereign states, and despite

---

[38] Robert D. Putnam, "*E Pluribus Unum*: Diversity and Community in the Twenty-first Century," *Scandinavian Political Studies* 30 (2007), 137–74.

[39] Daniel Phillpott, *Revolutions in Sovereignty: How Ideas Shaped Modern International Relations* (Princeton, NJ: Princeton University Press, 2001), pp. 75–96.

the changes which we have detailed, which placed secular authority in the most successful modern states increasingly in the hands of rationally ordered, constitutionally limited, and democratically elected governments.[40] The idea of unlimited sovereignty becomes a barrier to understanding, preventing us from looking behind the veil to see what is really happening to the powers of government within states and allowing us to ignore the emerging realities of globalization. David Held summarizes the situation in this way: "The world putatively 'outside' the nation state – the dynamics of the world economy, the rapid growth of transnational links and major changes to the nature of international law, for example – is barely theorized, and its implications for democracy are not thought out at all."[41]

Reinhold Niebuhr shared this focus on sovereignty with the rest of modern political thought, though he offered a more realistic political and social psychological account of how it works. The state, he suggested, does have a role that goes beyond providing order and security. It must be the organizing center of all the creative social forces that otherwise tend to break society apart into separate, uncontrolled enclaves of energy and experiment. The challenge here does not come from an alien enemy or from a rebellion seeking to overthrow the state. It is the natural outcome of social freedom, which culminates in anarchy unless its creative forces can be organized and limited.

Freedom, however, cannot be subdued by force, as though it were an invading army. When a government organizes freedom by force, the result is tyranny, and freedom is destroyed in the process. To maintain the necessary balance between order and freedom, the state requires a "majesty" that cannot be maintained by sheer power, nor easily explained by the rational consent of its citizens. "Majesty" elicits primitive awe, but it is essential to a modern state that seeks to control all the forces within its borders.[42]

Sovereignty and freedom thus coexist in an uneasy relationship which depends on a kind of necessary illusion. Those who hold power in states understand this at some level, so they exaggerate the majesty of the state to ensure that their power will not be questioned. If creative freedom in society necessarily tends toward anarchy, sovereign power inevitably tends toward tyranny. Tyranny, in turn, relies on an idolatry that makes the state the only worthy object of devotion and the goal of all individual and social effort. Niebuhr was no doubt thinking here of the propaganda spectacles

[40] See pages 58–61 earlier.
[41] David Held, "Democracy, The Nation-State, and the Global System," in David Held (ed.), *Political Theory Today* (Stanford, CA: Stanford University Press, 1991), p. 201.
[42] Niebuhr, *Nature and Destiny*, vol. II, p. 267.

which appeared to have led the German people to a point of blind devotion to the Nazi regime. Bonhoeffer wrote even more forcefully in *Ethics* about idolization of the successful Leader.[43] Although both of them saw what was happening in Nazi Germany as an idolatrous excess, they also saw that it spoke to realities in society and human nature that have to be addressed by every legitimate government. Niebuhr emphasized that this temptation to idolatry is an inevitable feature of political life, even in democratic states. Without the majesty that makes idolatry possible, freedom would end in anarchy.

Niebuhr's analysis suggests some things about realistic political leadership, but it even more clearly defines the task of the theological realist in relation to the state. Majesty is the source of idolatrous pretensions, but it is also a necessary feature of political order, national and international. The task of the political realist who is also a theological realist is to denounce the idolatry without denying the legitimacy.

When Niebuhr developed these ideas at the beginning of the Second World War, their application was clear to anyone who knew the rest of his Christian realism. The church must denounce the idolatry of totalitarian regimes without falling into self-righteousness, and it must remain vigilant against any attempt by anxious democratic leaders to counter the success of totalitarianism with an idolatry of their own. At the same time, the rejection of idolatry must not become a utopian disdain for the necessary illusions and the real exercises of power that allow free people to survive as an organized society. Restoration of global order depended on rejecting tyranny without succumbing to anarchy.

Subsequent history shows, however, that it is not so easy to maintain the coherence of this Christian realist analysis against the changing realities of an international order based on sovereign states. Perhaps because the disappearance of extreme forms of totalitarian idolatry makes the inevitable pretensions of all states seem more idolatrous, those who emphasize Christian Witness have in recent decades concluded that the most realistic course of action is to challenge the idolatry at its source and declare that faith has nothing to do with the exigencies of sovereign power and takes no responsibility for whether or not it works. Antiutopian Realists insist that this is unrealistic, and Counterapocalyptic Realists warn that the temptation to idolatry may be greatest precisely when a powerful state faces the limits of its global reach. The mysteries of sovereignty continue to defy consistent analysis, even when the analysis is a realist one.

---

[43] Bonhoeffer, *Ethics*, p. 89.

THE STATE IN CONTEXT

Perhaps, however, the problem lies with the assumption of unlimited sovereignty that the analysis seeks to explain. Pluralist political theory offers a different view, which David Held calls an "honorable exception" to the dominant understanding of the modern state.[44] In this account, the early understanding of unlimited secular authority gives way over time to one which is limited both by its own legal order and, more importantly, by the countervailing power of other social contexts which have their own history and legitimacy and cannot plausibly be interpreted as creations or instruments of the sovereign state.[45]

The result of these developments, as we have seen in the two preceding chapters, is an ordering of society in which contexts claim the resources and scope of action they need to provide specific human goods. In this process of claim and counterclaim, no one set of rules governs the resolution of conflicts. The remarkable thing, from the perspective of early modern political thought, is that none is necessary. This pluralism calls into question the idea that a single center of sovereignty is necessary for an ordered society, even when that ordering center is explicated with characteristic realism in Niebuhr's idea of the majesty of the state. It becomes unclear whether the necessary illusion is necessary to preserve order, or merely to explain the persistence of the idea of sovereignty in a modern world where the state's claim to unlimited power has evolved into more limited claims based on more specific goods and goals. Within the political pluralism of the successful modern state, government is one context among others. Some of its powers are unique, but none of them are unlimited.

With the end of superpower conflict and the globalization of contexts generally, the same realities now begin to impinge in obvious ways on the idea of sovereignty in the international order. Balance of power between sovereign states is no longer what insures global order. France and Germany are far less likely to go to war with each other in the next century than they were in the century just past, but this is not because they have arrived at a balance of power that is better or more durable than the one they had achieved before 1914. France and Germany are not thinking about going to war with each other because both of their governments are thinking about business. The political fortunes of governments in Europe today depend on how well they maintain the national interest in the world of global commerce, just as political fortunes used to depend on how well those

---

[44] Held, "Democracy, the Nation-State, and the Global System," p. 201.   [45] See p. 78 earlier.

governments maintained the strength of their navies. Progress toward that kind of order is less secure in other parts of the world than it is in Europe, but the European example suggests one path that the development of the successful modern state is likely to take in the future. In this emerging global order, government still has the essential role of maintaining peace and security within its territory, but that is less and less a function of military power that can be mobilized against other states. Security now requires governments to act as agents for the rights and interests of their people in global governmental forums, whether these are formal tribunals like the European Human Rights Court and the International Criminal Court, or negotiations about trade policy, wages, and working conditions that involve governments, corporations, and other stakeholders.

Pluralistic Christian realism thus raises quite different questions about the role of the state in global order from the ones posed by Niebuhr's carefully calculated balance between order and anarchy, in which the majesty of the state holds the key to the balance. Reinhold Niebuhr and the Christian realists in the ecumenical movement believed that the modern state was by far the strongest political reality in the global system of their day, and they worried that it might become so powerful that even in its democratic form, it would pose a threat to human freedom. As a result, they spoke out against totalitarianism, but they also took on the unwelcome task of reminding their fellow citizens in the Western democracies that their governments, too, could claim too much for their own majesty.

They were right about the perennial temptation of idolatry, of course. "The understanding that no political society can be entirely free of idolatry was Reinhold Niebuhr's most enduring insight," as Oliver O'Donovan puts it.[46] But idolatry ascribes to persons and institutions powers that they do not have as well as powers that they do not deserve. Given the emergence of religion and business as global contexts, we may now have to ask whether the modern state *is powerful enough* to perform its function in the global order. The weakness of the state in places where resources or people are exploited by business and the breakdown of government in places where religious movements have the capacity to make war are warning signs the state's place in the new global order is more fragile than it appears to be in Western Europe and North America. Yet because this emerging global order

---

[46] Oliver O'Donovan, *Common Objects of Love: Moral Reflection and the Shaping of Community* (Grand Rapids, MI: Eerdmans, 2002), p. 41.

is even more interconnected and interdependent than the one it replaces, instability anywhere puts the structure at risk everywhere.

New realities thus cast Christian political realism in the unlikely role of defender of the state. But who can deny that the people of Afghanistan or Lebanon would have been better off if they had stronger governments and weaker religious movements over the past couple of decades? Or that the citizens of developing countries might have better lives and a better future if they had governments capable of making and, especially, of enforcing labor and environmental laws?

To ask what the state *needs* is, in any case, to raise a realistic question about the idolatry of unlimited sovereignty. It suggests that government, like other contexts, has specific tasks and contributes specific things to the sum of human goods created and maintained by all of the contexts together. Instead of ordering and disposing all creative social forces, it depends on other contexts for the resources it requires to play its specific role, just as those other contexts depend on government for what it alone can provide.

Central to the specific task of government is providing security and order within a given territory. That was what defined the modern state at its beginning, and it is still what people want most when their state fails to provide it. It is also why people want a state when they do not have one. It is easy to lose sight of this where security and order can be taken for granted and governments do so many other things, too. It is in moments of crisis, when security and order are threatened, that we who live in the most successful modern states are reminded what governments are for, as Jean Bethke Elshtain remarked after September 11.[47]

The events of September 11 also call our attention to some new realities about the role of government. The need for security and order is now universal, not local. When security and order break down, the local population suffers, as we have seen in different ways in Bosnia, in Afghanistan and Iraq, and in Somalia and Sudan. But when security and order break down, forces are unleashed that result in terrorist activity, economic dislocations, or refugee crises in distant places, too. No government can be confident that it can maintain security and order in its own territory when these are absent in other parts of the world for extended periods of time. Provisions for external security must now include not only defenses against other states, but also defenses against the nonstate groups that have broken the modern state's monopoly on the use of mass violence and now deploy

---

[47] Jean Bethke Elshtain, *Just War against Terror* (New York: Basic Books, 2003), p. 46.

their own armed forces in service of political, religious, or even merely criminal purposes.[48] For the same reason, it is not only states which now need to defend themselves against these threats. Global security is increasingly a concern that business is reluctant to hand over to weak or unwilling governments, and religious and cultural institutions find themselves exposed to harassment, kidnappings, and terrorist attacks, with no government from which they can effectively seek protection.

Under these new conditions, sovereignty begins to look less like a power to be claimed by governments and more like an obligation imposed on them by other forces, including globalized business, religion, culture, and the global concerns of other governments. Sovereignty, as Elshtain puts it, is a way we name responsibility for what goes on within a given territory.[49] In a world of pluralistic societies, government cannot be held responsible for everything. That would be an invitation to totalitarianism. But as long as the powers of government remain associated with territory, and not, say, with religious affiliation, ethnic identity, or vocation, governments will bear a primary responsibility for security and order for all of the people who live within that territory, for making sure that they do not fall below the conditions for sustainable human life and that they do not escape the requirements of social order and become agents of terror or genocide.

Meeting that responsibility requires the exercise of power, to be sure, but in many cases it also requires empowerment of people and the creation of structures for participation in government and other contexts. States fail, order breaks down, and humanitarian crises ensue when people are denied participation in government for political reasons or because of ethnic or religious discrimination. Humanitarian crises caused by governments may require the same kind of massive international relief efforts that natural disasters elicit, but the prevention of these crises depends on enforcement of human rights and the creation of structures of political accountability. These are requirements of global security, as much as they are moral norms based on respect for the dignity of the persons involved.

At the same time, governments may also face long-term problems of poverty and political unrest because people lack ways to participate in shaping the conditions under which they work, or the education available to them and their children, or opportunities for meaningful religious life. The globalization of business, culture, and religion tends, as we have seen,

---

[48] Michael Ignatieff, *The Lesser Evil: Political Ethics in an Age of Terror* (Princeton, NJ: Princeton University Press, 2004), pp. 151–6.
[49] Elshtain, "Against the New Utopianism," p. 50.

to strengthen the private, internal forums in these contexts and isolate them from local conditions. Under these circumstances, governments which take responsibility for security and order for all people who live within their borders must take an interest in the public forums in all contexts, not just those that enable citizens to participate in their own government. Open public forums have characterized the differentiation of contexts in success- ful modern states,[50] but these forums have lagged behind the globalization of contexts, and governments must increasingly see their development as part of the requirements of order and security.

Political pluralism in a global order raises the expectations and more sharply defines the responsibilities that go with sovereignty. What we must add at once, however, is that a political realist will not leave sovereign states to face these increased responsibilities on their own. "Multilateralism in these matters," as Michael Ignatieff says, "has gone from being merely desirable to being a matter of life and death."[51] The number of weakened states will increase as the global forces of religion, commerce, and culture grow stronger. Their survival as successful modern states will require an increasingly vigorous international system of labor standards, human rights law, and humanitarian interventions.

In the past, states have generally resisted such regulation and interven- tion, and political realists have tended to accept that the scope and usefulness of international activity is limited by sovereignty. The realities of global- ization, however, have already begun to change the nature of sovereignty, not only through the pattern of international agreements and organiza- tions already in place, but even more through the globalization of business and culture that increasingly penetrates every aspect of life in supposedly sovereign states. Sovereign authority to make decisions about political and economic systems in isolation from these global systems may still exist in principle, but the range of actual choices is severely restricted by what has already happened in other places and what is probably happening now among people in even the remotest villages of the least developed countries. The alternative to globalization is not the kind of isolation that allowed Japan to become a world power with a quite different economic and politi- cal system during the nineteenth century. It is the isolation of North Korea or Belarus.

As globalization proceeds in other contexts, governments will increas- ingly have to adopt the pluralistic model of the successful modern state, because they will have to deal with the same forces that created the model in

---

[50] See pp. 136–37 earlier. [51] Ignatieff, *The Lesser Evil*, p. 162.

the first place. Contexts are interdependent, and the forms government can take are determined by the human goods it has to supply to keep the other contexts working and the resources it can command to get that distinctive job done. This does not mean that most people in the world now live in a successful modern state, or will live in one anytime soon. The resources required to be a successful modern state are large, slow to develop, and very unevenly distributed across the globe today. What it does mean is that there are few other models that are taken seriously as guides to the future for the worlds' governments, and most of these alternatives are propounded by people who are either obviously self-interested or certifiably mad.[52]

Under these circumstances, the assertion of sovereignty is increasingly a form of unapologetic politics, by which a government claims the authority and resources it needs to govern a successful modern state. It makes these claims not only on its own people, but also on the international community. It makes them not only on other states, but also on the corporations, universities, religious groups, and family networks whose global contexts overlap its territory.

GLOBAL PLURALISM

As the forces of globalization accelerate, the most plausible way to think of a global order to replace the balance of power maintained by the nuclear superpowers is a balanced relationship between globalized contexts analogous to the pluralism of successful modern states. This is a transition of some magnitude, built slowly for over a century, interrupted by war and challenged by totalitarian alternatives, but now rapidly changing the understanding of sovereignty, ideas of international law, and the relations between business, religion, and culture at a global level. This global order is not a new way of balancing states against one another, but a new way of relating the governments of states to everything else in an increasingly complex global system.

That is a substantial change in the global order that has prevailed over the past several centuries, but it is not anarchy, nor is it a "clash of civilizations." Like the pluralism within states, it allows for a level of conflict that some have argued the order cannot sustain, and it lacks the central authority

---

[52] The continued development of Marxist theory by the ruling parties in China, Cuba, and North Korea provide examples of the former. The regime of the late Turkmenbashi in Turkmenistan may be a paradigm example of the latter. See Paul Theroux, "The Golden Man," *The New Yorker* (May 28, 2007), 54–65.

whose final word some modern theorists have always regarded as necessary whenever there is real diversity. But it also suggests some new ways of resolving conflicts, and it imposes new constraints on the ambition of states and their leaders, which have been the primary sources of violent conflict in the past.

Although global pluralism has been underway for some time, its continuation is not inevitable. It could be interrupted by ecological catastrophes or global pandemics, as its early development was interrupted by global warfare. It could, for that matter, be interrupted again by global warfare, waged between resurgent states eager to demonstrate their majesty and restore unlimited sovereignty, although that seems far less likely than interruption by global terrorism, which might succeed in disrupting global commerce by making the costs of keeping it secure too high.

In addition to the threats posed by violence and disaster, there are real alternatives to global pluralism, presented by those who find its world too uncertain or too inefficient. Multinational corporations form a powerful force supporting a global order centered on corporations, as previous orders have been centered on states. Individual corporations and their leaders need not be ideologically committed to this solution to bring it about. It could be an unintended consequence of their efforts to seek competitive advantage and productive efficiency for their enterprises. Given their large and growing organizational resources, the relative weakness of many national governments, and the limited availability of public forums in globalized contexts in which other stakeholders might be heard, a global order based on the requirements of the market could prevail by default.

Religion, to the surprise of secularization theorists, emerges as the other primary contender for global dominance. For people in the Western democracies, this possibility is seen primarily as a threat posed by militant Islamist groups. Dissatisfaction with the culture of the modern world and government by nation states runs high among these factions, compounded by their dissatisfaction with prevailing politics in the Islamic world and by factional competition for attention through increasingly radical programs and actions. It is not inconceivable that a significant part of the globe could come under control of a transnational regime that would order its relations with the rest of the world around religious norms. Nor is it inconceivable that some of the same dissatisfactions with modern culture and modern politics could coalesce conservative religious commitments in the Christian West into a more powerful fundamentalist political movement, or that Orthodox Christianity in Eastern Europe could gradually emerge from the long period of Soviet repression as a powerful force in its own right, isolating a region from the Balkans to the Urals from outside influences in religion, culture, and commerce.

For a pluralist Christian realism, the key to both order and freedom lies in maintaining the balance between these competing forces, rather than choosing between them. That is not an easy thing to do, nor is it easy to persuade others to do it. The conjectural alternatives to global pluralism offer more complete and consistent answers to the question of the human good, and each suggests that this completeness and consistency renders its answer final. Make this choice, we are told, and no further choices of this scope will be necessary. Global pluralism, by contrast, can claim to be no more than a tolerable solution to the problem of order as we now find it.

In maintaining the balance between contexts on a global scale, the role of government poses particular difficulties. In many places, government needs to be significantly stronger than it is and provided with quite different resources from those it has in order to govern a successful modern state, but it is not clear that other governments can effectively provide these resources in the absence of local culture and contexts that support it. Despite the enduring historic connections between democracy and political pluralism, leaders of powerful democratic states may find it difficult to wait for these developments to happen. Because democracy makes global order possible, the argument goes, those who believe a global order is necessary must work aggressively to spread democracy.

What Christian realism counsels in these situations is both realism and restraint. It warns that we are apt to overestimate our ability to influence outcomes and that we do not need to use power merely because we think we have it. At the beginning of the Cold War era, realism tempered the calls for a decisive blow against totalitarianism with a watchful policy of containment and patience. The same advice might well apply today. There are real problems with global pluralism: the fragmentation of life among increasingly differentiated contexts, the loss of local ways of resolving conflicts between these contexts, the weakness or absence of public forums in globalized contexts, and above all, the tendencies toward global exploitation of the poor. Dissatisfaction with these elements of the global order may increase as we become more aware of them. The problems may eventually make this global order morally unacceptable, like the order provided by Mutual Assured Destruction during the Cold War. Global pluralism is not Utopia, but one thing that makes a tolerable solution tolerable is that it may last long enough to improve upon it.

CHAPTER 6

Human Goods and Human Dignity

THE IRONY OF MODERN POLITICS

Tracing the interactions between the contexts that provide human goods gives us a more complex and realistic picture of how the modern world creates social order, and unapologetic politics gives us a more complete account of public discourse. No single set of rules governs this discourse or regulates the relationships between competing contexts. The successful modern state has less need of shared ideas and a greater tolerance for conflict than the theologians and philosophers who envisioned modern politics at first thought.

This success, however, creates its own need for a unity that may not be supplied by political activity, even with the expanded scope that politics has in the unapologetic model. The contexts that make up a society are brought into a working relationship through politics. For our lives, it is a different matter. As we are led deeper into family, culture, government, work, and religion, our responsibilities seem more and more to conflict and compete. We acquire the knowledge and skills that make us effective at our work, good citizens, and responsible family members. More and more, we know how to shape the contexts where we live and work, at least on a local level. Colleagues and neighbors look to us for leadership. We know that many of them – our children, our students, the teams we lead, and the people we supervise – depend on us. So far, we have not disappointed them, but our attention is stretched and divided by the multiplicity of needs and possibilities, and we wonder if we are setting the right priorities.

Indeed, we wonder whether we *can* set the right priorities. The structure of our lives seems to isolate work, worship, home life, and public activities from one another. Each context demands our full attention, when it can get our attention at all. None is at the center telling us what it all means. We are not sure that all the goods that we help to create and maintain add up to a good life. We wonder whether we should be doing more things in fewer places, or whether we should be trying to strike a different balance between the contexts where our life is lived. We study time management, try to learn the right habits, and even read books on virtue.

Or does the problem lie in our society, and not in ourselves? Should our political energies be devoted to making workplaces more family-friendly, and schools more oriented toward workplace skills, and the public square more open to religion? Does liberal democracy, which allows all these diverse goods to be created and frees us to make our own choices between them, have anything at all to say about creating a way of life?

In such reflective moments, we also encounter a more serious problem. Although our multiple responsibilities are complex and our lives are divided, those who have opportunities to write and read books like this one have lives far easier than most of the people who share this modern world with us. Migrant workers, separated from home and family, work under conditions that leave them with few real choices about the rest of their lives and responsibilities. Factory workers in developing countries produce luxury goods for affluent consumers, but their productivity is limited by poor working conditions, poor education, and lack of technology, and they retain little of the wealth they are able to produce. Other people live under regimes that use the power of government to restrict worship and culture and to manipulate family loyalties for their own purposes, or in cultures where religion and family combine to keep women from becoming whole persons with lives and responsibilities that extend into society beyond the home. For people in these situations, the diversity of contexts has not delivered the freedom and abundance promised by the emergence of the successful modern state. The highly structured life of modern society has instead proved successful at keeping them in roles that limit their possibilities and prevent them from integrating their lives or taking responsibility for their situations.

At this point, the questions about priorities become even more unsettling than when they are only questions about ourselves. Now we are asking whether the best we can do with the many choices we have makes any difference at all in a world where so many people struggle for basic survival and minimal freedom. What happens to our ideas of human good in a world where our best possibilities seem to be islands of self-interest in a sea of need and oppression? What happens to our efforts to act responsibly when we repeatedly discover that results of those responsible choices become part of institutions and systems that turn our care for the people and places near us into self-interested exploitation of those farther away?

What emerges in our experience is a need for moral meaning that unifies the diversity of our responsibilities and acknowledges both the immediate and the more distant effects of our choices. The need is most acute precisely when we are most engaged with the multiple contexts where we have responsibilities and most aware of the global reach of the structures that shape life in the modern world. We cannot help but admire the almost living intelligence of well-constructed institutions and systems which engage our energies and loyalties in pursuit of the goods they provide, but we are not sure that all of this activity adds up to a meaningful life. Can we identify a way of relating to the goods we seek in various contexts that unites them all in what we would recognize as a good life? Or do our diverse responsibilities finally get the better of us, so that we cannot be responsible and live a good life at the same time? If the latter proves to be the case, then the modern search for the good life has become self-defeating, because it would not be possible to create and maintain the necessary conditions for a good life without giving up the opportunity to live it.

The irony of modern politics is that it creates this need for a meaning it is designed not to supply. The profusion of complex goods and specialized institutions requires us to create a way of life out of the abundant available resources, and to recreate it several times over the course of our lives. From the beginning of the modern period, this introduced a new level of complexity into personal life. Modern politics, however, was built on the assumption that the only way to maintain the security and order on which all this depends was to insulate the rules with which all must comply from the goods which each seeks in his or her own way. Order, peace, and possibly prosperity are public matters. Meaningful life is a personal choice.

This separation of the human good from political principle resonates historically with the growth of religious toleration and democracy. It seems connected with the end of an age of persecution and religious warfare, and it set the stage for twentieth-century struggles against totalitarianism.[1] What seemed of supreme importance in political experience, moreover, became axiomatic in political theory. Especially for John Rawls's theory of justice, the rationally necessary conditions of politics must be carefully distinguished from all other convictions about reality and the good, so that

---

[1] Reinhold Niebuhr, *The Children of Light and the Children of Darkness* (New York: Charles Scribner's Sons, 1944), pp. 119–24.

free and equal people may pursue whatever conceptions of the good they have within the framework of political justice.[2]

Almost from the first formulation of the theory, however, this exclusion of considerations about the good from public choice has seemed too extreme. As Michael Sandel observed in an early criticism, persons without some determinate identity and understanding of the good would not know enough to choose the neutral principles by which politics could operate on its own terms. Our political and our personal identities cannot be so neatly separated.[3]

We have seen that William A. Galston has addressed this problem by developing a political theory that is "comprehensive," rather than "free-standing."[4] Respecting the freedom of other participants and the integrity of public discussion does not require us to exclude ideas about the good from public consideration, but it does suggest that the practical relationships we build between different human goods will be shaped by the requirements of particular choices, and built around particular historical experiences, rather than deduced from comprehensive doctrine itself. The results of these public discussions will reflect the various goods involved and the changing conditions required to create and maintain them, and different solutions to different problems may not easily yield a complete account of the human good or a fully consistent comprehensive doctrine, despite the ways that those ideals have influenced particular historical choices. We might draw on a comprehensive doctrine to resolve a number of different problems and yet find ourselves unable to construct a fully consistent account of that comprehensive doctrine from the choices we have made.

This idea of a comprehensive political theory seems immediately closer to the questions of meaning and personal integrity, just as the ambiguity and incompleteness of the results reflects our experience in trying to make responsible decisions. We have ideas about the unity of the good that we bring to our choices about law and government, just as we bring them to all the other contexts, but we cannot apply our "comprehensive doctrine" in a complete and systematic way, even if we were capable of a complete and systematic formulation of it. Nor are we sure that we, or anyone else, could figure out what our comprehensive doctrine is by adding up the choices

---

[2] John Rawls, *A Theory of Justice* (Cambridge, MA: Harvard University Press, 1971), pp. 11–17; John Rawls, *Political Liberalism* (New York: Columbia University Press, 1993), p. 10.
[3] Michael J. Sandel, *Liberalism and the Limits of Justice* (Cambridge: Cambridge University Press, 1982). See also his more recent assessment of Rawls's work in Michael J. Sandel, *Public Philosophy: Essays on Morality and Politics* (Cambridge, MA: Harvard University Press, 2005) pp. 212–51.
[4] See p. 146 earlier.

we have made under its influence. The question is what we are to make of this ambiguity and incompleteness.

VALUE PLURALISM

For Galston, this political pluralism is the outcome of a consistent moral realism.[5] Because our moral concepts formulate ideas about reality that exists independently of our ideas about it, recognizing the variety in our moral concepts does not lead to relativism. Moral realism is not troubled by the idea that the human good is not completely known, or by the fact that our attempts to give a comprehensive account of it may be incomplete.

Galston, however, has a further explanation for the diversity. He connects political pluralism and moral realism to "value pluralism," a moral theory drawn from the closing section of Isaiah Berlin's essay "Two Concepts of Liberty."[6] Value pluralism suggests our disagreements about the good and our inability to give a fully consistent account of it derives in part from the fact that human goods are genuinely different, and incommensurable with one another. Sometimes, of course, moral disagreements are the result of mutual misunderstanding. There are reconciliations in which people revise their moral judgments. But we should not move from those happy occasions of concrete agreement to conclude that there could be a comprehensive agreement in which all moral differences are resolved. Every comprehensive doctrine is necessarily incomplete, inevitably in disagreement with other comprehensive doctrines, and indeed, all of them are at points internally inconsistent. There are different goods, and different kinds of goods, and there is no common standard by which they can all be measured.

For Galston, value pluralism and liberal pluralism form a complex of related ideas rather like the connection between moral realism and political realism in Niebuhr's Christian realism. Taken together, the moral theory and the political theory give direction to our efforts to deal with moral disagreement in political life. The connection is not one of tight logic. Being a value pluralist, or any other kind of moral realist, does not entail liberal pluralism, or any other form of liberalism. "My claim," Galston explains, "is rather that by itself, value pluralism functions as what lawyers would call a principle of estoppal: no political or moral argument that denies the truth of value pluralism can stand. One of my suggestions is that this negative

---

[5] Galston, *Liberal Pluralism*, p. 30.
[6] *Ibid.*, pp. 29–35. See Isaiah Berlin, *Liberty*, Henry Hardy (ed.) (Oxford: Oxford University Press, 2002), pp. 212–17.

argument does a great deal of work in the real-world, because many popular arguments tacitly or explicitly endorse premises that contradict value
pluralism."[7]

Thus, if value pluralism is correct, a "comprehensive" political theory
cannot be distinguished from a "freestanding" one because it culminates in
the acceptance of one comprehensive doctrine and the rejection of all the
rest.[8] That level of consensus is not possible, insofar as the real diversity of
human goods means that they cannot be ordered in a way that requires all
persons to arrive at the same ordering of good for themselves and others.
"If this is so, no amount of philosophical argument or cultural progress
can lead to the definitive victory of one account of value over all the rest.
Moral reflection is the effort to bring different dimensions of value to bear
on specified occasions of judgment and to determine how they are best
balanced and ordered, given the facts of the case."[9]

A comprehensive political theory allows for a good deal of interaction
between this moral reflection and the way a society orders its political
life. A decision to abolish slavery, protect workers from discrimination by
their employers, or intervene in the affairs of a sovereign state to prevent
genocide or terrorism could be defended on moral grounds that reshape our
understanding of prevailing political principles. Requirements of human
flourishing that are widely shared between different cultures and ways of
life can figure in our thinking about the purposes of government and about
the individual's rights.[10]

There is much in this combination of value pluralism and liberal pluralism that will sound familiar to readers who have followed the account of
Christian realism in this book. What we say about the human good refers
to a reality that exists apart from the words we use to speak about it. We
may organize moral concepts into moral theories, but our moral realism
primarily guides our thinking about responsible choices that involve specific goods in particular, local situations. Over the course of time, we take
responsibility for a multiplicity of real goods, so distinct from one another
that they require different forms of social organization to create and maintain them. We seek different goods in different contexts, and the conflicting
claims they make on our time, our care, and the resources at our disposal
provide all the evidence we need that they cannot easily be arranged in a
single system. A Christian realist who has understood the complexities of

---

[7] William A. Galston, "Liberal Pluralism: A Reply to Talisse," *Comparative Political Theory* 3 (2004),
144–5.
[8] Note again the distinction between a comprehensive doctrine and a comprehensive political theory.
See p. 146, note 47 earlier.
[9] Galston, *Liberal Pluralism*, p. 6.　　　[10] *Ibid.*, pp. 58–9.

responsible choice and unapologetic politics will be sympathetic with value pluralism as an account of ordinary moral experience.

The value pluralist, however, claims more than this. Value pluralism is "not a description of the perplexity we feel in the face of divergent accounts of what is valuable." It provides "an account of the actual structure of the normative universe."[11] The underlying reason why we experience this perplexity is that the things people value are genuinely different, and when these different values conflict, there may be no way to make a rational adjudication of the differences between them. Some moral conflicts are just inevitable, given the nature of moral reality.

Christian realism, by contrast, resists taking these differences as ultimate, at the same time that it insists on taking the experienced conflicts seriously. Conflicts between values not only give rise to tensions within the individual who is drawn to both of them. They lead to disagreements between the persons who incorporate these values into their lives and build their choices around them. To accept these conflicts as final seems at odds with the claim of prophetic faith that God is both creator and judge of the world, "the unity which is the ground of existence and the ultimate unity."[12]

This unity is important both to Reinhold Niebuhr's Christian realism and to the longer tradition of which he is a part. "Life must not be lived at cross-purposes," Niebuhr says. "The self must establish an inner unity of impulses and desires and it must relate itself harmoniously to other selves and other unities."[13] From this perspective, "all moral demands are demands of unity."[14] The moral imperative Niebuhr articulates here is to be distinguished from the wise counsel to seek inner peace and avoid picking quarrels with your neighbors. Love is the law of life, and it makes claims on us apart from any appeal to prudent self-interest.

Niebuhr sometimes treats this relation between unity and morality as if it were presupposed in the idea of morality itself, so that moral impera- tives only make sense if the unity of values is assumed. Even the minimal standards of morality necessary to make social life possible impose a moral obligation "only if it is assumed that life is related to life in some unity and harmony of existence."[15] Thus, every moral standard points beyond itself in a dialectic that leads toward more complete unity, and each approximation of justice gives rise to a more demanding standard of justice, whether or not society is actually capable of achieving it. This, of course, is a direct challenge to the idea of value pluralism. Either it is in the nature of moral values to refine themselves so that conflicts are resolved or it is not. Either

---

[11] Galston, *Liberal Pluralism*, p. 30.   [12] Niebuhr, *An Interpretation of Christian Ethics*, p. 22.
[13] *Ibid.*, p. 23.   [14] *Ibid.*   [15] *Ibid.*, p. 64.

value pluralism or *An Interpretation of Christian Ethics* has given a mistaken account of the structure of normative reality.

Niebuhr, however, appears to have become dissatisfied with his first explanation of the relationship between experienced conflict and ultimate unity.[16] In his later work, it is God's activity, rather than the experience of obligation, that brings unity out of conflict. It is not a matter of generating ever higher moral ideals to set against the self-seeking behavior of individuals and groups. The conflicts must actually be resolved. "Thus, the conflicts of history need not be accepted as normative, but man looks toward a reality where these conflicts are overcome in a reign of universal order and peace."[17] This, however, means that the unity can only be fully known from a point that lies beyond history and, to that extent, beyond reason as well. To understand the resolution of any historical conflict completely, we must view it from the end of history, where God completes what we cannot complete even in thought, much less in our history and in our own lives. The resolution is not dialectical, but eschatological.[18]

Galston also recognizes the dissatisfaction that remains after we have understood what value pluralism has to offer. Although we have been reassured that no one can legitimately impose on us a way of life based on their own way of ordering all human goods, it seems that we may never be able to make a unity of our own lives, given the irreducible conflicts between the different goods and goals that are available to be sought. This dissatisfaction fuels the ambition of moral theorists as it fires the eschatological hopes of the faithful. We want something more, and what the moral theorist wants is a theorization of liberal society that works, one that provides exceptionless rules, universal rights, or a strict hierarchy of goods, so that the conflicts are reduced to temporary perplexities about how to apply the principles that we know will resolve them. Galston is sympathetic, but not accommodating:

My response is simple: while we may want these more ambitious forms of theory, we cannot have them. The varieties of pluralism I have tried to describe and defend . . . are aspects of the moral universe we happen to inhabit. Pluralism is not a confession of philosophical incompleteness or incapacity; it is an assertion of philosophical truth.[19]

---

[16] This may explain why Niebuhr, late in his career, said that he had no interest in defending anything in *An Interpretation of Christian Ethics*. See Reinhold Niebuhr, "Reply to Interpretation and Criticism," in Charles W. Kegley and Robert W. Bretall (eds.), *Reinhold Niebuhr: His Religious, Social, and Political Thought* (New York: Macmillan, 1961), pp. 434–5.

[17] Niebuhr, *Nature and Destiny*, vol. II, p. 2.

[18] See Langdon Gilkey, *On Niebuhr: A Theological Study* (Chicago: University of Chicago Press, 2001), pp. 213–22.

[19] Galston, *Liberal Pluralism*, p. 130.

Thwarted ambition and hard reality are familiar to the Niebuhrian realist, but the impossibility of a certain kind of moral theory may not be the worst disappointment. If the moral universe we happen to inhabit will not support a certain kind of theory, will it nonetheless sustain a certain kind of hope?

THEOLOGICAL REALISM

That is the question that theological realism intends to answer. As we saw at the beginning of this book, Christian realism holds in tension three different realisms – political, moral, and theological.[20] A complete account of the moral universe we happen to inhabit requires all three of these realisms, and so Niebuhr turns to the reality of God to provide the meaning that is missing from moral experience and that value pluralism cannot supply. To a secular moral philosopher, this may seem to be little more than asking God to give us what philosophy says we cannot have, rather like a thwarted child appealing to mother for relief from the father's more consistent discipline.

Theological realism, however, is not a way of satisfying aspirations that have been disappointed by other aspects of our understanding of reality. Indeed, the understanding of human nature on which Christian realism relies emphasizes that ambition, pride, and anxiety distort our hopes and render us unrealistic.[21] One should not hang very much at all on the fact that people *want* a unity of the good that eludes them in ordinary moral experience. The question is what sort of unity the reality of God makes possible. The prophetic tradition suggests that this unity will stand in judgment on human aspirations as much as it fulfills them.

Because the resolution of history's conflicts and the fulfillment of history's hopes depend on God's action and lie outside of history itself, there are limits both to what we can know and to what we should expect within history. Acknowledging God's sovereignty over history and correctly locating God's judgment at the end of history gives us the unity that value pluralism says we cannot have, but not on the terms we wanted it. This is the lesson of the Hebrew prophets, who saw that God's sovereignty made Israel one among the nations subject to God's judgment, rather than designating their prosperity as the sign of God's justice. It was the false prophets who promised success on Israel's own terms, leading the kings to complain that you just could not get decent prophecy from people like Isaiah, Jeremiah, Joel, and Amos.[22]

---

[20] See pp. 6–11 earlier.   [21] Niebuhr, *Nature and Destiny*, vol. I, pp. 182–6.
[22] Reinhold Niebuhr, *Beyond Tragedy* (New York: Charles Scribner's Sons, 1937), pp. 93–110.

Where the true prophets came into their own, however, was after the disaster. Because they alone had not promised easy victory, it fell to them to make sense of defeat. They concluded that because the end of history is in God's hand, defeat within history does not destroy hope. They did not abandon the expectation of a messianic ruler who would resolve the conflicts between people and nations with a universal justice. The defeat of this expectation within history made possible its ultimate fulfillment.

Although the prophetic tradition understood that the final resolution of history's conflicts does not happen within history, it came to see – often precisely in the confounding of human expectations – signs that God's judgment and reconciliation are already underway, confronting us in the midst of everyday life with ultimate choices, but also offering redemption for our failures and consolation for our losses. This became the central theme of Christian theological realism, built on the memory of Jesus's blessing of the poor and the powerless, and the conviction that the reality of God's activity is seen most clearly in the life, death, and resurrection of Jesus Christ.[23]

The eschatological perspective of theological realism gives meaning to the historical events in which our lives are caught up, and offers hope for a resolution to conflicts that are more complex than we can understand. It also provides the basis for a theological interpretation of value pluralism. That interpretation is deeply rooted in the history of Christian realism, returning to Augustine's understanding of the earthly city where Christians live for the time being, which is neither the Christian Rome of Eusebius nor the apocalyptic Babylon.[24] In this city, those who know and love God are mixed up with those who love only themselves in complicated ways that do not allow us to separate them out, and for Augustine, the different understandings of the human good reflect this complexity. No doubt that is why he takes note of the report of Marcus Varro that there are a total of 288 different understandings of the supreme good to be found among the schools of philosophy.[25] Clearly, it is not possible to affirm all of these philosophies, and the very number of them makes us skeptical of their

---

[23] For Niebuhr's own statement of the Christian theological realism summarized here, see Niebuhr, *Nature and Destiny*, vol. II, pp. 1–119; also Reinhold Niebuhr, *Faith and History* (New York: Charles Scribner's Sons, 1949), pp. 120–38. Robert Song provides a detailed and perceptive account of Niebuhr's view of the meaningfulness of history, although Song himself remains unpersuaded by the theology. See Robert Song, *Christianity and Liberal Society* (Oxford: Clarendon Press, 1979), pp. 64–84.

[24] R. A. Markus, *Saeculum: History and Society in the Theology of St. Augustine*, (rev. ed.) (Cambridge: Cambridge University Press, 1988), p. 56. See p. 49 earlier.

[25] Augustine, *The City of God Against the Pagans*, R. W. Dyson (ed.) (Cambridge: Cambridge University Press, 1998), pp. 909–14.

claims, but neither should we suppose that those who share the earthly city are completely mistaken about what a good life looks like within its limitations. In explaining how human beings understand the human good, Augustine relies neither on a Stoic natural law that makes the good completely available to human reason, nor on a moral dualism that links good immediately and exclusively to God and rejects all other goals and values as evil.

People in the earthly city think that a great many things are good. That is why they pursue them, and compete with one another to obtain them. Above all, that is why they want to hold on to the goods they have, and why they seek a peace with their neighbors that will allow them to enjoy these goods in security. Nor are they mistaken in this. The goods they seek are good, because they have been created by God, and without that goodness these things would not even exist.[26] The problem is not that people love these things, but that they love them in the wrong ways, in ways that are not appropriate to the ways these goods are related to God. Their ways of loving human goods set those goods in conflict with each other and precipitate conflicts between the people who seek them.[27]

The human goods people seek are not rightly ordered in relation to each other, and indeed, they cannot be fully ordered except in relation to God. We understand human good correctly when we understand all goods in relationship to God. However, we do not receive this understanding as an orderly account of the hierarchy of goods, taught by philosophy or theology that we might learn for ourselves. We receive it by a life lived in relationship to God, "the way of life through which we may merit to know what we believe."[28] The meaning of the moral life, like the meaning of life as a whole, is eschatological. It is known in hope, but not reducible to theory. As Dietrich Bonhoeffer put it, "nowhere else but in the human person, in concrete life and human action, is the unity created of that which 'in itself,' that is, theoretically, cannot be unified."[29]

More needs to be said about how this eschatological unity is anticipated in "concrete life and human action," but the relationship between theological realism and value pluralism should already be apparent. As compared

---

[26] Augustine, *Confessions*, Henry Chadwick (trans.) (Oxford: Oxford University Press, 1992), p. 124.

[27] Augustine, *City of God*, pp. 918–42.

[28] Augustine, "The Catholic Way of Life and the Manichean Way of Life," in Boniface Ramsey (ed.), *The Manichean Debate*, The Works of Saint Augustine, vol. XIX (Hyde Park, NY: New City Press, 2006), p. 49.

[29] Dietrich Bonhoeffer, *Ethics*, Dietrich Bonhoeffer Works, vol. VI. (Minneapolis, MN: Fortress Press, 2005), p. 73.

to value pluralism, theological realism shifts the center of attention from human activity to God's activity, from the concrete details of life to the over-arching conditions that locate human life in a trajectory of history from creation to fulfillment. Theological realism sets the general conditions for meaning in all lives by locating the possibilities for human good and evil in relation to God's activity, showing that our choices are not lost in a universe of random events and that the goods we help to create and maintain are more than momentary triumphs of one interest in an endless competition with all the rest.

Theological realism is not the unified, comprehensive moral theory that value pluralism denied us. Value pluralism, in fact, survives as the theological realist's most judicious rendering of what our moral experience tells us about the human good, and what it does not tell us. Value pluralism is not to be dismissed because it is "secular," but affirmed precisely for that reason. Its secularity accepts that our understanding at any point in time will be incomplete, even when the subject is something so immediately human as the human good. To stop at that point, however, leaves the theological realist with "an intolerable tension between the need for meaning in society and the only partial capacity of society to satisfy that need."[30]

MEANING IN SOCIETY

If the value pluralist had the last word on meaning in society, then liberal pluralism might be the best way, after all, to organize society's political life. The effort to create a meaningful life out of the opportunities and responsibilities that the modern world offers can only go so far, before it encounters the real differences between goods that thwart our efforts to give one answer to the problem of human good as a whole. What commends a liberal society to those who continue to struggle with the problem of value pluralism is precisely liberal pluralism's refusal to provide a definitive answer. Recognizing that society has no solution to the problem of the human good, liberal pluralism puts as few obstacles as possible in the way of individuals who are doing the best they can by their own lights. "The value pluralist liberal state . . . will limit the agreement on principles and practices required of all citizens to constitutional essentials, parsimoniously understood. It will seek to create conditions within which, to the greatest extent possible, individuals and groups can lead their lives in

[30] Oliver O'Donovan, *Common Objects of Love* (Grand Rapids, MI: Eerdmans, 2002), p. 42.

accordance with their own understanding of what gives life meaning and purpose."[31]

Order, peace, and possibly prosperity are public matters. Meaningful life is a personal choice. So it has been from the beginning of the modern world, and so it is in other versions of political liberalism, too. Nor does this create an "intolerable tension" for the liberal pluralist. He or she may, in fact, breathe a sigh of relief, for as Isaiah Berlin pointed out, "the belief that all the positive values in which men have believed must, in the end, be compatible, and perhaps even entail one another" is the foundation for all the final solutions that have sacrificed individuals for some great societal purpose.[32]

The liberal theorist is therefore understandably somewhat nervous about religious groups that regard the loss of meaning in society as a problem, especially now that the political ideologies that so successfully carried out the sacrifice of persons to principle during the past century have largely lost their hold on the public imagination. We run the risk that in the twenty-first century religion will do to humanity what political ideologies did in the twentieth. John Rawls's transition from theological realist to the theorist of "freestanding" political liberalism makes sense against this historical background.[33] The comprehensive political theorist has a slightly more difficult problem, since it is not possible, in that account, to insulate our political principles completely from the influence of religion and other comprehensive doctrines. Even a secular political thinker might reflect that many citizens of liberal democracies are religious, and it might be politically important not to alienate them from liberal pluralism. Indeed, among the available comprehensive theories, the moral traditions of monotheism would seem to have much to commend them to a liberal pluralist over the principal political, ideological, and cultural alternatives, and there are many comprehensive political theorists who adhere to one or another of the Abrahamic faiths themselves. So William Galston suggests, briefly, that value pluralism and monotheism can, after all, be reconciled.[34] This is good news for liberal pluralists whose personal "understanding of what gives life meaning and purpose" includes a monotheistic religion, but it leaves the comprehensive political theorist, like her freestanding counterparts,

---

[31] Galston, *Liberal Pluralism*, p. 62.   [32] Berlin, *Liberty*, p. 212.

[33] Eric Gregory, "Before the Original Position: The Neo-Orthodox Theology of the Young John Rawls," *Journal of Religious Ethics* 35 (2007), 195.

[34] William A. Galston, *The Practice of Liberal Pluralism* (Cambridge: Cambridge University Press, 2005), p. 195. I accept for the moment Galston's assumption that it is *monotheistic* religion that is in prima facie conflict with value pluralism, and thus limit my comments here to those traditions.

with solid theoretical and historical reasons to question whether theological realism should enter into public life in ways that go beyond its influence on the individual search for meaning.

We should not exaggerate this problem, or pretend that the lack of a theological narrative turns liberal democracy into a moral wasteland.[35] A great deal of the moral life is concerned with specific choices about how people create and maintain goods in contexts. Our moral evaluations of people turn largely on how well and how conscientiously they do that, rather than on the theological commitments by which they give meaning to their choices. Nor should we suppose that religious people are always preoccupied with theological questions as they make their moral decisions. If theological realism is centrally concerned with God's activity, then it may often be the case that the most appropriate way to acknowledge theological realities in our choices is to trust that God's activity will continue as God intends it, whether or not we know how to relate our choices to it. It is often the mark of a totalitarian ideology that it insists that minute decisions about daily life have to be made in light of the class struggle or for the good of "the People." Weber regarded this focus on ultimate ends as the opposite of responsible action, and he feared that the religious person who says, "The Christian does rightly and leaves the results with the Lord," would be similarly irresponsible.[36] Bonhoeffer, however, understood that leaving the meaning of an action to God might have the effect of freeing the agent to be responsible, to think about foreseeable consequences in concrete circumstances, without claiming to determine ultimate good and evil. "Those who act on the basis of ideology refuse on principle to ask the question about the consequences of their action. This allows them to be more certain about their own goodness than those who act responsibly, within the limits of their abilities, after having seriously considered the consequences. Those who act on the basis of ideology consider themselves justified by their idea. Those who act responsibly place their action in the hands of God and live by God's grace and judgment."[37]

There are many reasons, then, to think that Christian realists and liberal pluralists will discover large areas of cooperation and agreement on specific moral choices. There is no reason for Christian realists to suppose that they

---

[35] Jeffrey Stout rejects this "traditionalist" criticism of liberal democracy in more detail and with more eloquence, but for some of the same reasons that I deploy here. See Jeffrey Stout, *Democracy and Tradition* (Princeton, NJ: Princeton University Press, 2004).

[36] Max Weber, "Politics as a Vocation," in H. H. Gerth and C. Wright Mills (eds.), *From Max Weber* (New York: Oxford University Press, 1946), p. 120. See p. 92 earlier.

[37] Bonhoeffer, *Ethics*, pp. 225–6.

must recalibrate every decision in light of their theology as they make it, or to fear that if they find themselves in agreement with others who do not share that theology, they must somewhere have been unfaithful.

Nevertheless, the question remains to be asked whether theological realism enters into public life in ways that impose constraints on how a society might combine and order human goods into a way of life. In light of God's ultimate judgment, will the Christian realist say that there are things that every way of life (not just every Christian way of life) ought to include? Are there ways of life that, on theological grounds, society should exclude or prohibit, so that no one is allowed to give life meaning and purpose according to that understanding?

These questions are specific. We are asking about Christian theological realism, which is a tradition of thought that has its own history, which we have traced, and its distinctive ways of understanding the reality of God. Like Rawlsian liberalism, the answers Christian realism will give to these questions "vary within a more or less narrow range."[38] We are not here concerned with hypotheticals about possible theological realisms. Could the Nazis have supplied their "German Christian" movement with a theological realism? Or, to use a favorite case for marking the limits of liberal toleration, could a cannibal cult of theological realists argue that their rites are sanctioned by theological reality in a way that makes their observance morally binding on society as a whole? There are reasons to think that both are implausible,[39] but we are not here concerned with those arguments. We are concerned with Christian theological realism, and we want to inquire specifically into its implications for society. We want to know whether there are ways of life that are not available, if Christian theological realism is a true account of the moral universe we happen to inhabit.

RESPONSIBILITY AND THEOLOGICAL REALISM

For both Reinhold Niebuhr and Dietrich Bonhoeffer, the first implication of theological realism is human freedom for responsible action. The general characteristics of responsibility have been described by social theorists such as Weber and exemplified by leading political figures.[40] It may be

---

[38] John Rawls, *Political Liberalism* (New York: Columbia University Press, 1993), p. 164.

[39] Christopher Insole suggests that theological realism provides a strategy of argument against absolutist, totalitarian, or repressive communities of belief and practice. See Christopher J. Insole, *The Realist Hope* (Aldershot, UK: Ashgate Publishing Company, 2006), pp. 191–3.

[40] Bonhoeffer mentions Gladstone and Bismarck as contrasting paradigms of political responsibility. See Bonhoeffer, *Ethics*, p. 274.

agreed that responsible action involves a limited sphere of responsibility in which decisions are made after considering the predictable consequences and with respect to a group of persons for whom one is acting and to whom one is accountable. Unlike a bystander or a critic from outside, the responsible person cannot avoid these decisions, but the authority that confers this responsibility for the decision never provides an absolute justification for one choice rather than another. For Niebuhr and Bonhoeffer, however, it is also important to understand these historical and social conditions that impose responsibilities in theological terms. When Niebuhr says, "We are men, not God; we are responsible for making choices between greater and lesser evils,"[41] he suggests that it is in relation to the reality of God that we understand our humanity. Apart from the historical and social circumstances of a responsible decision, responsibility must be defined negatively by saying that it is not a judgment about the ultimate meaning of our actions. That judgment belongs to God, and it is not ours to make.

This frees us, as Bonhoeffer said, to act responsibly. We can risk failure without risking meaning. But God's ultimate judgment also keeps us from claiming too much for our successes. Beyond historical conflicts and settlements, there is a divine justice in which all claims are satisfied and all needs are met. Beyond the conflicting and competing goods that we know, there is also a "theological *summum bonum*"[42] that ranks above all other goods and sets them in right relationship to one another. We cannot take responsibility for that good, but knowing that it exists should keep us from claiming that a moral theory based, say, on value pluralism tells us all there is to know about the moral universe we happen to inhabit. Christian theological realism keeps people who happen to be both responsible and comfortable from becoming too satisfied with their achievements. That is part of what connects it to the moral tradition of the Hebrew prophets.

Christian political realism warns political systems not to think too highly of themselves, but moral realism suggests that the human goods provided by liberal democracy are genuine achievements, and theological realism, taken by itself, does not determine how much satisfaction with those achievements is too much. It is understandable, therefore, that when liberal democracy enjoys such widespread global attention, political theorists and theologians

---

[41] Reinhold Niebuhr, "Theology and Political Thought in the Western World," *The Ecumenical Review* 9 (1957), 254.
[42] Cf. Galston, *The Practice of Liberal Pluralism*, pp. 194–5.

will spend some time arguing about its successes and its limits. That was not the situation when Niebuhr and Bonhoeffer wrote about politics in the 1930s and 1940s. The problem then was not how much democracy had accomplished. In Germany, particularly, those results were dismal, and even in the United States, the social order based on bourgeois democracy and capitalist economics seemed to many to be destined for replacement.[43] What the Christian realism of Niebuhr and Bonhoeffer faced were extravagant estimates of future success by ideologies that promised to escape history by abolishing the conditions that had led to the failures of capitalism and democracy. Private ownership of the means of production and the inevitable wars between competing bourgeois states were the sources of war and poverty, according to the communists, and once these were eliminated by a proletarian revolution, war and poverty would disappear, too. Individualism and the erosion of authority are the real problems, replied the fascists. Replace democracy and individualism with a strong leader and patriotic commitment and the weakness that allows outside forces to sap the nation's wealth and strength will disappear. Prosperity and imperial glory on a millennial scale will take their place.

The distinctive response of Christian realism to these ideologies was not a specific refutation of their political and economic theories, but a theological critique of their versions of human hope. Because we are, as Niebuhr said, responsible human beings who make choices between greater and lesser evils, we should be suspicious when someone offers us a choice that is not cast in these human terms, a political program that offers not more or less, but all or nothing. Because theological realism sees God's creation, redemption, and reconciliation of the world as the one final choice that determines the meaning of history, political programs that promise a final determination of history as the result of our choices cannot possibly be right.

Human nature is more durable than political systems, and the biblical understanding of human nature provides a better assessment of political possibilities and limitations than any of the ancient or modern utopias that offer a more flattering portrait of our humanity.[44] Known human goods are organized around the social contexts that Bonhoeffer called the "divine mandates," and these have a claim to integrity that goes beyond historical precedent. The differentiated spheres of life into which modern society is organized are not susceptible to abolition, recombination, or ordering

---

[43] See p. 19 earlier.   [44] Niebuhr, *Nature and Destiny*, vol. I, pp. 1–25.

into superior and inferior. They are unified only in Christ, that is, only as part of "the reality of the world that was reconciled to God in the manger, the cross, and the resurrection of Jesus Christ."[45] Any attempt to impose another unity on them, in service of some other purpose, will fail.

Bonhoeffer's claim here is a strong one, but it rests on a paradigmatic statement of theological realism. "The world stands in relationship to Christ whether the world knows it or not."[46] God and God's activity in history exist independently of our ideas about them. If the Christian's claim about God's activity is true, it is true for everyone, not just for those who believe it to be true. If it is God's activity that unites the disparate, often competing realms of effort that make up modern life, then claims that they can be unified on other terms are mistaken.

Niebuhr, as we have seen, worried that these claims about the importance and permanence of the contexts of responsible choice could too easily be bent to the support of existing institutions and social hierarchies, and he no doubt found Bonhoeffer's claims for the divine mandates overstated.[47] He would not have argued with the theological point behind Bonhoeffer's insistence that the mandates are unified only in Christ, however. The reality of God's ultimate judgment renders all human judgments partial and provisional. Niebuhr would add that this includes judgments about the permanence and completeness of an inventory of "divine mandates," but Bonhoeffer's aim was to put the unity of human good beyond the reach of the ideologies and revolutionary movements of his time. Niebuhr would agree with that completely.

The first effect of theological realism for Niebuhr and Bonhoeffer was thus to limit the scope of all political claims about the future. Because the point is theological, it remains valid against all political systems and relevant to public life even after the specific ideologies which they addressed have disappeared from history or have been discredited by more specific criticisms of their historical and economic theories. Analyses that promise the end of evil cannot be correct, if theological reality is anything like the way it is represented in Christian eschatology.[48] Those analyses, therefore, cannot serve as the starting point for responsible action.

Theological realism, however, also suggests a certain restraint in the scope of theological claims. Theology must not simply try to fill the place it has denied to ideology. The full reality of God's activity in history transcends

---

[45] Bonhoeffer, *Ethics*, p. 73.   [46] *Ibid.*, p. 68.   [47] See pp. 103–04 earlier.
[48] Cf. David Frum and Richard Perle, *An End to Evil* (New York: Random House, 2003).

any ideological system that reduces history to orderly principles of action of which we are the primary agents. That is why all such ideologies are false. But the full reality of God's activity in history transcends theological systems, too. Theology must not falsify itself by posing as a better ideology.

For Niebuhr, "the real point of contact between democracy and profound religion is in the spirit of humility which democracy requires and which must be one of the fruits of religion."[49] Theological realism focuses our immediate attention on responsible choices, giving meaning to those choices without fostering the illusion that we could explain or justify them completely. It allows us to take our situation seriously, without requiring it to be perfect, and to speak meaningfully of good and evil in this life, even though we know that meaning finally depends on realities that are beyond our knowing and our doing. "From a Christian perspective," Bonhoeffer writes, "the fallen world becomes understandable as the world preserved and maintained by God for the coming of Christ, a world in which we *as human beings* can and should live a '*good*' life in given orders."[50]

Both the "can" and the "should," are important in Bonhoeffer's statement. The structures of social life summed up in the mandates of work, family, church, and government allow us to live a life that deserves to be called "good." We should therefore devote ourselves to that task and not abandon this life to God's judgment or postpone living until after the revolution. Greater justice is always possible, as are more complete community and more sustainable culture, but the obligations we have to work for these things must, for a Christian theological realist, be compatible with a good life in the present.[51]

No single ordering of human goods within history emerges from this provisional affirmation of the structures of social life. Efforts to create a way of life by simply abolishing the existing structures are foreclosed, but no claims are made for the perfection of work, family, church, and government as we have them. They exist in a certain tension with one another, under the conditions of history in this fallen world. The boundaries between them are subject to constant testing and renegotiation, and if those tensions are ignored or those boundaries are erased, we are no longer speaking of the divine mandates.[52] The mandates are not ultimate, but they have a certain presumptive authority, based on the penultimate good they make possible. This cannot be arbitrarily sacrificed to idealized claims about the future,

---

[49] Niebuhr, *The Children of Light and the Children of Darkness*, p. 151.   [50] *Ibid.*, p. 165.
[51] See p. 108 earlier.   [52] *Ibid.*, pp. 370, 393–4.

even when the mandates are not functioning as well as they should in the present.[53]

THE TASK OF THEOLOGICAL REALISM

A way of life shaped by theological realism thus fits comfortably into a society organized by the principles of liberal pluralism. Both regard the variety of existing social institutions as a reflection of the variety of real human goods. Both reject ideologies that would replace these institutions with a new, unified social order that refers all choices to some single good or goal. Neither requires that the systems of family, government, faith, or commerce function perfectly or even supposes that they are perfectible. A Christian realism formulated along the lines suggested by Niebuhr and Bonhoeffer does not contradict the political principles of a liberal society and may, in fact, hold liberal pluralism more closely to its own purposes.

Still, there is more to be said. The negative, critical task of eliminating proposals that impose an ideological unity on ideas or a revolutionary unity on institutions is one that liberal political theory and theological realism can share. It is appropriate to a successful liberal democracy in which the important historical choices have largely been acceptable. If we were not tempted to be satisfied with things as they are, we would not need theological realism's reminder that something better is possible. It also assumes a free political system, open to correction when utopian aspirations or apocalyptic self-righteousness get the better of its grasp of reality.

In those fortunate and relatively rare historical circumstances, some important theological considerations fade into the background of ideas that need not be challenged, even if they are not universally shared. In a liberal democracy with a long history and strong religious traditions, it is easy to slip into the assumption that everybody really believes the same thing, but some people like to get together and sing hymns about it. It is important for the theologians, at least, to keep the differences between theological realism and political liberalism in mind, to study the points at which theological realism has come into conflict with other forces shaping the direction of society, and to work continually at restating its implications for our present situation.

This is in some respects an intellectual exercise, but it is an important one. It is a task better suited to the lecture hall and the symposium than to

---

[53] *Ibid.*, p. 70; See also Reinhold Niebuhr, *Christian Realism and Political Problems* (New York: Charles Scribner's Sons, 1953), pp. 110–11.

the street demonstration or the campaign rally. In those venues, it is often more important to know what we share with the people on either side of us than to know where we differ. Focusing on the differences need not turn the Christian realist into a cultural pessimist, as though it were clear from the outset that society has always already lost touch with theological reality or become incapable of understanding it. But we will want to be alert to the points where that may be happening. Otherwise, we may fail to recognize a decisive moment of conflict when it comes.

That was the situation that Dietrich Bonhoeffer faced, especially in the German churches at the beginning of the Nazi era, because National Socialism took other forms besides a revolutionary ideology that sets out to abolish the existing social order. Nazism could also present itself as a conservative movement. At the same time that Hitler was destroying conventional social forms of rank and power to appeal to a younger generation disillusioned by German defeat, he promised the established leaders of business, church, and culture that he would secure the German order against the threat of Soviet communism. It was that conservative side of Nazism that often attracted the pastors and people of the German churches.[54]

In the face of these anxieties, business, church, and culture could each be promised that it would become a bulwark against revolutionary change through cooperation with the new Nazi political order. Traditional authorities were, in fact, strengthened, and their control over German institutions provided additional channels for directing workers, parishioners, and students in the ways the new regime required. Thus, the distinction between the "orders" was at least superficially maintained in ways that proved attractive to a conservative theology.

The difficulty Bonhoeffer had in formulating a theology within his tradition that would be adequate to distinguish the Christian confession from its Nazi corruption is a reminder why the ongoing critical work of theology is important at all times. The most difficult task is not to formulate a theology that explains the evil in an external enemy without falling victim to our own illusions of righteousness. That was Niebuhr's task, and he did it so well that his insights still illuminate the relationships between Christianity and democracy half a century later. The most difficult task, however, is to isolate the central convictions of Christian faith from the

---

[54] Bonhoeffer, by contrast, learned from early experience in a working-class parish in Berlin about the distance between the privileges of the established church and the insecurities of most Germans during the Weimar era. See Eberhard Bethge, *Dietrich Bonhoeffer: Man of Vision, Man of Courage* (New York: Harper and Row, 1970), pp. 168–74.

shared assumptions of a culture, so that what supports a social and political order at one point is kept available for use against it, if necessary. That was Bonhoeffer's task, and it may at any point become ours: To use the terms that belong to what has been an "overlapping consensus" of important shared values to explain why we now must call the consensus into question.

THE PERSON AND THE GOOD

Bonhoeffer thus begins his ethics by "renewing and reclaiming the old concepts of order, estate, and office."[55] This work of renewal is difficult to get right, and each of the many ways it can be wrongly done appeals to particular social and political interests for their own reasons. The whole idea of social "orders" seems to some inherently conservative, which makes the concept suspect to those who want change and attractive to those who do not. The division of society along vocational lines suggests to many a hierarchy of authority and a narrowing of attention that serves to keep people from raising questions that those in authority do not want to hear. The theologies of the Protestant Reformation raised the appreciation of secular callings to a higher level, but they could also limit an individual's moral life to that narrow vocational context. The goods pursued by the merchant or the carpenter were as real and as worthy as those pursued by the pastor, but they did not fit a person for judgments about matters that fell outside of his vocational competence. The ruler, as we have seen, had a specific calling to provide an order that was largely independent of other goods. For other people, the appropriate way to seek the goods government provides was "obey and suffer."[56]

Bonhoeffer, moreover, understood that modern lives are not so easily lived in a single vocation. The craftsman or merchant in Luther's time might easily live a whole life around the workshop or the warehouse, with family and workers living on the premises, and the parish church and school nearby. Such a person might even enjoy a sense of identity and freedom greater than those a few generations back who toiled as peasants on the land. Our life cannot be lived that way. Its settings are more differentiated, and anyone who lives what could be called a good life draws identity from several different places. In such circumstances, it does not take the intrusion of a totalitarian government to introduce tensions between work, faith, and family. The conflict is part of life.

---

[55] Bonhoeffer, *Ethics*, p. 390. See pp. 101–03 earlier.   [56] See p. 69 earlier.

In its original form, the doctrine of orders threatens to treat the separation of these spheres of activity as a religious obligation, and thus to introduce a dangerous unreality into our attempts to deal with these tensions.[57] So the mandates must be unified in some way, if people are to have lives that can be called good, but everything depends on how that unity is understood. For Bonhoeffer, the theological understanding must be Christological. That is, it must engage us with God's activity in history as it is fully present in Jesus Christ. "Human beings as whole persons stand before the whole earthly and eternal reality that God in Jesus Christ has prepared for them."[58]

Like other assertions made by Christian theological realism, Bonhoeffer's affirmation is eschatological. As we have seen, the unity of the mandates in Christ cannot be anticipated by a social theory or a political program. There is no authority to whom we can listen who will prepare us to stand before this whole earthly and eternal reality. Nor should we mistake this assertion of the eschatological unity of reality in Christ for some claim about the historical Jesus, as though his words and actions give us a model of this unity which we can attempt to follow, even if from a distance. The sayings of Jesus, as we have seen, become relevant precisely as they direct us to concrete realities and present responsibilities.[59] The unity of all things in Christ is something else again. We anticipate it as the completion of God's work which gives meaning to our attempts at responsible action. We cannot grasp it by asking what Jesus would do.

Nevertheless, this unity is not solely eschatological. Jesus Christ is the presence of God within history and not only beyond it. Through Christ, God's grace and judgment become available in our lives, and we are enabled to see glimpses of the meaning that those lives have in this larger reality. Here, Bonhoeffer closely follows Karl Barth's idea of election: By entering into history in Jesus Christ, God chooses all humanity to participate in God's activity of creation, redemption, and fulfillment.[60]

To say that the mandates are unified in Jesus Christ is thus to say both that the differences between them cannot be erased prematurely by human activity and that they are already brought together in the human person. It is not for some other part of God's creation that these orders, goods, and values exist, but precisely so that human life may be preserved for God's ultimate redemption. This allows Bonhoeffer to establish the relationship between the "ultimate" and the "penultimate," between eschatology and

---

[57] Bonhoeffer, *Ethics*, p. 74.   [58] *Ibid.*, p. 73.   [59] See p. 97 earlier.

[60] Karl Barth, *Church Dogmatics*, G. W. Bromiley (trans.) (Edinburgh: T. & T. Clark, 1957), II/2, 94–145; Cf. Bonhoeffer, *Ethics*, pp. 301–02, especially note 13.

the field of human activity that precedes God's judgment and redemption.[61] What can be done to restore human life to its proper orientation in each of the mandates is not, in itself, capable of restoring the right relation between persons and God, but it prepares the way for the ultimate. It is part of creating the space in which judgment and redemption happen. It is in this connection that Bonhoeffer says that human beings "can and should live a '*good*' life in given orders."[62]

The hungry person needs bread, the homeless person needs shelter, the one deprived of rights needs justice, the lonely person needs community, the undisciplined one needs order, and the slave needs freedom. It would be blasphemy against God and our neighbor to leave the hungry unfed while saying that God is closest to those in deepest need. We break bread with the hungry and share our home with them for the sake of Christ's love, which belongs to the hungry as much as it does to us. If the hungry do not come to faith, the guilt falls on those who denied them bread. To bring bread to the hungry is preparing the way for the coming of grace.[63]

It is in acts of service "for the sake of Christ's love" that make good lives in given orders possible that our diverse responsibilities and the competing goods they seek become unified in Christ.

WAYS OF LIFE

In these reflections on the penultimate, Bonhoeffer returns us to more general questions about ways of life and their relation to the order of a society. No single way of life follows from this understanding of how our concrete responsibilities are unified, but we learn what gives a life meaning in any historical or cultural setting. To be sure, Bonhoeffer's reflections are tied very closely to the German reality in which he lived and wrote, and the terms of his reflections on the penultimate are addressed principally to those who share his Christian faith. Attending to the penultimate is, as he says, "a commission of immeasurable responsibility given to all who know about the coming of Jesus Christ."[64] At a personal level, therefore, this commission ought to resolve some of the questions about a meaningful life that modern politics throws back on the individual to resolve.

Is there anything more to be said if we take this seriously as theological realism? If the way that human goods and the institutions that create them come together in the human person as known through Jesus Christ is not only a confession of faith, but also an aspect of "the moral universe

---

[61] Bonhoeffer, *Ethics*, pp. 146–70.   [62] *Ibid.*, p. 165. See p. 199 earlier.   [63] *Ibid.*, p. 163.
[64] *Ibid.*

we happen to inhabit," does anything follow for the ordering of society generally? Are there, to repeat the question with which we began, things that every way of life (not just every Christian way of life) ought to include? Are there ways of life that, on theological grounds, society should exclude or prohibit, so that no one is allowed to give life meaning and purpose according to that understanding?

If human goods are unified in persons, that aspect of the moral universe might call into question ways of life that treat persons as instrumental to the creation of goods. It is not immediately obvious that value pluralism can exclude values that some people might want to pursue at great cost to the welfare and opportunities of others. Liberal pluralism addresses this problem by using political principles of consent and freedom to rule out such ways of life on political grounds, despite the fact that someone might come up with a comprehensive doctrine that includes them.[65] For Christian theological realism, the comprehensive doctrine itself rules out aristocratic ways of life, in which large resources are devoted to creating certain goods and providing leisure for persons of special talent to enjoy those goods and refine them. In such a life, the good itself becomes the source of meaning, and even those who enjoy, understand, and cultivate it become its servants. This is especially problematic if the nature of this good or the state of development in the society requires large numbers of people who are literally servants to those who serve the good. But Christian theological realism raises the question whether such an aristocracy is an acceptable way of life, even when technological development and a generally prosperous society minimize the exploitation of others. Imagine a society in which a large number of people were paid good wages and otherwise treated well in return for devoting their working hours exclusively to attending to the needs of a class of experts who, in turn, gave their lives without reservation to solving complex technical problems which they alone had the ability and the desire to master. Would that be an acceptable way of life? Would it be so different from the way of life at the upper levels of a large corporation, a major law firm, or a research university?

The idea that human goods are unified in the person precludes social and institutional arrangements that subordinate persons to particular goods or to the contexts where those goods are created and maintained. This principle is easily stated, but it is difficult to uphold in practice, because creating and maintaining human goods does require discipline and even sacrifice on the part of those who are responsible for them. Regular hours of work,

[65] Galston, *Liberal Pluralism*, p. 62.

study to acquire knowledge and skills, and the postponement of present enjoyment to invest in future productivity all will seem oppressive at times, but we must subordinate ourselves to them up to a point, if we are to have any goods beyond those that are found lying about in nature or left over from previous generations. More difficult situations arise when the burdens of discipline fall unevenly on the people involved. Competition and profit are measures by which the business context disciplines itself to produce goods efficiently and in proportion to the demand for them. It is, however, harder to affirm those disciplines if your job has been outsourced or downsized than if you are in one of the positions that remains at the end of the adjustment. We cannot replace those disciplines with a utopian idea: "From each according to his ability, to each according to his needs!"[66] The unity of the good in the person does, however, tell us that disciplines essential to the creation of particular goods must be subject to critical examination of their effects on persons.

We see a recent example of this theological realism in the papal encyclical *Centesimus Annus*. In that commentary on the hundredth anniversary of Leo XIII's *Rerum Novarum*, John Paul II begins by acknowledging efficiency of free markets and the role of profit as an indicator of economic efficiency. Nonetheless, despite the legitimacy of profit and efficiency as a rule of economic life, a profitable and efficient business may operate in ways that leave its workers without a living wage or means to make a contribution to the common good beyond their labor that goes into the business. Social and governmental forces thus appropriately limit the disciplines of the market to ensure that there is provision for the dignity of the people involved, in addition to a fair and efficient exchange of goods. "It is a strict duty of justice and truth not to allow fundamental human needs to remain unsatisfied, and not to allow those burdened by such needs to perish. It is also necessary to help these needy people to acquire expertise, to enter the circle of exchange, and to develop their skills in order to make the best use of their capacities and resources."[67] The ways that social and governmental forces limit the operations of the market will vary with circumstances, but they must consider the good of the people concerned and engage their active participation. No ideal patterns or absolute rules can be laid down

---

[66] Karl Marx, "Critique of the Gotha Program," in Robert C. Tucker (ed.), *The Marx-Engels Reader* (2ed.) (New York: W. W. Norton, 1978), p. 531. Marx, of course, thought that this ideal state of affairs could only be reached when capitalism and socialism had been superseded by genuine communism.

[67] John Paul II, "Centesimus Annus: On the Hundredth Anniversary of Rerum Novarum," in David O'Brien and Thomas Shannon (eds.), *Catholic Social Thought: The Documentary Heritage* (Maryknoll, NY: Orbis Books, 1992), p. 464.

for this. The point is rather that the rules of economic order must not themselves be treated as absolute.

When laws passed by a legislature protect workers from harm by the laws of economics, something more is at work than the process of claim and counterclaim by which a modern, pluralistic society fixes the boundaries between contexts. The same is true when historical investigations in universities and other institutions of culture are used to demand reparations on behalf of those who have been harmed by acts of government, or when the church protests culturally sanctioned prejudice and discrimination, or when, to complete the circle, government protects children from exploitation by their parents or by religious groups. Each of these developments marks a recognition that persons should not be treated as mere means to the goods they can create, whether those goods are the products of a business, the care of a family, an artistic creation, or a piece of legislation. Nor can the claims of persons be limited to mere survival, just enough so that they can be productive again, or to what will make them even more productive at the tasks someone else has assigned to them. The unity of persons transcends their social roles and is not exhausted by what they have to contribute to any one context, or to all of them together.

THE INTEGRITY OF THE PERSON

There is, then, an integrity of persons that gives meaning to the integrity of contexts which we considered previously.[68] The claims any context can make are limited not only by the claims of other contexts, but by the integrity of the persons who participate in them. Without this integrity, persons would have no more than the space which happened to be left to them by the particular juxtaposition of contexts in the place and time where they live.[69] They would have just as much religious freedom as the church happened to wrest from the state, just as much responsibility for their children as the family successfully claimed against church and state, just those economic rights which the collective influences of church and culture could soften the hearts of business and government to provide. That something is missing from such an account of persons and their rights is obvious when we look at it in this comprehensive way. The idea of a person

---

[68] See pp. 126–32 earlier.

[69] William Schweiker argues this point specifically with reference to economic life. See William Schweiker, "Responsibility in the World of Mammon," in Max Stackhouse and Peter Paris (eds.), *Religion and the Powers of the Common Life*, God and Globalization, vol. 1 (Harrisburg, PA: Trinity International Press, 2000), pp. 105–39.

completely subordinated to the laws of economics sends us scurrying to government to try to limit the economic context and fix the problem. But the idea of a person subordinated simultaneously to the laws of economics, the laws of the state, the doctrines of the church, the expectations of culture, and the demands of family is absurd. What we need to fix in that case is our understanding of the person who exists in the center of these contending social forces.

This is an important point in relation to versions of liberalism that identify it closely with the freedom of individual choices, so that the distributive results of democratic choice and market mechanisms are not subject to moral criticism.[70] It also implies a criticism of those earlier versions of political pluralism which suggested that the integrity of the various social spheres provides all the protection needed for the integrity of the person. Abraham Kuyper, for example, regarded each of the spheres of social life as having a kind of sovereignty, in the sense that there was no power above it except the power of God.[71] This is an answer to those who would make everything dependent on the positive law of the state, but it may not adequately address the integrity of the person, who in the modern world may be caught between the competing claims of these sovereign spheres rather than protected by them.

This integrity of the person seems to be the point of Bonhoeffer's theological claim that the mandates are unified in Christ. He understood that people can be divided by the different mandates in which they live and thrown into conflict within themselves by the claims that the mandates make against one another. Older ideas in the tradition had contributed to this fragmentation, but Bonhoeffer does not intend to continue it. Instead of separate estates or realms each conveying a command of God to the person, the mandates come together in the reality of God become human.

This is the witness the church has to give to the world, that all the other mandates are not there to divide people and tear them apart but to deal with them as whole people before God the Creator, Reconciler, and Redeemer – that reality in all its manifold aspects is ultimately *one* in God who became human, Jesus Christ. The divine mandates in the world are not there to wear people down through endless conflicts. Rather, they aim at the whole human being who stands in reality before God.[72]

---

[70] See, for example, Robert Nozick, *Anarchy, State, and Utopia* (New York: Basic Books, 1974), pp. 149–74.

[71] Abraham Kuyper, *Lectures on Calvinism* (Grand Rapids, MI: Eerdmans, 2000), p. 91. See also John Neville Figgis, *Churches in the Modern State* (London: Longmans, Green and Co., 1913), pp. 49–53.

[72] Bonhoeffer, *Ethics*, p. 73.

Instead of subjecting each person to the duties of separate and distinct mandates, Bonhoeffer reverses the traditional understanding of the orders. The person is now where these distinct goods, with their different and possibly conflicting imperatives, must come together. "God has placed human beings under these mandates, not only each individual under one or the other, but all people under all four."[73] The diversity of contexts and the variety of human goods they create and maintain make possible a wholeness of life, in which all goods can be enjoyed in appropriate relations to each other and in relation to God.

The placement of all persons in all contexts seems to require active participation in each of them. Simply enjoying the goods that a context makes possible does not contribute to the wholeness of a person. The point is to be a part of the creating and maintaining of these goods. Programs that rectify distributive injustice without correcting the marginalization that limits participation accomplish only part of what justice requires. David Hollenbach summarizes recent Catholic social teaching on social justice in these terms, but his point applies to all forms of pluralistic realism: "Persons can only live in dignity when they are capable of interacting with others in society, whether in the economic, political, and cultural spheres."[74] Those who are full participants in public life do not merely create and distribute goods according to an ideal plan maintained by some other authority. They have that authority among themselves, and they reshape the goods as they create and maintain them. A way of life which respects human dignity seeks that full participation for all persons in all contexts. Then, the diversity of goods no longer threatens irreconcilable conflict, but promises fulfillment.

People enter the context of business and economics because each person needs goods that can be adequately supplied only by complex, organized systems of production that utilize limited resources in the most efficient way. By subjecting ourselves to those disciplines, we gain the freedom to enjoy a level of material well-being far beyond what our own efforts at subsistence could provide, but we also acknowledge our solidarity with everyone else who shares this productivity, our dependence on economic systems and technologies inherited from the past, and our responsibility to pass them on in sustainable forms to the future. The economy becomes a vast cooperative effort with its own order and even beauty. It is a system within which competition has a place, rather than a system of competition. By tempering

---

[73] *Ibid.*, p. 69.
[74] David Hollenbach, *The Common Good and Christian Ethics* (Cambridge: Cambridge University Press, 2002), p. 198.

the requirements of efficiency to the realities of human need, work becomes a part of the common good, rather than a mechanism for acquiring goods for ourselves from which we might share a portion, elsewhere and later. Each person needs to be connected to others, immediate and more remote, by these systems of shared work.

People enter into the context of government because each person needs security, order, and a predictable framework for settling disputes that inevitably arise in the other contexts of work, family, faith, and culture. Not to participate in these decisions with all the other people who happen to share a part of the earth with us would be a denial of our common humanity. It would either express the hope that conflict will not come near to those who refuse to defend themselves or proclaim to the world that all these goods are so indifferent to us that protecting them from destruction and observing justice in their exchange are matters beneath our notice. Those are positions toward secular authority which Christians have taken in times of apocalyptic crisis or utopian optimism, but they are not the theological realism of a whole person who stands in Christ before the whole of reality. In light of God's ultimate judgment, each person needs the penultimate security and order that government alone can provide, and each thus has a concern for how that government understands justice.

The context of family begins at birth, for parents and children alike. People sustain and nurture those relationships beyond the dependence of childhood and expand them beyond biological connections because everyone needs a context in which dependence is not exploited and acceptance is not conditional upon past achievements or future promise. That is why families do not conduct tenure reviews.

Or perhaps we should say that family is to be found in relationships where such reviews are not done. There is much controversy today in church and society over which relationships should be called "marriage" and what groups are suitably called a "family." The idea of persons whose whole lives are related to all of reality in Christ suggests to me at least that alongside relationships where justice is important, everyone needs loving relationships where they willingly give more than they receive, and alongside relationships where shared productivity is important, everyone needs relationships where they have gratuitous enjoyment of another person's companionship. It is sentimental to think that those relationships just happen, without the support of social structures that recognize and respect them, or that they will sustain themselves through good times and bad without public commitments that raise them above the level of personal convenience. A way of life that omits such relationships is incomplete, however successful it may be in other contexts. A way of life that organizes itself to despise some of these relationships or prevent others from having them is perverse.

Beyond the structured contexts of economics and government and the intimate relationships of family, people also require a variety of more fluid, elective relationships that we may loosely group together in the context of culture. In these ways, they pursue knowledge, acquire new skills, share the enjoyment of art and music, and connect with other parts of the world and other ways of life through media and communications. Although these activities in today's world are severely limited for many people by lack of access, lack of resources, or the competing demands of work and family, this is the context in which we most clearly experience those specific human goods and excellences that Alasdair MacIntyre called "goods internal to practices."[75] For many, of course, research, art, or teaching is also their work, but these persons have a particular obligation not to allow the disciplines and satisfactions of that work to become subordinated to economic necessity. To call the relationships we have in culture "elective" is accurate, since it is here, especially, that we pursue interests and passions and follow lines of inquiry as far as we choose to take them. At the same time, the goods created in culture impose their own rules and methods and create communities of evaluation and criticism appropriate to their specific fields. To participate in culture, rather than merely to consume its products, involves learning the rules and methods and participating in the communities of evaluation and criticism. That is why universities *do* conduct tenure reviews, and why cultural organizations generally should not be confused with families.

Finally, there is religion, for although we stand before God as whole persons in Christ in every context, there is also a context in which we reflect on that reality and acknowledge it, the place of theology and prayer, of worship and discipleship. It is difficult to speak of religion in general terms. A multiplicity of states, corporations, and cultures pose no problem when we speak of government, work, and culture, but each community of faith seems to want to represent all persons before the whole of reality on its own terms. Religious pluralism makes it difficult even to find a language for the religious context.

It is important to remember that for Christian theological realism, each person stands before God in Christ whether or not she knows it, and regardless of how truthfully his language represents that reality. To call the

---

[75] Alasdair MacIntyre, *After Virtue*, 2nd ed. (Notre Dame, IN: University of Notre Dame Press, 1984), pp. 188–9.

context in which we reflect on this relation to reality as a whole "religion" recognizes those who would not call that place a church, but it also means to include those who would insist that they have no religion. For purposes of understanding society, theological realism includes within religion all those places where people seek meaning and unity in life beyond the multiplicity of goods and contexts. This does not imply a commitment by the theologian to treat them all with the even-handed neutrality that is appropriate to a government. Some efforts to seek meaning and unity fail, and it is important to point that out when we see it. Nor is the theologian required to leave these failed efforts alone simply because they do not acknowledge that they are religions.[76] By contrast, there are engagements with the penultimate needs of the neighbor that deny any religious motivation which stand in judgment on the failures of organized religions. Theologians who seek to explore what it means to stand before God in Christ will miss much of what they are looking for if they organize their search for religion according to the labels chosen by the participants.

We might, then, be tempted to say that the context of religion is like the context of family, that we each just happen to have the one we have. But faiths are not families. Most faiths are rather clear about that, despite the tendency of congregations in a society where faith is often privatized to speak about "our church family."[77] In order to be whole persons before God, people need traditions that lift them out of the circle of the familiar and connect them with patterns of history that transcend their own doing and acting. Otherwise, the responsible person disappears in the web of responsibilities. That is the main point to Bonhoeffer's statement that the witness of the church is to deal with people as whole persons who stand in reality before God.

Speaking as I do in the tradition of Christian realism, I cannot avoid talking about the church, and my ways of discussing religion in society will no doubt seem sometimes to mean "church," even when I do not say it. I cannot claim to do theology for other traditions, but I invite readers to test what is said about the religious context in relation to other contexts against their own theology, tradition, and experience.

Work, government, family, culture, and religion thus provide a summary understanding of the contexts that must be unified in a person to give life meaning that comes to fulfillment in God's activity within and

---

[76] Cf. Niebuhr's critique of Marxism in Reinhold Niebuhr, *Moral Man and Immoral Society* (Louisville, KY: Westminster John Knox Press, 2001), p. 155.

[77] See, for example, Luke 14:25–27.

beyond history. It is worth repeating here that these contexts are not onto-logical structures that reappear on the same list in every society at every point in history. We have, in fact, again substituted five contexts for Bon-hoeffer's four mandates, in order to provide a more complete statement of how the forces with which whole persons have to deal are differentiated in our time.[78] The key point is not in the list of contexts or in their number, but in Bonhoeffer's insistence that we deal with all people under all of them.

No one should choose a way of life that omits some of these contexts or withdraws into any one of them. Such a way of life may be easier than doing difficult things that we do not do well. It may seem to have virtues of simplicity that are superior to a life that tries to attend to culture, work, and government as well as family and faith. It may receive praise from those who admire the results of our single-minded devotion. It may win tenure and promotion. But it is not the life of a whole person.

More relevant to the life of the whole society is that no context should create such a way of life and make it available for people to choose. A way of life that cuts people off from other contexts cannot be justified by the goods it creates, even if it devotes many of those goods to rewarding the isolated and incomplete persons who have chosen it. Nor should people choose for themselves a way of life that allows them to live as whole persons, but exists only by depriving others of the opportunity. Exploitative systems of labor are excluded, as we suggested earlier, even if the laborers wear white collars. Aristocratic societies which devote all their resources to the cultivation of an elite that creates and maintains specially favored goods are likewise morally impermissible, even if those who limit their own lives to make the elite possible are otherwise well treated.

NEW DIRECTIONS

The Christian realist's theological claim that the unity of human goods is found in the person before God changes our ways of thinking about the fragmentation of life and the conflict of responsibilities with which we began this chapter. It is no longer what political theory makes it, a personal problem to be solved on terms of our own choosing. The conflict between goods is a human and historical problem, which can ultimately be resolved only by God's activity, but which impinges on all the decisions we make about our life together within history.

---

[78] See pp. 104–06 earlier.

The value pluralism that seems to be as far as moral realism can take us toward unity of the good is from this theological perspective a judgment. It marks the penultimate failure of efforts to unify the good on our own terms. But it is a judgment with which we must live. We will not succeed in unifying the good within history, either personally or ideologically. Far from failing to take the realities of pluralism seriously, as liberal theorists fear, the Christian realist treats "conditions of reasonable pluralism" as an historical manifestation of a basic human reality. The limits that social diversity imposes on our efforts to do good and seek justice in modern liberal democracies are part of the conditions of sin which every realistic approach to ethics, especially social ethics, must take into account.

Nevertheless, theological realism rescues the problem of the unity of human good from personal and ideological futility and returns it to the public discussions of modern pluralistic societies in the form of a question: "How do we treat persons as the image of God, taking form in history in the person of Christ?"

The language, of course, is confessionally Christian, but it is not the purpose of theological realism to draw everyone into a particular doctrinal "grammar." Theological realists are talking about reality, and they have the usual responsibility of persons who want to talk about reality to find a way of speaking that communicates with those to whom they want to involve in the discussion.[79] A decent respect for the sensitivities of their conversation partners and an adequate knowledge of history will keep Christian theological realists from relying exclusively on the language of Christian tradition.

In the public forum of every context the Christian realist seeks a recognition of the image of God that refuses to reduce persons to the good they can create and finds meaning in human activity that orders goods toward enabling persons to live responsible lives as full participants in all contexts. That reality sets limits on the available ways of life. These limits do not apply only to those who are seeking to live a Christian way of life. They are part of "the moral universe we happen to inhabit," to return to William Galston's phrase.

Theological realism thus supplies an idea of human dignity that is intelligible and accessible in a public forum that can grasp its political implications, even if many of the participants do not share the theology. This idea of human dignity is not, in itself, a theory of human rights, but it could easily

---

[79] Insole, *The Realist Hope*, pp. 190–3.

become one.[80] It takes only a little familiarity with the accounts of human rights developed over the last several centuries to translate the contexts in which all persons must participate in order to lead whole human lives into various kinds of rights. Negative rights – right of liberty or freedom – require that persons remain undisturbed in their pursuit and enjoyment of the human goods that the contexts provide. Positive rights – welfare or social rights – assert the claim that persons have on society for the opportunity to participate in each context and on the resources they need to make use of that opportunity. Rights of participation, or social justice, require that all persons be received on equal terms as participants in the contexts, so that they not only enjoy the goods created and maintained, but have a share in shaping them.[81]

If Christian realists developed such an account of human rights and made it law, they would have a system of law and government based directly on an understanding that human beings are created in the image of God, as that image takes form in Jesus Christ. Judging from the requirements of human dignity as we found them in the theological realism of Niebuhr and Bonhoeffer, it would be a political system that resembles in many ways the combination of rights, freedoms, and democratic participation we find in liberal democracy. It would also be a political system that contradicts liberal political theory. Rawls, certainly, would reject the use of this comprehensive image of human good as the basis for the formulation of political principles. Galston, who allows comprehensive doctrine to influence the understanding of political principles, would no doubt object in this case that the theology had simply replaced those political principles. There would also be questions about pluralism, which might not be fully answered by the theological realist's claim that it is reality that dictates this way of respecting human dignity, not the confessional theological language we are using here to talk about it. At the very least, Galston might ask if he could substitute a different confessional language, perhaps that of Abrahamic monotheism, for Bonhoeffer's Christological terminology on which I have relied here.

Let us concede the point about language for present purposes. Theological realists are subtle enough about the meaning of words to recognize that different systems of words convey different meanings, but they also

---

[80] On the transition from human dignity to human rights, see Michael Perry, *Toward a Theory of Human Rights: Religion, Law, Courts* (Cambridge: Cambridge University Press, 2007), pp. 33–6.

[81] David Hollenbach, *The Common Good and Christian Ethics* (Cambridge: Cambridge University Press, 2002), pp. 159–64.

recognize that there are a variety of ways to refer to the same divine reality, within each religious tradition as well as in the differences between them. Theological realism is not so committed as some versions of unapologetic theology to a specific Christian language, especially for these purposes of unapologetic politics.[82] Beyond the important questions about pluralism and how choices of theological language might affect possibilities for full participation on equal terms in the political discussion, how might we reconcile theological realism and political theory on this question of the political implications of human dignity?

One possibility might be to construct a liberal account of human dignity, beginning with political premises internal to liberal political theory itself. Although liberal theory is intended as an account of how a liberal political community should be organized, even its minimal premises about human nature might suggest ways that persons should be held inviolate in any political system. Rawls in his later work suggests at least that liberal societies will extend a minimal set of human rights to all persons, including those who choose not to organize themselves into a liberal society.[83]

If it could be demonstrated that political liberalism has an account of human dignity very similar to the one provided by Christian theological realism, the question whether this dignity is derived from politics or theology could be reduced to a historical question. Liberalism and religious traditions could compete, as it were, for the honor of having introduced the idea to the world. But "human dignity" is useful precisely because it is a very elastic term, and there is little reason to suppose that efforts to specify it in liberal theory and Christian theology would end up in exactly the same place, or even in a very similar one. Liberal theory, in any case, seems to face the problem that the more specific it becomes about persons and what their dignity requires, the more liberalism begins to look like the comprehensive understanding of human good it has sought to avoid. Even a comprehensive political theory seeks to minimize what it requires in the way of substantive moral commitments, in order to give persons maximal freedom to construct their own idea of a meaningful life. That freedom seems central to the liberal pluralist's idea of exactly what it is that gives persons dignity. Locating dignity in that freedom seems, however,

---

[82] This is not, however, a point that can be answered only in theory. The theological realist would have to be prepared to discuss in some detail what meanings might be gained or lost by these shifts of language, and to argue over whether or not the difference makes a difference in the discussion at hand.

[83] John Rawls, *The Law of Peoples* (Cambridge, MA: Harvard University Press, 1999), pp. 78–81. See p. 157 earlier.

incompatible with locating dignity in a more specific idea of what human nature is and how human beings are fitted by that nature for a particular way of life. This would be true, even if, as seems to be the case, the Christian realist's idea of human nature required a great deal of political freedom.[84] Political liberalism and Christian theological realism may share the idea that human beings are inviolable in ways that give them certain rights in any form of organized political life. If that is what is meant by human dignity, then political liberalism and theological realism each has an idea of human dignity, but it seems unlikely that both of them have the same idea.

A more promising reconciliation of theological realism and political liberalism might be to show that they arrive at the same results. We have already noted, for example, that certain aristocratic ways of life ruled out by theological realism might also be rejected, for different reasons, by liberal pluralism.[85] One could attempt to develop these points of agreement by demonstrating that all or many of the ways of respecting persons required by theological realism are also required by political liberalism, so that what is guaranteed them in one way by the idea that they are persons in the image of God is also guaranteed for other reasons by the political principles of a liberal democracy, and vice versa.

This sort of reconciliation is suggested by the way Rawls's later work develops the idea of overlapping consensus in relation to specific traditions. It may be the case, he proposes, that political liberalism rests not on a single set of principles supported by different traditions for different reasons, but on a family of more or less closely related principles. In that way, a religious or philosophical tradition might develop a set of political principles distinctive to its own tradition, not merely compatible with it. If the political organization that followed from these principles were sufficiently like Rawlsian liberalism, it could be regarded as a fully qualified liberal society, not merely as a decent society whose distinct arrangements deserve respect under the Law of Peoples. Rawls specifically suggests the Catholic moral theologians' idea of the common good as such a tradition.[86]

Galston makes the argument in more specific terms, developing a point-by-point comparison of liberal pluralism and Catholic social ethics in *Public Matters*. Although there are areas of disagreement along with the

---

[84] Niebuhr, *The Children of Light and the Children of Darkness*, p. 3. See also Robin Lovin, *Reinhold Niebuhr and Christian Realism* (Cambridge: Cambridge University Press, 1995), pp. 119–57.

[85] See p. 205 earlier.

[86] Rawls, *Law of Peoples*, p. 142n; Paul J. Weithman, *Religion and the Obligations of Citizenship* (Cambridge: Cambridge University Press, 2002), pp. 196–200.

convergences, the comparison reflects favorably on either liberal pluralism or Catholic social ethics, depending on where you are standing when you start making the comparison, and it suggests that the two ways of thinking have more to learn than they have to fear from one another. Galston's suggestion that liberal pluralism may also require something like participatory justice is particularly interesting in this respect.[87]

There may, nonetheless, be important differences in both content and scope between political liberalism and the respect for persons derived from theological realism. David Hollenbach begins his systematic treatment of the common good by pointing out the problems that a tolerant liberalism fails to solve.[88] Hollenbach may have too expansive a notion of the common good. His libertarian Catholic critics would no doubt think so. Or Rawls may have too restricted an idea of political liberalism. Galston's liberal pluralism would suggest that. In either case, a reconciliation of the content of the requirements of theological realism and political liberalism would appear to be an ongoing discussion, both within and between the two ways of thinking about persons in society.

The question of scope is also important. Theological realism makes universal claims about how persons should be treated under any system of government. The difference between the minimal human rights that are part of Rawls's Law of Peoples and the somewhat more expansive political rights that people have in liberal democracies makes it unlikely that the liberal theorist would regard the full requirements of human dignity spelled out by theological realism as universal in scope, even if a careful reconciliation showed that they were, indeed, requirements of life in a liberal democracy. Rawls's emphasis on the conditions of freedom and equality under which persons consent to political arrangements requires that even their rights, beyond the most basic, must be the rights they choose for themselves.

The liberal theorist might argue then that this more restricted scope is a good thing, since it would make liberal democratic governments less likely to adventure the enforcement of these requirements on other, non-democratic states. Theological realists might respond that powerful liberal democracies have not been notably eager to enforce international human rights agreements where their interests were not also involved, and in any case, the theological realist might say, the respect we think that persons are

---

[87] William A. Galston, *Public Matters: Politics, Policy, and Religion in the 21st Century* (Lanham, MD: Rowman and Littlefield, 2005), p. 153.
[88] Hollenbach, *Common Good and Christian Ethics*, pp. 32–61.

due should not vary with the kind of government they have, even if we recognize that under certain kinds of government, it may be very difficult for them to get that respect.

Such discussions might continue for some time without arriving at definitive conclusions. The important point to note is that in the recent literature, we seem to have moved beyond the assumption of incompatibility between religious comprehensive doctrines and political liberalism toward a recognition of common objectives both for politics and for persons. Liberal theory begins to speak of rights in terms of a dignity that requires political participation as well as a theoretical presumption of equality. Moral theologians practice what David Hollenbach calls "intellectual solidarity," entering into the exploration of concrete social and political problems in secular terms and minimizing explicitly theological claims where these are not essential to arriving at practical agreement.[89]

On each side, there will be those who are wary of the rapprochement. Christian pacifists will continue to argue that any accommodation to secular reason compromises the nonviolent Christian witness.[90] Philosophers committed to the rigorous exclusion of religious and metaphysical claims from political discussion continue to regard religion, and especially religious authority, as a "conversation-stopper."[91] Still, the distance between the two sides now appears less than it did at the high point of the contemporary theorization of liberal politics. Recent discussions have more in common with the joint effort of theology and democracy at the middle of the twentieth century to clarify what distinguished them from alternatives that had no respect for political freedom or human dignity.

POLITICS, FAITH, AND A MEANINGFUL MORAL LIFE

These developments in the current discussion are an important recognition of the history that has linked Christian realism and the development of modern politics for more than five centuries. The relationship has frequently been adversarial, with political liberalism and Christian tradition both claiming to be the origin of modern democracy and each suspecting the other of undermining it. "The debate has been inconclusive," Reinhold Niebuhr wrote well before the current episode began, "because, as a matter

---

[89] Hollenbach, *Common Good and Christian Ethics*, pp. 137–70.
[90] Hauerwas, *With the Grain of the Universe*, pp. 218–21.
[91] Richard Rorty, "Religion in the Public Square: A Reconsideration," *Journal of Religious Ethics* 31(2003), 141–9.

of history, both Christian and secular forces were involved in establishing the political institutions of democracy; and the cultural resources of modern free society are jointly furnished by both Christianity and modern secularism."[92] That recognition of shared origins and continued collaboration is all that history suggests and all that a prudent Christian realism wants.

Christian realism does not seek to conform society as a whole to a religious ideal, because it has no such ideal. It does not ask how society would look if everyone shared its theology, because its theology includes an understanding that not everyone will. From the time that Augustine sat down to write the *City of God*, Christian realism has rejected both withdrawal from the complexities of social life and utopian solutions that claim to dissolve them. Christian realism seeks today what it has always sought: A responsible engagement with a society that creates and maintains the human goods that everyone requires for this life, whatever they believe about their ultimate destiny. In modern times, Christian realism has been a participant in the search for a form of government that neither claims too much for itself nor expects too much of human nature. The political task of Christian realism today is not to offer an alternative to the liberal democracy that has emerged from that collaboration, but to keep it sufficiently realistic.

So what we have – what Christian realism seeks and what it has helped to create – is neither a religious ideal of social life nor a religious constitution, but a system of unapologetic politics. Faith influences the shape of social life by bringing to the public forum of each social context a comprehensive idea of the human good, centered in the person as the image of God in whom these diverse goods are united. Those responsible for law and government respond to this unapologetic account of human dignity by finding ways to formulate its requirements in terms acceptable in the forum of public reason. That is where government's work is done. But democratic government also presses back with the requirements of its own integrity, refusing to become simply the instrument of a theological proclamation. The church, in turn, rejects the demand for apology and persists in formulating the requirements of Christ's presence in history in its own terms.

If this process goes well, both church and state will be satisfied that they have preserved their separate integrities, assessed in the private forums of theologians and liberal theorists. More important, in the interaction between these contexts, without any single set of rules to govern the discourse, on terms that no context taken by itself can dictate, people will lead meaningful lives. For what we know is that meaning in life comes not from

---

[92] Niebuhr, *Christian Realism and Political Problems*, p. 95.

the goods we create, but from responsibilities accepted before God in creating them. As we participate in the contexts in which human goods are created and enable others to participate in them – not each individual under one or the other of them, but all people under all of them – we anticipate God's judgment and mercy. As we accept our responsibilities and entrust the results to God, Christ takes form in history and action takes on meaning that thought cannot supply.

Select Bibliography

Ambrose, *De Officiis*, Ivor J. Davidson, ed., Oxford: Oxford University Press, 2001.

Augustine, *The City of God against the Pagans*, R. W. Dyson, ed., Cambridge: Cambridge University Press, 1998.

Ballor, Jordan J., "Christ in Creation: Bonhoeffer's Orders of Preservation and Natural Theology," *Journal of Religion* 86 (2006), 1–22.

Barry, Brian R., *The Liberal Theory of Justice*, Oxford: Clarendon Press, 1973.

Beinart, Peter, *The Good Fight*, San Francisco: Harper Collins, 2006.

Beitz, Charles R., *Political Theory and International Relations*, Princeton, NJ: Princeton University Press, 1979.

Berlin, Isaiah, *Liberty*, Henry Hardy, ed., Oxford: Oxford University Press, 2002.

Berman, Harold, *Law and Revolution: The Formation of the Western Legal Tradition*, Cambridge, MA: Harvard University Press, 1983.

Bernstein, Richard, *The Abuse of Evil: The Corruption of Politics and Religion Since 9/11*, Cambridge: Polity Press, 2005.

Bonhoeffer, Dietrich, *Creation and Fall: A Theological Exposition of Genesis 1–3*, Dietrich Bonhoeffer Works, vol. III, Minneapolis, MN: Fortress Press, 1997.

_____, *Ethics*, Clifford J. Green, ed., Dietrich Bonhoeffer Works, vol. VI, Minneapolis, MN: Fortress Press, 2005.

Brink, David O., *Moral Realism and the Foundations of Ethics*, Cambridge: Cambridge University Press, 1989.

Brown, Peter, *Augustine of Hippo: A Biography*, Berkeley: University of California Press, 2000.

Brunner, Emil, *The Divine Imperative*, Olive Wyon, trans., Philadelphia: Westminster Press, 1947.

Brunner, Emil & Karl Barth, *Natural Theology*, Peter Fraenkel, trans., Eugene, OR: Wipf and Stock, 2002.

Bull, Hedley, *The Anarchical Society: A Study of Order in World Politics*, 2nd ed., New York: Columbia University Press, 1995.

Carter, Stephen, *The Culture of Disbelief*, New York: Basic Books, 1993.

_____, "The Religiously Devout Judge," *Notre Dame Law Review*, 64 (1989), 932–44.

Chambers, Simone & Will Kymlicka, eds., *Alternative Conceptions of Civil Society*, Ethikon Series in Comparative Ethics; Princeton, NJ: Princeton University Press, 2002.

Craig, Campbell, *Glimmer of a New Leviathan: Total War in the Realism of Niebuhr, Morgenthau, and Waltz,* New York: Columbia University Press, 2003.

Cuddihy, John Murray, *No Offense: Civil Religion and Protestant Taste,* New York: Seabury Press, 1978.

Deede Johnson, Kristen, *Theology, Political Theory, and Pluralism: Beyond Tolerance and Difference,* Cambridge: Cambridge University Press, 2007.

Dobson, William J., "The Day Nothing Much Changed," *Foreign Policy* 156 (September/October 2006), 2–25.

Dorrien, Gary, *The Making of American Liberal Theology,* vol. II, Louisville, KY: Westminster John Knox Press, 2003.

Douglas, R. Bruce & David Hollenbach, eds., *Catholicism and Liberalism: Contributions to American Public Philosophy,* Cambridge: Cambridge University Press, 1994.

Elshtain, Jean Bethke, "Against the New Utopianism," *Studies in Christian Ethics* 20 (2007), 52–4.

———, *Augustine and the Limits of Politics,* Notre Dame, IN: University of Notre Dame Press, 1995.

———, *Just War Against Terror: The Burden of American Power in a Violent World,* New York: Basic Books, 2003.

Eusebius, *The History of the Church,* G. A. Williamson, trans., London: Penguin Books, 1989.

Ferguson, Niall, *The War of the World: Twentieth-Century Conflict and the Descent of the West,* New York: Penguin Press, 2006.

Fergusson, David, *Church, State, and Civil Society,* Cambridge: Cambridge University Press, 2004.

Figgis, John Neville, *Churches in the Modern State,* London: Longmans, Green and Co., 1913.

Forrester, Duncan B., *Apocalypse Now?,* Aldershot, UK: Ashgate Publishing, 2005.

Fox, Richard, *Reinhold Niebuhr: A Biography,* Ithaca, NY: Cornell University Press, 1996.

Fukuyama, Francis, *America at the Crossroads,* New Haven, CT: Yale University Press, 2006.

———, *The End of History and the Last Man,* New York: Free Press, 1992.

Friedman, Thomas, *The World Is Flat: A Brief History of the Twenty-first Century,* New York: Farrar, Straus and Giroux, 2005.

Gaddis, John Lewis, *The Cold War,* London: Penguin Books, 2007.

Galston, William A., *The Practice of Liberal Pluralism,* Cambridge: Cambridge University Press, 2005.

Gamwell, Franklin, *Politics as a Christian Vocation,* Cambridge: Cambridge University Press, 2005.

Gordis, Robert, *The Root and the Branch: Judaism and the Free Society,* Chicago: University of Chicago Press, 1962.

Grewe, Wilhelm G., *The Epochs of International Law,* Michael Byers, trans., Berlin: Walter de Gruyter, 2000.

Gustafson, James, *Ethics from a Theocentric Perspective*, Chicago: University of Chicago Press, 1981.

Halliwell, Martin, *The Constant Dialogue: Reinhold Niebuhr and American Intellectual Culture*, Lanham, MD: Rowman & Littlefield Publishers, 2005.

Hauerwas, Stanley, *A Community of Character*, Notre Dame, IN: University of Notre Dame Press, 1981.

_____, *The Peaceable Kingdom*, Notre Dame, IN: University of Note Dame Press, 1983.

_____, *With the Grain of the Universe: The Church's Witness and Natural Theology*, Grand Rapids, MI: Brazos Press, 2001.

Held, David, ed., *Political Theory Today*, Stanford, CA: Stanford University Press, 1991.

Herberg, Will, *Protestant, Catholic, Jew*, New York: Doubleday and Company, 1955.

Himmelfarb, Gertrude, *The Idea of Poverty: England in the Early Industrial Age*, New York: Alfred A. Knopf, 1983.

Hirst, Paul Q., ed., *The Pluralist Theory of the State: Selected writings of G. D. H. Cole, J. N. Figgis, and H. J. Laski*, London: Routledge, 1989.

Hollenbach, David, *The Common Good and Christian Ethics*, Cambridge: Cambridge University Press, 2002.

Höpfl, Harro, ed., *Luther and Calvin on Secular Authority*, Cambridge: Cambridge University Press, 1991.

Hughes, Emmet John, *The Church and Liberal Society*, Princeton, NJ: Princeton University Press, 1944.

Huntington, Samuel P., *The Clash of Civilizations and the Remaking of World Order*, New York: Simon and Schuster, 1996.

Hutcheson, Francis, *An Inquiry into the Original of Our Ideas of Beauty and Virtue*, Wolfgang Leidhold, ed., Indianapolis: Liberty Fund, 2004.

Ignatieff, Michael, *The Lesser Evil: Political Ethics in an Age of Terror*, Princeton, NJ: Princeton University Press, 2004.

Insole, Christopher J., *The Politics of Human Frailty: A Theological Defense of Political Liberalism*, Notre Dame, IN: University of Notre Dame Press, 2005.

_____, *The Realist Hope*, Aldershot, UK: Ashgate Publishing, 2006.

James, William, *Pragmatism: A New Name for Some Old Ways of Thinking*, New York: Longmans, Green, and Co., 1907.

Juergensmeyer, Mark, *Terror in the Mind of God: The Global Rise of Religious Violence*, Berkeley: University of California Press, 2000.

Kaplan, Lawrence F. & William Kristol, *The War Over Iraq: Saddam's Tyranny and America's Mission*, San Francisco: Encounter Books, 2003.

Keller, Catherine, *God and Power: Counter-Apocalyptic Journeys*, Minneapolis, MN: Fortress Press, 2005.

Kennan, George, "Morality and Foreign Policy," *Foreign Affairs* 64 (1985), 205–18.

Kraynak, Robert P. & Glenn Tinder, eds., *In Defense of Human Dignity: Essays for Our Times*, Notre Dame, IN: University of Notre Dame Press, 2003.

Lieven, Anatol & John Hulsman, *Ethical Realism*, New York: Pantheon Books, 2006.

Locke, John, *A Letter Concerning Toleration*, James Tully, ed., Indianapolis: Hackett Publishing, 1983.

———, *Two Treatises of Government*, Peter Laslett, ed., Cambridge: Cambridge University Press, 1988.

Lovin, Robin W., *Reinhold Niebuhr and Christian Realism*, Cambridge: Cambridge University Press, 1995.

Magid, Henry M., *English Political Pluralism: The Problem of Freedom and Organization*, New York: Columbia University Press, 1941.

Morgenthau, Hans J., *Politics Among Nations: The Struggle for Power and Peace*, 4th Ed., New York: Alfred A. Knopf, 1967.

Morrison, Jeffrey H, *John Witherspoon and the Founding of the American Republic*, Notre Dame, IN: University of Notre Dame Press, 2005.

Murray, John Courtney, *We Hold These Truths: Catholic Reflections on the America Proposition*, New York: Sheed and Ward, 1960.

Naveh, Eyal, *Reinhold Niebuhr and Non-Utopian Liberalism: Beyond Illusion and Despair*, Brighton, UK: Sussex Academic Press, 2002.

Neuhaus, Richard J., *The Naked Public Square*, Grand Rapids, MI: Eerdmans, 1984.

Niebuhr, Reinhold, *The Children of Light and the Children of Darkness*, New York: Charles Scribner's Sons, 1960.

———, *Christianity and Power Politics*, New York: Charles Scribner's Sons, 1940.

———, *Christian Realism and Political Problems*, New York: Charles Scribner's Sons, 1953.

———, *Essays in Applied Christianity*, D. B. Robertson, ed., New York: Meridian Books, 1959.

———, *Faith and History*, New York: Charles Scribner's Sons, 1949.

———, *An Interpretation of Christian Ethics*, New York: Seabury Press, 1979.

———, *The Irony of American History*, New York: Charles Scribner's Sons, 1952.

———, *Love and Justice: Selections from the Shorter Writings of Reinhold Niebuhr*, D. B. Robertson, ed., Louisville, KY: Westminster John Knox Press, 1992.

———, *Moral Man and Immoral Society*, Louisville, KY: Westminster John Knox Press, 2001.

———, *The Nature and Destiny of Man: A Christian Interpretation*, Louisville, KY: Westminster John Knox Press, 1996.

———, *Reflections on the End of an Era*, New York: Charles Scribner's Sons, 1934.

———, *The Self and the Dramas of History*, New York: Charles Scribner's Sons, 1955.

———, *The Structure of Nations and Empires*, New York: Charles Scribner's Sons, 1959.

Nurser, John, *For All Peoples and Nations: The Ecumenical Church and Human Rights*, Washington, DC: Georgetown University Press, 2005.

O'Brien, David & Thomas Shannon, eds., *Catholic Social Thought: The Documentary Heritage*, Maryknoll, NY: Orbis Books, 1992.

O'Donnell, James J., *Augustine*, New York: HarperCollins, 2005.

O'Donovan, Oliver & Joan Lockwood O'Donovan, eds., *Bonds of Imperfection: Christian Politics, Past and Present*, Grand Rapids, MI: Eerdmans, 2004.

_____, *From Irenaeus to Grotius: A Sourcebook in Christian Political Thought*, Grand Rapids, MI: Eerdmans, 1999.

Patterson, Eric, ed., *The Christian Realists: Reassessing the Contributions of Niebuhr and His Contemporaries*, Lanham, MD: University Press of America, 2003.

Perry, Michael, *Toward a Theory of Human Rights*, Cambridge: Cambridge University Press, 2007.

Petro, Nicolai N., *The Rebirth of Russian Democracy: An Interpretation of Political Culture*, Cambridge, MA: Harvard University Press, 1995.

Phillpott, Daniel, *Revolutions in Sovereignty: How Ideas Shaped Modern International Relations*, Princeton, NJ: Princeton University Press, 2001.

Placher, William, *Unapologetic Theology: A Christian Voice in a Pluralistic Conversation*, Louisville, KY: Westminster John Knox Press, 1989.

Plant, Raymond, *Politics, Theology, and History* Cambridge: Cambridge University Press, 2001.

Ramadan, Tariq, *Western Muslims and the Future of Islam*, New York: Oxford University Press, 2004.

Ramsey, Paul, *Deeds and Rules in Christian Ethics*, New York: Charles Scribner's Sons, 1967.

Rauschenbusch, Walter, *Christianity and the Social Crisis*, New York: Macmillan, 1907.

Rawls, John, *Justice as Fairness: A Restatement*, Cambridge, MA: Harvard University Press, 2001.

_____, *The Law of Peoples*, Cambridge, MA: Harvard University Press, 1999.

_____, *Political Liberalism*, New York: Columbia University Press, 1996.

_____, *A Theory of Justice*, Cambridge, MA: Harvard University Press, 1971.

Roy, Olivier, *Globalized Islam: The Search for a New Ummah*, New York: Columbia University Press, 2004.

Sandel, Michael J., *Public Philosophy: Essays on Morality and Politics*, Cambridge, MA: Harvard University Press, 2005.

Schlossberg, Herbert, *The Silent Revolution and the Making of Victorian England*, Columbus: Ohio State University Press, 2000.

Schweiker, William, *Theological Ethics and Global Dynamics*, Oxford: Blackwell Publishing, 2004.

Shafer-Landau, Russ, *Moral Realism: A Defence*, Oxford: Clarendon Press, 2003.

Skillen, James W. & Rockne M. McCarthy, eds., *Political Order and the Plural Structure of Society*, Emory University Studies in Law and Religion, No. 2, Atlanta, GA: Scholars Press, 1991.

Skinner, Quentin, *The Foundations of Modern Political Thought*, Cambridge: Cambridge University Press, 1978.

Slaughter, Anne-Marie, *A New World Order*, Princeton, NJ: Princeton University Press, 2004.

Stackhouse, Max, ed., *Christian Social Ethics in a Global Era*, Abingdon Press Studies in Christian Ethics and Economic Life, No. 1, Nashville: Abingdon Press, 1995.

――――, "Public Theology and Political Economy in a Globalizing Era," *Studies in Christian Ethics* 14 (2001), 70–1.

Stiglitz, Joseph E., *Globalization and Its Discontents*, New York: W. W. Norton, 2002.

Stone, Ronald H., *Prophetic Realism*, New York: T. & T. Clark, 2005.

Taylor, Charles, *Modern Social Imaginaries*, Durham, NC: Duke University Press, 2004.

Tinder, Glenn, *The Political Meaning of Christianity: An Interpretation*, Baton Rouge: Louisiana State University Press, 1989.

Trigg, Roger, *Religion in Public Life: Must Faith Be Privatized?*, Oxford: Oxford University Press, 2007.

Waldron, Jeremy, "Religious Contributions in Public Deliberation," *San Diego Law Review* 30 (1993), 817–48.

Walzer, Michael, *Spheres of Justice*, New York: Basic Books, 1983.

Warren, Heather, *Theologians of a New World Order: Reinhold Niebuhr and the Christian Realists, 1920–1948*, New York: Oxford University Press, 1997.

Witte, John, *Law and Protestantism: The Legal Teachings of the Lutheran Reformation*, Cambridge: Cambridge University Press, 2002.

Index